The Economics of Violence

How do we understand illicit violence? Can we prevent it? Building on behavioral science and economics, this book begins with the idea that humans are more predictable than we like to believe, and this ability to model human behavior applies equally well to leaders of violent and coercive organizations as it does to everyday people. Humans ultimately seek survival for themselves and their communities in a world of competition. While the dynamics of "us vs. them" are divisive, they also help us to survive. Access to increasingly larger markets, facilitated through digital communications and social media, creates more transnational opportunities for deception, coercion, and violence. If the economist's perspective helps to explain violence, then it must also facilitate insights into promoting peace and security. If we can approach violence as behavioral scientists, then we can also better structure our institutions to create policies that make the world a more secure place, for us and for future generations.

Gary M. Shiffman, Ph.D., a veteran of the US Departments of Defense and Homeland Security and the Senate, teaches at Georgetown University and explores the science of behavior, particularly the ways in which we can understand illicit behaviors. At Giant Oak, he creates software to make the world safer and more secure.

"*The Economics of Violence* is a pathbreaking work that argues how a more rigorous understanding of human behavior can be harnessed to counter violence more effectively. Drawing on his formidable intellect and experiences in the military, as a Senate staffer, a homeland security executive, an entrepreneur, and a security studies scholar, Shiffman makes a powerful case for this unique approach to strengthening US national security."

Bruce Hoffman, Professor, Georgetown University,
author of *Inside Terrorism*

"Understanding political violence requires turning away from simplistic labels – 'ethno-nationalist', 'narco-terrorist', 'religious radical' – toward the scientifically grounded concepts of scarcity, markets, and firms. Shiffman's enlightening and accessible prose demystifies today's national security threats with precise logic, careful case studies, and wide-ranging pop-culture references. A brilliant ground-breaking book that every national security professional should read."

Jacob Shapiro, Professor of Politics and
International Affairs, Princeton University

"Gary M. Shiffman uses the science of economics as a tool for understanding violent human behavior, and he shows us how better to understand those who would harm us. Gary brings provocative, innovative, and exciting ideas to those seeking knowledge, clarity, and peace of mind in the promotion of freedom and security. *The Economics of Violence* is an exciting new book from an established and important voice in national security."

Senator Connie Mack, III

"This is a valuable book that should set records straight about stereotypes, identity, politics, and misleading assumptions. I have been disabused of some of my assumptions, and the reader will find the recipe for combatting violent groups in the last chapter."

HRH Prince Turki Al Faisal Al Sa'ud, former
Director General of the General Intelligence
Directorate of the Kingdom of Saudi Arabia

"Gary Shiffman has always been a clarion voice in understanding the importance of behavioral science and economics in national security – never more so than in this work. In this book, Shiffman has provided a seminal study of how economic dynamics and individual decisions affect the manifestations of violence and the evolution of terrorist, militant, and criminal movements in a changing global landscape. By using an economic lens, he breaks down the orthodoxy between traditional disciplines and rigid categories of identity to understand sources of violence and how non-state actors emerge, adapt, and compete. By examining the cases of Pablo Escobar, Joseph Kony, and Osama bin Laden in this way, he is able to explain how each have acted as 'entrepreneurs' using force and forms of coercion to capture markets, each in his own way. This should become required reading for those seeking to understand how individual decisions drive sub-state groups and violence, and how we might use these insights to counter this violence and fight like entrepreneurs."

Juan C. Zarate, former Deputy Assistant to the President and Deputy National Security Advisor for Combatting Terrorism (2005–2009)

The Economics of Violence

How Behavioral Science Can Transform Our View of Crime, Insurgency, and Terrorism

Gary M. Shiffman
Georgetown University

CAMBRIDGE
UNIVERSITY PRESS

University Printing House, Cambridge CB2 8BS, United Kingdom

One Liberty Plaza, 20th Floor, New York, NY 10006, USA

477 Williamstown Road, Port Melbourne, VIC 3207, Australia

314–321, 3rd Floor, Plot 3, Splendor Forum, Jasola District Centre,
New Delhi – 110025, India

79 Anson Road, #06-04/06, Singapore 079906

Cambridge University Press is part of the University of Cambridge.

It furthers the University's mission by disseminating knowledge in the pursuit of
education, learning, and research at the highest international levels of excellence.

www.cambridge.org
Information on this title: www.cambridge.org/9781107092464
DOI: 10.1017/9781316136072

First published 2020

Printed in the United Kingdom by TJ International Ltd. Padstow Cornwall

A catalogue record for this publication is available from the British Library.

ISBN 978-1-107-09246-4 Hardback
ISBN 978-1-107-46575-6 Paperback

To Sarah Ann Chance Shiffman, 1940–2015.
I'll be talking to you and Dad often.

CONTENTS

ACKNOWLEDGMENTS

I am grateful to my amazing family for remaining patient during the times when writing this book may have seemed a priority. Jeanne, Phoebe, and Belle, you are my everything.

Thanks to Cambridge University Press' Chris Harrison. When we met a few years ago, I had something important to say, and you expressed enthusiasm for the project and remained patient as life's many other priorities competed for my time. Thanks to Philip Good for your creativity and passion.

More than any one person's work, this book reflects the ongoing dialogue I've had with amazing classes of Georgetown University students. During all of those hours of classroom dialectic, reading your point papers to and about various rebel leaders, discussing *The Wire* over pizza and beer, and getting your feedback at The Tombs, we've learned together. I absolutely could not have written this book without you, students and alums.

Many graduate research assistants have my gratitude, to include: Wilson Co, Meredith Burkart, Harsh Pandya, Berfu Kizitlan, Michael Gee, Roya Solamani, Prabin Khadka, Hugh Brooks, Holly Ghali, Ravi Gupta, Alex Kisselburg, Michael Counihan, Sarah Beane, Danile Lim, Diogo Ide, Taylor Teaford, Max von Bargen, David Sterman, Allison Hawkey, Andrea Clabough, Audrey Hsieh, Sarah Welsh, Jillian McGhan, Christopher Wall, Kathleen Walsh, and Kristina Drye. And thank you Carole Sargent, Georgetown's Director, Office of Scholarly Publications, for great support to me and the entire community. Lisa Hacken, my friend for many years, provided fantastic freelance editorial support. My daughter Phoebe provided valuable feedback at the right time.

I continue to gain intellectual energy from the research of Jacob Shapiro, Dan Byman, Eli Berman, and many others who toil in the fields of organized violence. This book reflects my most ambitious efforts at narrative, and I thank Tim White and members of Washington, DC's Literary Society for the inspiration to take on this challenge.

Partial funding for the research in this book came from the Center for Risk and Economic Analysis of Terrorism Events (CREATE), an organization whose members have improved security through the development of advanced models and tools for the evaluation of the risks, costs, and consequences of terrorism.

I am grateful to all of these people and more, but, of course, all errors and failures reflect only on me.

INTRODUCTION

During the first year of my transition from military service to staffing US Senate leaders on Capitol Hill, I began working on how to counter acts of terrorism. The year was 1996, and I had served on active duty as a Surface Warfare Officer in the US Navy since 1988. I understood important military concepts such as the capabilities of various Russian-made weapons systems and the impact of Tomahawk cruise missile technology on air superiority. Still, my experience did not help me comprehend how to tackle suicide terrorism. In July of 1997, two people walked into the Mahane Yehuda Market carrying backpacks full of explosives and nails, detonating the bombs and killing themselves and 15 people around them, wounding 170 more. Just a few months later, in September 1997, the horrors were repeated on Ben Yehuda street, where three suicide bombers killed seven people, including three 14-year-old girls, and wounded more than 190 others.[1] The people who killed themselves and others created horrific spectacles. I read of both events from my desk in the Senate Hart Office Building in Washington, DC, feeling angry and frustrated that my national security training had not prepared me for dealing with these acts of terrorism. This launched my search to understand organized non-state violence. By "organized" I mean non-random – the ability of some person or group to produce acts of violence over time. By "non-state" I mean groups of people we don't traditionally think of in the context of state-on-state warfare: global terrorist groups, insurgents, and criminal groups such as drug traffickers and mafias.

I began my academic career studying psychology, reflecting my interest in human behavior. I began my professional career by serving in the military, reflecting my belief in the importance of public service. In 1996, after eight years on active duty in the US Navy, during which I served in the Gulf War during Operations Desert Shield and Desert Storm, and earned a graduate degree in Security Studies from Georgetown University in Washington, DC, I began working on national security issues in the US Senate. I had moved from military combat operations to national security policymaking at the highest levels of the US government. My psychology and military backgrounds gave me a perspective that was well suited to combatting the issues of war where the belligerents were clearly identified by the uniforms worn and the turf occupied. However, when faced with the issue of suicide bombings and terrorism, I felt underprepared, and I found myself in the midst of a national security community facing the same struggle.

I accepted a position working for Senator Connie Mack, who served on the Foreign Operations Appropriations Subcommittee, the Banking Committee, and the Joint Economic Committee, and who chaired the Republican Conference – the third-most-senior position in Senate leadership. I was his National Security Advisor, and I was not going to waste a moment of this opportunity. I dug into US–Cuba relations following Fidel Castro's shooting down of two unarmed Cessna aircraft in the Florida Strait, leading to legislative and policy changes to the Foreign Sovereign Immunity Act. I developed plans to support the peace processes in the Middle East and Northern Ireland, and to support democratic leaders in Hong Kong during the process of reversion of Hong Kong from UK sovereignty to the People's Republic of China. As a war veteran with a graduate degree from Georgetown University, I possessed experience, knowledge, and motivation; however, at my Senate desk in 1997, I struggled with my inability to address non-state violence. One cannot stop a suicide terrorist in a crowded market by launching cruise missiles at that same crowded market. As a member of the national security policymaking community, I was unprepared.

In the two decades since my transition from the Navy to the Senate, I've worked in industry, government, and academia, and I've learned a great deal from these experiences. I ran an operational business unit at L-3 Communications, a large defense and government contractor. During the administration of President George W. Bush, I was appointed Chief of Staff of US Customs and Border Protection (CBP) in the US Department of Homeland Security (DHS); CBP is the largest law enforcement agency in the world and has the responsibility of securing the country's borders while facilitating trade and travel. I have also had the great privilege of leading research initiatives sponsored by the Defense Advanced Research Project Agency (DARPA) and the DHS Science and Technology directorate (DHS S&T). During the transition from thinking about Tomahawks to thinking about terrorism, I have explored and grown skeptical of many popular theories of non-state organized violence. For example, I question policies based on slogans such as "radical Islam" and other national or religious identities. Instead, I've come to appreciate science-based approaches to national security, particularly those based on social science and economics.

One thing I've learned, and a major theme of this book, is that assigning identity labels to groups who commit violence hinders effective policymaking. My experience leading government-funded research has allowed me to realize that we need more scientific work on human behavior as it relates to organized violence. While massive investments dating back to at least 1914 have profoundly transformed the world, we've focused on engineering and weapons technologies and not on human behavior. My experience has convinced me that violence does not emanate from religion, ethnicity, or poverty, and that entire groups of people do not act as a mass. I've also learned that military operations do not always lead to successes over violent adversaries.

Throughout history and throughout the world we witness violent acts committed by members of the secular, the sectarian, the majority, the minority, the poor, and the wealthy. Of the countless stories of violence we read about, it is important to note that only a limited number of individuals, and not an entire identity group, commits the acts. One person carried the explosive backpack into the crowded Israeli marketplace, but the other thousands of Palestinian people did not. If only a small fraction of Muslims commits acts of terrorism, then it is inaccurate to conclude that those who do engage in violence do so as a result of Islamic doctrine. Dylann Roof claimed that he shot and killed nine people in a Charleston church in 2015 in order to start a race war. His act of violence against civilians for political reasons undoubtedly meets the generally accepted definition of terrorism, even though his skin color and religion do not resemble the popular media portrayal of a terrorist. Despite this, Dylann Roof's proclaimed ideology was hardly unique: the bulk of the Southern Poverty Law Center's designated hate groups similarly advocate for violence against minority groups.[2] Hardly anyone would argue that white supremacist groups represent the majority of white Americans. As we invest in science in support of national security, we need to look beyond simple markers of identity and better understand and examine the human decision-making process behind all those who engage in violence.

Interestingly, piercing the veil of the common identity language of national security allows for new perspectives of organized violence – new categories for organizing and understanding. For example, if we see a person selling drugs in order to make money, purchase weapons, and kill innocents in order to raise more money, buy more weapons, and take on a state militia, have we seen a "terrorist," "insurgent," or "criminal"? If that person is Catholic or Muslim, Mexican or Pakistani, do we know if that fact of identity influenced the violent acts? These terms, "terrorist," "insurgent," and "criminal," simplify the chaos of the world, allowing us to organize what we see and read about in buckets that seem orderly. At the same time, however, these simplifications also mislead us. Our long wars since September 11, 2001, in part, can be explained by this misleading simplification. We are not at war with Radical Islam.

Over the past decade, while engaged in armed conflict in Iraq, Afghanistan, Syria, and Libya, members of US national security leadership have witnessed debates over proper strategies: *counter-terrorism* (CT), *counterinsurgency* (COIN), or *law enforcement* (LE) with respect to *transnational criminal organizations* (TCOs). When we add these terms to identity labels, we get digestible news but, perhaps, flawed policy. That is, the term *Islamic terrorism* describes what we see, but when we conflate the term with the causes of violence, we have confused correlation with causation. The killers were Muslim and did engage in an act of terror (correlation), but did Islam cause the act of terror?

Readers of this book will hear a perspective of organized violence that is different from what is popular in the media and among national security intellectuals. This perspective matters because we err when policymakers or pundits assign a label to an act and then refer to the associated library of policy responses. We fight a terrorist as if the person is not also an insurgent, criminal, spouse, parent, business person, consumer, and friend. We bypass the individual when we rush to create a story about the group. This book asks you, the reader, to consider one idea at the outset: violence does not emanate from a person's group identity. Because policies of the past decade have been based on the faulty logic of identity-based collective violence, they have been wrong.

To better keep us safe, we've got to ask, "where does violence come from?" Organized violence lies along a spectrum of human actions and human choices – a continuum of possible decisions made by individuals within competitive markets, by people with goals and ambitions, and also by individuals confronting scarcity of time, wealth, information, and freedom. This book will explore the lines that separate crime, insurgency, and terrorism, as well as the role of identity in understanding organized violence. The result of this exploration will have significant consequences for policymakers: by better understanding the nature of human violence, we can better understand threats to our safety and security and make the world a more difficult place for illicit actors and groups to operate.

In addition to anecdotes from recent history, this book uses narratives from fictional stories to help unpack theories and material that can be dense and fact-laden. When pursuing my graduate degree in National Security Studies in the early 1990s, I felt the need to give up on fiction; I believed that I could not afford time off for the luxury of a novel or a movie. Over time, however, I've come to appreciate the value and relevance of literature. As ascribed to Ralph Waldo Emerson, "fiction reveals truth that reality obscures." A good book or film help can help us understand complex issues and thereby provide valuable insight to people concerned with national security. In my work, I've explored how literature can illuminate organized violence in ways that are relevant to my day jobs. By weaving in references to fiction throughout this book, the reader will join this exploration of the value of a tale well told.

Understanding terrorism helps us to understand insurgency, civil wars, and criminal violence. Rather than separate, unrelated categories, these forms of violence share common drivers. By looking beyond the labels often ascribed to these acts of violence, such as "religious sect" or "ethnic tribe," a different and powerful story of organized violence emerges. By peering orthogonally at the long-held canons of national security, we can begin to understand the story behind horrific market bombings. Viewing violence as a human choice, rather than an inevitable result of religion or ethnicity, is essential to countering it. This book was written with the goal of articulating a new social-science-based analysis of violence and inspiring readers to seek out new approaches to national security.

1 VIOLENCE

Imagine a man taking a moment, between the first dance and the cutting of the cake at his daughter's wedding, to order an act of extreme violence. In the opening scene of Mario Puzzo's *The Godfather*, we see the Sicilian-American immigrant named Amerigo Bonasera, a legitimate business owner, asking Don Vito Corleone, the boss of the Corleone crime family, to commit murder.

Bonasera offers to pay cash in exchange for the murder of two boys who assaulted his daughter. Don Vito negotiates with him in the library of the family home, where just through the window we see and hear the music and dancing of Connie Corleone's wedding party. Steeped in culture and highly stylized, this moment reinforces Puzo's statement that "no Sicilian can refuse any request on his daughter's wedding day." Bonasera requests revenge for two young men's violent actions against his daughter after a New York City courtroom acquitted the culprits, humiliating and enraging Bonasera. Failed by the official system, he turns to the Mafia and seeks to hire Don Corleone to kill the boys.

The head of the Corleone crime family sees this as an opportunity to pick up a loyal constituent and negotiates on two fronts. He counter-proposes to cause the boys "to suffer," but refuses to "do murder." In exchange for this act "of justice," Don Vito requests Bonasera's loyalty, not his cash. Bonasera agrees and demonstrates his assent in Sicilian style – with a bow and a kiss on Don Vito's ring.

Now, imagine that the Governor of New York tasks you with bringing an end to Don Vito and the Corleone crime family. You might take the generally accepted approach to addressing organized violence: identify the associated identities by race, religion, ethnicity or tribe; then ascribe a category to the act such as crime, insurgency, or terrorism; then, finally, ascribe motive to identity-category before responding. You might first try to understand the Sicilian Mafia, the Cosa Nostra, then compare and contrast with the Corleone family specifically. You might examine how the Catholic religion and Sicilian culture, as practiced by Italian-American crime bosses, impacts their organizations. You would likely build an organizational chart highlighting familial and other relationships.

Like the Senator Pat Geary character in *The Godfather: Part II*, you might make generalizations about Italian-Americans and the crime syndicates that they run. You might target the leadership of the Corleone family, arresting Don Vito himself. Those familiar with Mario Puzo's *The Godfather* story understand the likely unintended consequences of taking out Don Vito, either making way for Sonny to rise to leadership and perhaps expand into the heroin trade, or allowing the other crime families to take over more of the New York marketplace. Through your thoughtful and respectable approach, you may have exacerbated and worsened the public safety and security of the people of New York.

This example of organized crime abstracts well to insurgencies and terrorism. If one were to counter actors in these other categories, one would use kinetic force (law enforcement or military) to take key targets out of action. In the national security profession, we assiduously measure numbers of key targets killed or captured, and acts of violence occurring in specific geographic areas. At some point, based upon these metrics, we declare victory. The standard of victory can be as low as *no acts of known violence in a location on a map*, or at least none that we observe. But what "victory" did we actually accomplish? Did we allow for a next-in-line to rise up, a new, more dangerous leader? Did we clear out one boss to the advantage of others? Judging by recent history, such as policy responses following the 9/11 attacks on the United States, and responses to the Islamic State, Al Qaeda, and the Taliban, we seem to do exactly this. We have some metric of violent acts committed and look for a change in those measures so we can feel good about our contribution, only to feel pangs of anxiety when the near-future headlines admonish us: the same people are back, but following a different leader.

This generally accepted identity-category approach (e.g., Sicilian crime syndicate, Islamic terrorism) to understanding organized violence jeopardizes our safety and security by neglecting the stories of individual people and the markets in which they make decisions. Explaining an individual's behavior must require more than a label or two – Arab, Jew, Muslim, Protestant, Catholic, black, white, Hispanic, Russian, American, etc. The war in Afghanistan provides a great example of why it is dangerous for us to use these terms to define a conflict. The way in which we went to war was impeded by a fixation on terms like *drug trafficker, terrorist*, and *insurgent*. Policy leaders at the most senior levels of US government could not agree on whether we were fighting a criminal organization, an insurgency, or a terrorist group, and this debate bogged down the establishment of a comprehensive military and policy approach to the conflict. This is because different federal agencies are set up to combat different kinds of threats based on the terminology used. The US Drug Enforcement Administration (DEA), for example, combats global drug trafficking. Immigration and Customs Enforcement (ICE) and US Customs and Border Protection (CBP) combat criminals, weapons, drugs, and cash moving across borders into the United States. The Federal Bureau of Investigation (FBI) exerts preeminence on counter-terrorism cases from a law enforcement perspective. US Special Operations Command claims the same alpha status within the US Department of Defense. Assigning tasks to a particular agency within the government often follows which terms one uses to describe the task: crime, insurgency, or terrorism. Avoiding this language and turning to the language of economics instead will better inform our decision-making.

By moving to the language of markets, we can see conflict more clearly. For example, instead of seeing Islamic terrorism, a Mexican cartel, or a white supremacist, can we see entrepreneurs using force and coercion, as well as other goods and services, in competition, to exert dominance in efforts to capture markets? Seeing the conflict from this perspective allows us to better understand the nature of the violence, the source of the violence, and the methods to undermine and deter the violence.

As human beings, we share something seemingly basic, yet more powerful and profound than the different colors of our skin and the languages we speak. We share a desire to thrive and to find meaning as individuals and betterment for ourselves and for our kin.

Our behaviors, although often correlated with the aforementioned identity-category labels, ultimately take shape at a much more fundamental level; that is, we make choices based on our goals, resources, constraints, threats, and concerns. Observing violent conflicts while appreciating and even embracing the complexity of individual human behaviors in this way reveals a powerful perspective on organized acts of violence.

As wars between states decline, violence within states (e.g., insurgents like the Taliban) and across states (e.g., transnational movements like Al Qaeda and ISIS) evolves, seemingly complicating the national security landscape. More and more, sub-state actors like organized criminals, insurgents, and terrorists threaten national security. Status quo policymakers and scholars attempt to divide the response to the threat into self-contained fields of: (1) law enforcement (LE) (e.g., to counter TCOs), (2) counterinsurgency (COIN), and (3) counter-terrorism (CT), with the well-intentioned goal of imposing order and context on the messiness of violent relations below the state level. However, in so doing, these elites of the national security institutions, lamenting the lost simplicity of the bipolar world, introduce misleading analytical tendencies. This clean dissection of organized violence into self-contained identity-categories and response categories (LE, COIN, CT) leads to a comforting conclusion. What feels like knowledge is misunderstanding, and subsequently jeopardizes our own safety and security. We gain simplicity but give up insight. We address nothing short of life and death for ourselves, our families, and our communities when we combat organized violence. With conflicts resurging in Syria, Iraq, and Afghanistan, with racial violence in the United States spiking in prominence, and with organized criminal groups globalizing, now seems an appropriate time to reconsider the way in which we view organized violence.

By seeking to impose an identity-category order on violence using broad terms, scholars and policymakers bypass the relevance and role of the individual in a market – behind every act of sub-state violence lie individuals making decisions in a world of scarcity. Each violent actor is motivated by individual goals, constrained by circumstances, and has determined that his or her interests would be best served through violence. In essence, sub-state violence is an economic problem – not in the sense that all violent actors seek monetary gains, but, rather, in the sense that organized violence, when it occurs, results from a market in which individuals rationally pursue their self-interests. Violent groups like the FARC in Colombia, Boko Haram in Nigeria, and the Yakuza in Japan all defy ready categorization, and attempts to assign identity-categories to them can be misleading when it comes to understanding their origins and growth. The FARC, for example, started out under a Marxist-Leninist banner, but through consolidation of political power gradually became one of the largest drug trafficking organizations in the world. Boko Haram and the Yakuza also began as political groups, but Boko Haram evolved into a jihadist militant organization and the Yakuza became a transnational organized crime syndicate.

Framing violence in terms of individual human behavior allows us to move from aggregated characteristics to individual behavioral terms and provides two immediate benefits. First, we know this to be intuitively correct: people choose to commit acts of violence. But individual-level analysis seems overly complicated for national-level policymakers, so we simplify our method of examination by grouping violence into identity categories. Second, we have scientific methods applicable to human behavior, and, therefore, national security practitioners can approach individual-level analysis through the application of social and behavioral sciences. This approach gives us a science of human violence.

Identifying Pablo Escobar, Joseph Kony, and Osama bin Laden as merely the heads of organized criminal networks, insurgents, and terrorists, for example, limits our understanding of these men and their actions. Focusing on these divisions misses the key similarity between the three and the many others who have resorted to sub-state violence throughout history; they are individuals who, like most people, have goals and desires but face constraints in achieving them. The stories in this book will seek to demonstrate how violent actors fit core behavioral science models as they conform to expectations of human behavior. Examining the patterns of behavior of these three with social science concepts, we will see the unity of organized violence.

While the notion that behind each act of violence is a human decision seems like common sense, failure to examine sub-state violence in economic terms has thus far limited our understanding of it. We have too often divided sub-state violence into separate categories of crime, insurgency, and terrorism, each with their own community of experts, theoretical languages, and public perceptions.

Indeed, if an alien from outer space were to land in the United States and read only US newspapers, one might expect it to conclude that terrorism is a religious phenomenon primarily related to Islam; civil wars occur over aspects of identity such as religion and ethnicity; and crime relates simply to wealth – those who have it, and those who do not. These sub-fields we have developed are counterproductive myths that belie an essential clarity.

Discussions of organized violence often focus on the macro-level, rather than on the stories of individuals or on an understanding of how self-interest motivates and is best served by the consistent provision of coercion. The study of violence has proliferated discourse on the clashes of ideologies, cultures, and civilizations. Debates often focus on the language of -ism (Islamism, communism, nationalism) rather than that of personal quests for wealth, power, and revenge. Similar organizational structures, recruitment methods, and ways of referring to violence reappear across the separated disciplines. Instead of recognizing that fact and its rootedness in the way human nature expresses itself in social environments, practitioners and policymakers have often lost themselves in the specifics. We create "buckets" of knowledge and then lose perspective with our heads in one particular bucket. Religious justification for violence and fundamentalism becomes an issue of radical Islam for those studying Al Qaeda, Catholicism and secret societies for those studying the Mafia, and a mix of Christianity and local ideologies for those studying Kony's Lord's Resistance Army. Missing is the understanding that the particular religion is merely a title for a fundamental form of expression rooted in its value in the marketplace of all human interactions.

The failure to approach violence through economic analysis is not merely an issue for our hypothetical alien. The identity-category approach, meaning the tendency to view sub-state violence as distinctly different phenomena – crime, insurgency, and terrorism – has pervaded decision-making and policymaking processes throughout the various organizations tasked with protecting national security. When I first began working at the Department of Homeland Security, I raised the issue of how drug cartels on the Mexican border displayed similar traits to the insurgencies and terrorist campaigns the United States was battling elsewhere in the world. Many responded negatively, refusing to acknowledge that the two phenomena, drug trafficking and insurgency, in two separate parts of the world, involved similar decision patterns. I discussed how illicit entrepreneurs everywhere choose to use violence, but others wanted to defend the view that Mexican drug smugglers posed unique problems that were unrelated to the Iraqi insurgencies. These policy leaders insisted that seeking knowledge from issues across the globe – that is, looking for answers to one problem in the seemingly unrelated problems elsewhere – would waste valuable time.

My experience with leaders at the Department of Homeland Security is far from unique. In Afghanistan and Pakistan, the market for heroin has played an important role in funding militant groups. Yet for many years, scholars and journalists overlooked the role of drug trafficking and protection rackets in the region. Gretchen Peters, reporting from Afghanistan and Pakistan, described how top officials resisted examining the role of the drug trade in financing the Taliban because they were afraid it would blur the lines between terrorism and drug trafficking, as if there were ever a clear line to begin with.[1]

In his memoir, *Duty*, former Defense Secretary Robert Gates recalls a briefing from Michele Flournoy, Under Secretary of Defense for Policy at the time, upon her return from Afghanistan: "I saw little to convince me that we have a comprehensive interagency plan or concept of operations. I still believe that many competing – and often conflicting – campaigns are ongoing in Afghanistan: counter-insurgency, counter terrorism, counter narcotics, and efforts at nation building. Interagency planning, coordination and resourcing are, by far, the weakest link."[2]

Yet, despite recognizing the failure to establish a unified effort and an inter-agency plan, the more fundamental lesson appears to have largely eluded decision-makers throughout discussions of Afghanistan policy. Policy debates revolved around terms that only served to assert false divisions. Gates recalls considering *counter-terrorism, counter-terrorism plus* or *counterinsurgency minus*, and *fully funded counter-insurgency* as three distinct courses of action.

The absurdity of how our collective confusion forms the division of concepts along the lines of counter-terrorism, counterdrug, and counterinsurgency quickly becomes obvious. If the need for the concept of counter-terrorism plus/counterinsurgency minus does not reveal it, one only needs to listen to Gates himself:

> I wrote that all three of the mission options we had been discussing were "doomed to fail, or already have." Counterterrorism focused solely on al Qaeda could not work without a significant U.S. ground presence in Afghanistan and

the opportunity to collect intelligence that this would afford us. "We tried remote-control counterterrorism in the 1990s, and it brought us 9/11." "Counterterrorism plus," or "counterinsurgency minus," was what we had been doing since 2004, and "everyone seems to acknowledge that too is not working." Fully resourced counterinsurgency "sounds a lot like nation-building at its most ambitious" and would require troop levels, time, and money that few in the United States or in the West were prepared to provide.[3]

Criticizing the identity-category approach to national security counters popular convention but also appeals to our innermost thoughts. Gates, after recounting the various acrimonious aspects of the debate over strategies, notes that in the end they were hardly different. He writes,

> I believe, for example, that my view of a geographically limited counterinsurgency, combined with aggressive counterterrorism and disruptive Special Forces attacks on Taliban leaders, emphasizing expansion and training of the Afghan security forces, was actually pretty close to what Biden had in mind. The difference between his recommendation for increased troops and mine was the difference in total force between 83,000 to 85,000 troops and 98,000 troops. His number was far above what was required for counterterrorism, and mine was far too small for a fully resourced counterinsurgency strategy.[4]

Gates continues, "Contending teams presented alternatives to the president that were considerably more black and white than warranted." By Gates' own accounting, the administration got caught up discussing false dichotomies between forms of organized violence and the respective fields or teams associated with countering each form.

The failure to connect various forms of illicit and violent substate activity extends beyond the bureaucracy in Western capitals. According to Gretchen Peters, soldiers in Afghanistan often had significant information on the intersection of markets and the insurgency; a soldier might know which stalls in a marketplace belonged to the Haqqanis, for example. Yet rarely would the information make it into official records.[5] The reason, in large part, was a lack of understanding of the information's relevance to the conflict. When she asked one soldier why information on Haqqani-operated businesses did not appear in the official system, he responded, "Why ma'am? Do you think this is interesting?"

Even the counterinsurgency doctrine taught to our soldiers creates artificial divisions. At the core of counterinsurgency doctrine is the call to separate the "insurgents" from the "population," yet forgotten is that insurgents are not barbarians separate from the society in which they operate but, rather, members of that very society who have found it in their interest to commit violence.

David Kilcullen recounts a story regarding a reconstruction liaison team in Iraq in 2007.[6] The unit, which had recently rotated into the new area, became the target of mortar fire from a previously stable district. The unit quickly learned that the mortaring was not part of an upsurge in what is typically understood as insurgency. Instead, it was the result of the new unit's failure to fulfill a construction contract to a local company that the previous unit had promised. As Kilcullen notes, the loss of the contract exacted real costs for the sheikh who had negotiated it, depriving him both of the contract's resources and of the prestige that resulted from his ability to negotiate such a contract. Under these conditions – the loss of the contract having imposed significant reputational and financial costs – the sheikh found violence to be a rational choice. As Kilcullen puts it, "in a chaotic country with little rule of law and no welfare safety net, [losing the contract] was a potential death sentence."[7]

The story of the construction dispute in Iraq reflects a larger pattern. The prevalence of this form of violence calls into question the divisions that policymaking and scholarly community draw between types of sub-state violence. Although some may consider the Iraqi sheikh attempting to enforce a contract by mortaring an American base an insurgent, his actions represent the story of not just Iraq's insurgency, or insurgency elsewhere, but also of economic exchange through violence that is visible throughout the world. Little distinguishes him from the crime boss in New York City offering protection against his own violence. The classic protection racket of a mob goes something like this: pay me to protect your store, and nothing will happen; fail to pay me, and I cannot guarantee your safety (read: "my people will be back to burn your store to the ground"). What separation does exist is not the result of the ethnicity, religion, or identity of an insurgent, but of scarcity, perceptions of scarcity, and preferences.

Although the sheikh's story represents merely one more person making economic decisions, public discourse, policymaking discourse, and academic discourse try to force these stories into particular types of sub-state violence. Like me, Kilcullen has noted the tendency to divide sub-state violence into separate disciplines, writing "for various institutional reasons, governments, military forces, law enforcement agencies, and even (perhaps especially) university faculties tend to prefer theories of conflict framed around a single threat–insurgency, terrorism, piracy, narcotics, gangs, organized crime, and so on."[8]

The artificial walls between the disciplines studying organized crime, insurgency, and terrorism overly complicate the world of sub-state violence in which we live. While the United States used drones to pursue Al Qaeda members in Pakistan, China planned to use an armed drone to kill a Southeast Asian drug smuggler who had killed 13 Chinese sailors.[9] Forms of violence associated with one category also occur in others, sometimes to higher degrees. According to the New America Foundation, Al Qaeda, its associated forces, and those inspired by bin Laden's ideology have killed 45 people inside the United States from 9/11 to 2015.[10] Pablo Escobar, on the other hand, killed over 100 people when he bombed Avianca Flight 203 in November 1989 in an attempt to coerce the government into stopping its war on his criminal enterprise.[11] The point is not to compare the deadliness of Al Qaeda to Escobar, but rather to highlight that labeling either's actions as "terrorism" or "crime" does not further our understanding of or approach to the violence.

Similarly, although the narco-violence in Mexico ranks among the most deadly intra-state conflicts, categorizing it as crime discourages our better understanding of violence.[12] Although the Mexican cartels engage in drug trafficking, they simultaneously engage in activities commonly thought to be unique to insurgency, such as guerrilla warfare and political violence against the state. In addition, these organizations engage in acts of terrorism. They have demonstrated ties to Hezbollah, a terrorist organization with a political wing and insurgent roots, and they coerce law enforcement through targeted attacks.[13] Beyond violence, the cartels frequently compete with the government for control of the population by providing social services and jobs.[14] Focusing on the cartels' drug trafficking ignores their other activities – both legitimate and illegitimate – that might lead policymakers to classify them as insurgencies or terrorist groups, for example, if they professed a radical political or religious ideology.

The lines blur not only between crime, insurgency, and terrorism, but also between illicit and licit activity. Just as we do not assume a murderer does nothing but murder, we must not assume a trafficker only traffics. We know that the best money launderers maintain legitimate businesses to provide cover, an appearance of legitimacy, and a nice way to clean dirty money. One individual engaging in criminal violence often owns a legitimate business, simultaneously! Why spend time debating which category the sheikh mentioned by Kilcullen belongs to? None of the categories will capture the sheikh's complexity, because people do not live their lives as confined actors who never deviate from the label we so conveniently place on their dossiers. People are born and live as individuals who may, at times, participate in violence. They might get a job, open a business, and hold up a liquor store at various times in their lives. At a certain point, the category itself loses meaning, leaving policymakers, practitioners, and scholars to wrestle with the true root of violence – the conditions under which rational individuals find it in their interest to commit violence. Focusing upon the more basic foundation of sub-state violence requires a turn toward economic theory.

Interestingly, academics have long examined various forms of sub-state violence through an economic lens, but this exploration has yet to make it to mainstream approaches to violence, for two reasons. First, those studying crime, civil wars, and terrorism have produced a wealth of theories, models, and data based in social science (economics, anthropology, sociology, psychology, etc.); however, these theories have not sufficiently crossed the borders dividing the applied domains. The knowledge has not flowed into the world of national security and law enforcement policymakers and practitioners. Second, the talented academics who have taken the economic literature to studies of violence focus on one category. The work often provides an economic explanation of organized crime, an economic explanation of insurgency, or an economic explanation of terrorism. This book benefits from the previous work; however, it focuses on the application of ideas by the practitioners, and tries to forcefully highlight the continuity of violence – the blurring of the lines distinguishing crime from insurgency from terrorism.

This book seeks to break down the artificial distinctions between the treatment of crime, insurgency, and terrorism, to assert the primacy of understanding individual decision-making as the starting point for any analysis of sub-state violence, and to present scholarly analyses on the topic to practitioners and policymakers in an easily digestible form so that future responses to organized violence are better informed and more effective. We will examine the stories of Pablo Escobar, Joseph Kony, and Osama bin Laden and the violent organizations they controlled. In doing so, we will see how the attempt to divide their stories into the disciplines of organized crime, insurgency, and terrorism fails to address the central commonality between their stories. However, before turning to the stories of our three central characters, we step back from the loaded contexts in which these stories occur and introduce some foundational concepts. Our inquiry into organized violence must start with questions about what motivates human violence, in context. We will view Escobar, Kony, and bin Laden as individuals with goals and desires consistent with basic human nature and demonstrate the commonality each has with the other, as well as with you and me. We will understand the logic of violence, and therefore understand the relationship between identity and violence, as well as the counterfactuals – why violence may not occur.

Chapter 2 explores human behavior within an economic framework to reveal a science of humans choosing violence. Chapter 3 uses the story of Pablo Escobar to explore organized crime. Chapter 4 looks at civil war and insurgency through the actions of Joseph Kony and the Lord's Resistance Army. Chapter 5 examines how Osama bin Laden used terrorism as a tool to strengthen his firm and achieve his goals. Chapter 6 expands on the terrorism discussion to include a focus on how Abu Bakr al Baghdadi led the Islamic State to become a household name. Finally, Chapter 7 gets us to the "so what?" question: if we can see the unity of the different manifestations of organized violence, must we organize our counter-violence efforts differently? When beginning an analysis of organized violence with an inquiry into the human condition, the lines separating three disciplines of organized violence diminish, leaving only a spectrum of one violence.

In my own thinking about this issue, I've evolved from categories of violence to hybrid organizations. Boaz Ganor defines a hybrid terrorist organization as having two or three legs: terrorist activity, political organization, and service provision to constituents.[15] Discussions of Lebanese Hezbollah, for example, have expanded this definition to include the group's global illicit trafficking and criminal activity.[16] Despite this, analysis of the Lebanese Shia group still breaks down its activities into separate categories: insurgent against Israel, political power in Lebanon, narco-trafficker in South America, and religious terrorist group worldwide. Dividing the essential elements of the group into separate phenomena, however, limits our ability to understand, and therefore counter, the institution's managing elite.

Here I suggest a different concept – unity. There never was a difference between criminal, insurgent, and terrorist violence, so they are not now merging in our generation. If this assertion sounds bold, then keep reading. The justification comprises the content of this book. In this context, we must ask why we maintain security and law enforcement organizations designed to address distinct phenomena: drug trafficking versus weapons trafficking versus insurgents versus terrorists. The laws, policies, and institutions that counter violent threats matter. Better understanding these threats will improve our efforts to counter all visible manifestations of organized violence.

It is all too easy to dismiss the behavior of violent actors as irrational. To put this into context, we can take an extreme case – suicide terrorism. Recalling the Mahane Yehuda Market and Ben Yehuda Street bombings, we struggle to understand why people would walk into crowded marketplaces in the middle of the day and kill civilians. In trying to analyze and understand such seeming acts of barbarity, taking simple explanations such as "crazy," "brainwashed," and "drug-induced" off the table leaves us with rational actors – human beings. This book journeys to the frontiers of applied economics in order to explain how sane and rational people can walk into crowded marketplaces surrounded by children and families and detonate explosives, killing themselves and those around them. If we can observe, describe, and explain these actions, we can better deter them.

2 THE HUMAN CONDITION

"Hate Crime:" A Mass Killing at a Historic Church. A man suspected of killing nine people at the Emanuel African Methodist Episcopal Church, including a state senator, will be charged with nine counts of murder.[1]

The Atlantic, June 19, 2015

An apparent bomb blast tore through a mosque in Kuwait's capital during Friday prayers, killing at least 27 people and wounding at least 227 others, state media reported, citing a security official. ISIS claimed responsibility for what it called a suicide bombing at the Shiite-affiliated Al-Sadiq mosque.[2]

CNN, June 26, 2015

We witness evil acts in the world. Even when we can make sense of them, they are only locally explainable. For example, talking about global terrorism committed in the name of Islam does not help us understand violent acts in the United States perpetrated in the context of white supremacy. The inexplicability of violence hinders our peace of mind: if I cannot understand it, how can I be safe from it? The lack of clarity about who perpetrates violence and why also hinders our ability to deter and respond.

In this chapter we will discuss what drives human behavior and how the theory of kinship explains how individuals link together into groups or firms. But before we navigate toward clarity and meet the characters who will lead our journey, we must lay a sound foundation on which to examine organized violence. This chapter covers the principles of economic science to provide a base for analyzing organized violence. In later chapters it will become clear that criminals, insurgents, and terrorists all act in ways that we can easily comprehend using these tools. The economic lens erases, or at least blurs, the sharp distinctions between crime, insurgency, and terrorism, and clarifies the unity of the phenomena of organized violence. By illuminating similarities between the patterns of behavior in organized violence, we can achieve greater insight and improve security.

While it is important, to be sure, to understand the political, regional, or religious influences from which individuals act, this book examines and explains violence in terms of what motivates individuals to choose violence as the best option. For this approach, it is necessary to look at participants in organized violence as human beings with needs who make decisions in conditions of scarcity, and interact with others in order to satisfy these needs and meet their goals.

The foundation of human interaction rests upon the decisions individuals make about how to allocate time and other resources. Coordinating the division and distribution of resources and labor through trade gives rise to the market. Think of a market as a place where people can engage in trade. A store is certainly a market, but so is a place where people trade ideas or agree to do one thing in exchange for another. In this sense, almost any place where two or more people communicate with each other represents a market.

Within the market, entrepreneurs develop firms within which the allocation of resources is coordinated in a top-down manner by a centralized leadership. In a market with limited resources, the firms compete with each other. If the stakes are high enough and violence promises a benefit, the firms will compete violently. As firms grow, entrepreneurs are forced to engage in governance, collecting rents and coercing compliance. Whether it is a cupcake company in Washington, DC, Pablo Escobar's international drug cartel, Joseph Kony's Lord's Resistance Army, or bin Laden's Al Qaeda network, we can see all organized human activity as a story of individuals, goods, collective action, rules, enforcement, markets, and competition.

My good friend and colleague at Georgetown University, a well-known political scientist, once commented, with a tone of concession, "You economists are right – it is all about the money." This is amusing, because economists do not actually think this way. Economics is often misunderstood as the study of money and its exchange. In fact, the study of economics is, at its root, a scientific story of human behavior, about how humans behave and why. In other words, economics is the study of individuals making decisions in conditions of scarcity. By beginning our story with an examination of what drives human behavior, we will begin to see how the distinct categories of organized violence easily adhere to rules of behavior derived from economic theory. In later chapters, we will test this theory with empirical observations.

Human Behavior

Let's begin with Adam Smith, whose 1776 edition of *An Inquiry into the Nature and Causes of the Wealth of Nations* has formed the core text of economics for two-and-a-half centuries. In *The Wealth of Nations*, Adam Smith argues that humans demonstrate a unique trait in their ability to engage in trade and, thereby, in the coordination of a division of their labor. The ability to divide labor expands the overall wealth for those who can engage in trade, as each individual no longer has to do everything. To eat, one does not need to farm but can, instead, repair timepieces and pay the farmer. The significant and heroic idea here in these early days of behavioral science is Smith's articulation of the fundamental and universal aspect of all human nature. Smith writes:

> This division of labour, from which so many advantages are derived, is not originally the effect of any human wisdom, which foresees and intends that general opulence to which it gives occasion. It is the necessary, though very slow and gradual, consequence of a certain propensity in human nature which has in view no such extensive utility; the propensity to truck, barter, and exchange one thing for another.

The concept of the economic agent who makes decisions based on self-interest is inherent in the classical economist's approach to understanding almost everything. Voluntary trade leaves both parties in a transaction better off than they were before. A party to the trade may not have everything he or she wants, but they gain something of value – otherwise, they would not have engaged in the trade. If trade did not leave both parties better off, the ability to trade, barter, and exchange would be ignored in favor of personal efforts to obtain all necessities in life by oneself.

Individuals who come into the world equal in their potential will specialize in particular fields. In doing so, individuals develop separate identities and ways of acting in and viewing the world. Consider a worldview where the way that people act or think is not a product of differences in their essential identity. In this worldview, fundamental human nature transcends race, religion, culture, geography, and historical placement. The differences we discern in this worldview are the product of exposure to the human propensity to truck, barter, and exchange, and the subsequent specialization that these motivations impose. Smith writes:

> The difference of natural talents in different men is, in reality, much less than we are aware of; and the very different genius which appears to distinguish men of different professions, when grown up to maturity, is not upon many occasions so much the cause, as the effect of the division of labour. The difference between the most dissimilar characters, between a philosopher and a common street porter, for example, seems to arise not so much from nature, as from habit, custom, and education. When they came into the world, and for the first six or eight years of their existence, they were perhaps, very much alike, and neither their parents nor playfellows could perceive any remarkable difference. About that age, or soon after, they come to be employed in very different occupations. The difference of talents comes then to be taken notice of, and widens by degrees, till at last the vanity of the philosopher is willing to acknowledge scarce any resemblance. But without the disposition to truck, barter, and exchange, every man must have procured to himself every necessary and conveniency of life which he wanted. All must have had the same duties to perform, and the same work to do, and there could have been no such difference of employment as could alone give occasion to any great difference of talents.

The human tendency to trade gives rise to the market, the place where individuals trade and interact, not the other way around. As individuals become wealthier through trade, their continued interaction with the market increases the overall wealth of the market. Additionally, the market's size impacts wealth. Division of labor between 200 people, for example, creates greater opportunity than the division of labor between two people. Trade between a watchmaker and a farmer increases the wealth of each; while one repairs watches, the other grows vegetables, and both have timekeeping devices and vegetables to eat. But trade among 200 people provides more variety of goods in the marketplace and on the dinner table.

Modeling Human Behavior

To illuminate and clarify the concepts of human nature and the benefit of trade, behavioral scientists build models. How do we model this? Economists tend to apply these concepts with a discussion of the simplest example of an economy – the story of Robinson Crusoe, his island, and his trading partner Friday.

Daniel Defoe's *Robinson Crusoe* allows us to start with a simple story, of one person and two goods, and increase complexity from there. The first economic concept to learn is the idea of production possibility, the range that defines the greatest productive output from a combination of activities. To illustrate this fundamental idea of a production possibility, we can take Daniel Defoe's hypothetical scenario where a man, Crusoe, is alone on an island. Crusoe has two possible pursuits: he can harvest bananas, or he can fish. Alternatively, he can allocate his time to some combination of these two acts. This island has a remarkable consistency in its bounty, so Crusoe is guaranteed to gather a certain number of bananas or fish per day based upon the labor hours he allocates to each task. If he devotes all of his time to gathering bananas, he will harvest 24 bananas by the end of the day, but no fish. If he devotes all of his time to fishing, he will catch 12 fish by the end of the day, but he will harvest no bananas. If he splits his time, he will have some combination of the two.

Crusoe's preferences determine his choices – that is, whether to climb trees for bananas or to go fishing. In this example, we can see Crusoe's preferences, given his constraints, at least as they relate to bananas, fish, and labor hours. More generally, this concept conveys both goals and constraints. If we can understand an individual's goals and constraints, we can go a long way toward understanding and predicting that individual's behavior – a nice step toward understanding decisions resulting in violence.

We often hear of scarcity in the central narrative around wars and other conflicts: fighting over access to water or fishing, for instance. In our example, Crusoe cannot gather bananas and fish at the same time. He must choose to do one or the other. When Crusoe chooses to spend his time harvesting bananas, he is leaving fish in the sea that represent the opportunity cost of his choice. We can think of cost as the next-best option not chosen. In our case, since Crusoe can only choose between two commodities, he chooses fish at the cost of bananas, or bananas at the cost of fish. When Crusoe makes the choice to either gather fish or bananas, he makes a definitive choice as to his expected utility from this action; this is called a revealed preference.

As social scientists, we must highlight two key terms from this discussion: revealed preferences and expected benefits. We know someone's preferences when these preferences are "revealed" to us through their behavior and actions. We observed Crusoe's choice; we did not ask him to state it. In addition, an individual makes decisions based upon expected outcomes, sometimes referred to in academic literature as "rational expectations." We have an expected benefit in mind when we take an action. When Crusoe makes a choice to invest an hour harvesting bananas, he expects to gain a certain amount of utility from that activity. He might expect that when he goes to eat the banana later that it will taste good, give him the nutrients he needs, and not make him sick. But because we do not know the future, every choice carries risks. We can only create an expectation of the utility we will gain from an action based on probabilities. In a more realistic scenario, Crusoe would have to contend with the risk that he would not catch any fish, or that there would be no ripe bananas. Inherent risks in any particular action will affect an individual's expected utility, affecting the individual's subsequent choices. If Crusoe does not believe that he will catch any fish if he goes out today, he will probably choose to harvest bananas instead.

We can start to understand criminal acts through this economic analysis. The decision to rob a liquor store assumes a probability and an outcome. In the Crusoe example, in order to make inferences about his preferences from observed behavior, we need to make assumptions about the maximum possible output he can achieve. If we apply this economic perspective to the phenomenon of violence, we understand that we have to make assumptions about people's goals; that is, why did they decide to engage in violence? Economists tend to prefer to use revealed preferences to make those assumptions explicit. We will spend much more time on this in later chapters, but for now the key concept to introduce is that all human acts, violent or not, are influenced by expectations of a desired outcome.

To increase wealth in an economy (visualize expansion of the range of possible production), economists argue that we must increase the input of labor and/or capital, and/or advance technological methods.[3] To expand his wealth, Crusoe can work more hours. If he had previously been working 12 hours each day, he can decide to work 15 hours a day. In this case, Crusoe has expanded his possible production by increasing the input of labor. Now imagine that Crusoe brings a second identical fishing rod when he goes fishing, wielding one in each hand. By doubling the capital employed, Crusoe can increase the number of fish he catches. In this case, Crusoe has expanded his possible production by increasing the capital he has available. Finally, let's give Crusoe credit for inventing a new, more efficient method of catching fish or harvesting bananas. Perhaps he has fashioned a net that allows him to catch 18 fish a day instead of the 12 he caught with a rod. Or perhaps he builds a tool that allows him to gather bananas more quickly, such as an extended hook, so he can collect 50 percent more in a day. By devising new, technologically improved methods to complete his work, he increases his *wealth* in terms of products he values and his ability to produce them.

Leaving the island for a moment, we can see that this dynamic is also at work in the production of border security. The US Border Patrol, which is tasked with producing border security in the same way that Crusoe has tasked himself with producing fish or bananas, can increase its production of security in a couple of ways. It can increase the number of hours border agents work by hiring more agents or lengthening the workday. The Border Patrol can also expand the use of cameras or drones to monitor the border, and thus by increasing capital allow one border agent to produce more security for each hour worked. Finally, the Border Patrol could also develop and deploy new sensors capable of covering more area per sensor, and thus increase the productivity of border agent hours by improving technological tools. Whether looking at fishermen, illicit drug cartels, or law enforcement providing public safety and security, the production of goods and services can be understood in terms of the inputs of labor, capital, and technology.

Having established the basic parameters for the simplest economy, that of one person and two commodities, we now add a new dynamic – trade. What happens to Crusoe if another person, whom we will call Friday, appears on the island? We know that humans seek to barter and trade with other humans to better their situation. If we placed a wild boar on the island, Crusoe would likely hunt the boar and roast it for dinner, but it would be absurd to posit that Crusoe would hunt Friday and roast him for dinner. Why is that?

Crusoe does not hunt Friday but teams up with him because he expects trading with Friday will increase his chances of survival. Friday's arrival results in the presence of two people on the island capable of production – harvesting and fishing. In the absence of the ability to barter in this case, another human would be, at best, a non-issue; but he could also, perhaps, present a problem, as scarcity of food might cause competition and lead to violence. However, Crusoe and Friday are humans and are differentiated from other animals by their innate understanding of the benefits of trade and cooperation. So when the weaver of this fictional tale, Defoe, illustrates the choice of cooperation and not conflict between the two, we as readers readily accept the progression of the story. In all my years of telling this story at Georgetown University, never once did a student object with the claim that Crusoe or Friday surely would have preferred a week's worth of good human steak over long-term cooperation. Certainly, some might suggest constraints on human behavior that make cooperation difficult or impossible. In fact, much of the organized violence we witness in the world will be explained in terms of rules that make cooperation difficult. This I develop in later chapters. For now, I ask you to simply accept the tendency to seek trade pervades humanity.

The decision to trade – to collaboratively establish a market – does not come from benevolence or empathy. Trade benefits all parties involved (provided it is voluntary). Trade is not zero-sum; both sides must expect to increase wealth or utility from the exchange, thereby benefiting all parties involved. This helps explain an individual's natural inclination to trade. For example, Crusoe may value bananas more than fish, so he will attempt to trade a certain amount of fish to Friday for a certain amount of bananas. Friday will accept or decline the trade based on two factors: his preferences for bananas and fish, and the relative scarcities of these two goods. Once a trade is accepted, *both* parties will be better off because each has exchanged something they value less for something they value more. Since both sides are better off after the exchange, they are collectively and individually wealthier than if they had not traded.

Economic growth depends upon the size of the available market, and trade addresses scarcity. Rather than being limited to 24 person-hours per day, which one can allocate to either labor or leisure, the island's economy now has 48 potential hours of harvesting per day. Instead of one individual harvesting or working on developing technological breakthroughs, there are two individuals with ideas, experiences, and the opportunity to collaborate on technological innovation. The economy of the island has grown because its inputs to production – labor, capital, and technology – increased.

Crusoe's decision to trade with Friday also expands wealth by enabling a division of labor. Originally, Crusoe had to both catch fish and harvest bananas himself. Each time he switched between the two tasks he paid a transition cost in lost productivity. He would have to put away the canoe and fishing rod before going out to harvest bananas. With the ability to trade with Friday, Crusoe can now minimize these costs and still receive his optimum balance of bananas and fish.

Moreover, by enabling a division of labor, trade allows Crusoe to specialize in fishing, hone his skills, and expand the amount of fish he can catch each hour. By addressing scarcity and enabling the division and specialization of labor, trade expands the wealth of the economy as well as that of the individuals who contribute to it. This is the principle of comparative advantage – the ability of an individual to carry out a particular economic activity more efficiently than others. If Crusoe is better at fishing and therefore has a comparative advantage in fishing, while Friday has a comparative advantage in harvesting, they will allocate their labor hours accordingly, and will both have more bananas and more fish than they would have had otherwise. In a criminal organization, comparative advantage is at play as well. Some people, for example, may be better at bookkeeping while others are better at committing violence; if an organization allows people to specialize in different tasks, the organization will achieve greater gains.

We see the role of specialization in the debate over the use of the US Marine Corps to conduct counterinsurgency operations in Iraq and Afghanistan since 2003. Some have argued that the Marine Corps has become accustomed to fighting for long periods on land, losing some of its amphibious capabilities. Defense Secretary Robert Gates voiced such an opinion in a speech at a Navy League Sea-Air-Space exposition.[4] While noting that the Marines had been a "game-changer" in Iraq and elsewhere, he stated, "For years now, the Corps has been acting as essentially a second land army. As General Conway has noted, there are young, battle-hardened Marines with multiple combat tours who have spent little time inside of a ship, much less practicing hitting a beach."[5] Secretary Gates continued, "We must always be mindful of why America built and has maintained a Navy, Marine Corps, and Coast Guard." This is an argument about specialization. The marine splitting his time between training for counterinsurgency and amphibious assault faces the same transition costs and lack of development of expertise as Crusoe does when he switches between harvesting bananas and fishing.

Where Violence Comes From

We have used the simple story of trade and labor division common among economists to start our conversation, but so far we have only discussed peaceful cooperation and trade. Where do violence and conflict come from? Economists have addressed this question. Jack Hirshleifer, for example, develops a theory of conflict in "The Bioeconomic Causes of War." His fundamental contribution is that the final causes of war are the same as the causes of peace: those that promote survival in conditions of scarcity.[6] Thus, if Friday has a good that he is unwilling to trade with Crusoe but which Crusoe needs to survive, hence creating a condition of scarcity, Crusoe may use violence to take the good. Crusoe's violence is not an irrational break from economic calculation of his preferences, but merely a different decision of how to act based on the result of those calculations. Although both Crusoe and Friday want to maximize their own incomes, Hirshleifer points out that, because war is costly and can damage the value of the sought-after goods, there is always the option for collaboration over war. The potential settlement

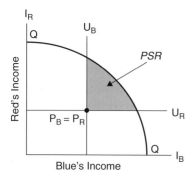

Figure I Potential settlement region: moderate complementarity, agreed perceptions.[9]

region – shaded in Figure I – demonstrates the range of "possible peaceful arrangements that both sides perceive as yielding a better outcome than war."[7] As long as both sides can accurately assess the potential outcomes for either collaboration or combat, "peace always has the edge on war."[8]

Contingent causes like opportunity, preference, and perception, however, determine how both sides assess their outcomes, and therefore determine when wars take place. Crusoe will not use violence if he does not perceive himself as having an opportunity to be successful, or if he believes that trade is more likely to promote his preferences.

Individuals will choose violence or cooperation depending on how each contributes to achieving goals. Hirshleifer also identifies proximate causes of war as expected benefit and cost, confidence of success, the existence of benevolence or malevolence, and if cooperation expands economic opportunity. The fundamentals of war and peace thus boil down to opportunities, perceptions, and preferences.

Our example of Crusoe needing an object that Friday is unwilling to trade, and thus resorting to violence, only addresses individual violence. In order to understand competition and war between groups, as opposed to individual violence, we need to think about collective action and kinship.

Kinship and Radicalization

To understand kinship, let us remove Crusoe and Friday from the island. Imagine that they have been rescued and survive, and now live in the same town where Friday reunites with his family. Back with his family, Friday no longer uses the skills he developed on the island to feed only himself. He now shares his wealth with his family. Why does he do so if economic theory tells us humans are self-interested?

He does so because, according to Adam Smith, humans are biologically programmed to promote the self-preservation of our kin and the survival of our species:

> Self-preservation, and the propagation of the species, are the great ends which nature seems to have proposed in the formation of all animals ... But ... it has not been entrusted to the slow and uncertain determinations of our reason, to find out the proper means of bringing them about. Nature has directed us ... by immediate and original instincts. Hunger, thirst, the passion which unites the two sexes, the love of pleasure, and the dread of pain, prompt us to apply those means for their own sakes, and without any consideration of their tendency to those beneficent ends which the great Director of nature intended to produce by them.[10]

In addition to fulfilling a biological need, kinship eases transaction costs. For example, Friday's kinship with his family establishes a fundamental trust that allows his children to rely upon him to provide food rather than hedge against the risk that he will simply abandon them to their fates. This allows Friday's children to focus on their education and their own pursuits, encouraging further economic development.

Kinship does not have to be understood in biological terms. Friday's bonds with non-familial members of his village serve as a form of fictive kinship, which also eases transaction costs. In decreasing transaction costs, kinship also expands the potential market, thereby increasing wealth. Rather than isolated individuals crying out in the wilderness, we get communities in which individuals exercise the core human tendency to truck, barter, and exchange identified by Smith, sometimes called the affiliative instinct.

This reflex to affiliate relates back to fundamental human nature, the propensity to trade, and the importance of market size. In a competitive world, I need to know who supports me and my people, and who opposes us. In a world of scarcity – the world we inhabit – everyone cannot have everything. So individuals divide into "us" and "them" and work to ensure survival for self and kin. Sometimes "kin" refers to blood relatives but sometimes to other definitions of "us."

To understand the power of non-biological kinship and the affiliative instinct, take, for example, prison gangs. Prison populations often break down into gangs along racial lines. Part of the reason for this is that individuals enter prisons with few or no kinship ties to other prisoners, but still have a need for the support of others to survive. In order to find protection from looting and physical violence, prisoners quickly affiliate with an established group.[11]

Since trust develops over time, and a new inmate needs protection immediately, initial affiliation occurs at the most basic level – with the physically obvious traits of ethnicity such as skin color. Division into groups is easily established by skin color: I have found my people, because they look like me.[12] These initial bonds then grow over time. By affiliating by physical appearance, a fictive kinship is established that requires few interactions to develop the initial bonds of trust. Think about walking into a crowded room of strangers; you immediately look for "your people," asking yourself, "Who do I know here, or who do I have something in common with – who are my people?" We participate in the same phenomenon as the individual prisoners seeking a group: "Who do I know? Who knows me? Who can I trust?"

David Skarbek identifies this dynamic in his discussion of prison gangs, noting how authorities have sought to utilize supply-side solutions, identifying high-risk individuals and segregating them from the general population. These efforts typically have little effect because gangs arise out of the existence of a market and the gang's rules provide governance within that market. He writes, "This strategy will only be effective … if supply-side factors drive gang activity entirely. If violence serves an end – such as resolving a drug debt or establishing property rights – then removing the people who participate in violence does not remove the underlying dispute that gives rise to violence. The unmet need for governance still exists."[13]

Indeed, as Skarbek points out, supply-side efforts have a dismal record in combating prison gangs: "A former warden with 30 years of corrections experience writes, 'If a gang leader is neutralized by transfer or long-term lockup, the group names new leadership; like corrections officials they are prepared for succession.' Likewise a Department of Justice survey concluded that isolating gang leaders simply leaves a void for new leaders to emerge and fails to eliminate gangs. Breaking up one gang opens the door for another to form or for young members to step into leadership roles."[14]

The reason behind this failure is that prison gangs are a product of a market. When changes in the market cause an increase in the prison population, and competitive groups begin to form and accumulate power within that population, prisoners must join groups, usually selected by race or other outwardly identifiable traits, in order to find security – another example of the kinship principle. We will see similar market dynamics in the upcoming chapters in our examination of Pablo Escobar, Osama bin Laden, and Abu Bakr al Baghdadi. Skarbek documents how gangs arose in American prisons following and in response to a degradation of prison norms, driven in part by rising incarceration levels and greater diversity of prisoners, in order to maintain governance and enable the support structures necessary for the continuation of markets within the prison. Tellingly, just as Al Qaeda and other terrorist movements had members produce paperwork on their recruits and activities due to bureaucratic needs within a competitive labor market, so do prison gangs. Skarbek writes: "Many gangs have elaborate written constitutions that guide their operations."[15] Prison gangs' leaders also maintain detailed lists of members as well as new prisoners' identities, using them to confirm that people are who they say they are and to identify who ought to be punished.

Kinship can also explain behaviors that would otherwise seem irrational. Such behaviors are often a result of the production of social kinship, rather than irrationality. Let's examine the issue of radicalization in prison and Islamist terrorism. Islam promises a social kinship, and, as we have seen, kinship is important in prison. If the individuals responsible for Islamic religious practice in a prison subscribe to a version that accepts or promotes violence, that conversion into the kinship group will often imply or require a responsibility to also support violence. As Peter Neumann notes in his report on prison radicalization, many countries have sought to address the risk of prison radicalization by institutionalizing and promoting professionalized prison imams.[16] Yet in many countries, and in particular in the non-Western countries with the most severe prison radicalization problems, the provision of Muslim services often remains the province of extremist inmates.[17]

The root of the radicalization, in this example, is not an irrational violence based in Islamic teachings, but the need for kinship and the economic benefits it brings. By affiliating with the violence-embracing

Which came first, the violence or the religion?

But what made this kinship violent?

group, one might find his "in" group, a sense of belonging, safety, and protection from others. The same preferences that promote peace and development in one context act upon human nature differently in another to promote conflict and violence. The issue in prisons prone to violent extremism is that individuals who perceive opportunities for membership and belonging in a Muslim group pass through routes controlled by individuals who promote violence. Someone not attuned to the economics of affiliation might view this as a story about Islam, but in fact this is a story of self-preservation in which Islam-as-Islam plays a secondary role to universal elements of human interaction, survival, and wealth. Failing to understand this distinction can lead to problems for policy development and implementation. In the coming chapters, we will see versions of this story repeated across regions, religions, ethnicities, and categories of violence.

The creation of groups does not end scarcity, and inter-group competition requires effort to govern as well. We see the tendency to affiliate, to divide into "us" and "them," but we can face challenges and competition and scarcity even within "our" group. While a family may almost innately know its internal division of labor, a larger grouping is less likely to be able to rely on such innate ties. The ties across larger groups necessitate some form of rules and enforcement, leading to the creation of a "firm" and presenting opportunities for entrepreneurs.

Firms

In 1937, Ronald Coase proposed that, where the transaction costs in negotiating contracts between individuals are high, entrepreneurs will seek to establish firms in which the direction of the individual replaces negotiated market transactions.[18] Bringing more activities under the umbrella of the firm can reduce costs of determining and negotiating price and therefore increase profits.[19] These firms are tightly bound by a form of kinship among their members. These market concepts, firm and entrepreneur, apply across commercial and governance domains of human interaction. The theory of contract enforcement applies equally well in illicit economies as it does in licit economies. If a firm that engages in illegal activities has outsourced a certain function, and that subcontractor fails to perform as expected (the contract is breached), the illicit firm does not have recourse to government-sponsored enforcement of civil law. Drug traffickers cannot sue distributors in state courts, for example. Therefore, firms decrease contract costs and avoid the complications of contract enforcement through kinship or fictive kinship, and illicit repression. If it keeps activities within the firm, and members of the firm are family or feel as if they are family, contract violations diminish and collective action is sustained.

One way that firms motivate loyalty is through the promise of repeated exchange. In a repeated exchange (or, as game theorists say, a repeated game), incentives change because of the dimension of a time horizon. In a classic example (perhaps unkind to auto mechanics), the car of a local resident will get a better price for a repair than a tourist's because the mechanic has an incentive to entice the local customer to return for future services. She will never see the tourist again, so must maximize profit on the first visit. The lifetime value of the repeat customer far exceeds that of the one-time customer. In the context of violence, if there is an enduring marketplace for violence and coercion, a firm can incentivize its members to engage in that marketplace. On the other hand, if the market is volatile and might not exist for an extended period of time, a member might choose not to participate.

While the firm usually offers the promise of expanded wealth, the promise of tight bonds of kinship – family-style relationships – can often improve the efficiency of recruiting and retaining works in violence. Conversely, a leader sometimes gains efficiency by avoiding the restrictions of the strong bonds of kinship on the leader's future direction of the firm within a market. When a leader faces low transaction costs in hiring workers to engage in violence, she may prefer to engage in short-term, or one-time, games, buying the needed services from others.[20]

Indeed, sometimes a decentralized network of individuals is more powerful because it is resilient to disruption. A decentralized network finds power in its ability to cross boundaries and borders. Without a leader to rely upon, individual participants (nodes) in the network need not fear losing the leader.

Having introduced the concepts of kinship and the firm, we can now return to Hirshleifer's theory of violence and see the roots of inter-group and inter-state violence. These wars are merely the expression of the same competitive forces in a context of scarcity that we examined with the example of Crusoe and Friday fighting over a good required for survival. The difference is that, in the Crusoe example, we spoke of individuals in violent competition. In Hirshleifer's theory, we begin to view groups of people as firms. For example, states are firms, and competition between states defines what we traditionally consider to be war. At the sub-state level, the firms may be criminal enterprises, insurgent organizations, or terrorist networks. A simplistic separation between these types of firms is illusory and leads to confusion, while clarity comes from seeing the unity of the market dynamics.

While violent competition between firms defines the traditional concept of war, we must acknowledge that competition – and violent competition – occurs at all levels of human interaction. Stathis Kalyvas argues that this messy combination of competing forces that emerges in wars is too often reduced to a single master cleavage, such as a territorial disagreement or ideological dispute.[21] For Kalyvas, individuals in conflict respond to the micro-foundation or more individualized and local disputes, resulting in the ambiguous and complex mixture of motivations, alliances, and goals that define violent conflict.[22] Kalyvas concludes that the study of civil war can neither focus solely on the micro-level, as individual private violence is constrained by the opportunities presented by the master cleavage, nor on the master cleavage alone, without missing the critical importance of local disputes.

Bandits and Governors

We have now seen how individuals seek to trade with each other; why, in certain circumstances, they may opt for violence rather than trade; and how kinship, real and created, links the actions of individuals together into groups or firms. However, we have yet to consider the issues of governance in detail. If we create a group of ten people, governance may not be difficult, but we now must address the collective actions of a large group. Mancur Olson's story of roving and stationary bandits provides a useful starting point to understand how individuals' decisions lead to governance by sub-state actors.[23]

The roving bandit represents a figure similar to the image of an isolated town plagued by bands of outlaws.[24] The 1964 Clint Eastwood movie *A Fistful of Dollars* presents a classic example. The town of San Miguel is caught between bandits known as the Rojo brothers and the family of the local sheriff. In Olson's telling of the story, the roving bandits (i.e. the Rojo brothers) randomly take at will from the population. The roving bandit presents an economic problem for the development of wealth in a society. When people expect that increasing their wealth may consequently lead to their losing their livelihood in an encounter with a roving bandit, they produce and invest less because they become more pessimistic about their future.[25] For example, a farmer who believes that his crops will be stolen will not build a new irrigation system or purchase fertilizer to increase his yield. The threat of crime causes the farmer to produce less, which makes both him, and society as a whole, less wealthy. Instead of developing an expertise and specializing in it, individuals will focus on subsistence farming to avoid the risk of losing investment to a roving bandit. As a result, they experience little accumulation of wealth and trade, leading to poor economic growth.

This roving status also presents an economic problem for the bandit. The decline in society's wealth diminishes the available wealth from which he can steal. Over time, a roving bandit will realize that he is earning less than he could if his behavior did not discourage economic growth. Therefore, a utility-maximizing bandit will, if possible, opt to become a *stationary* bandit.

A stationary bandit is a person, such as a ruler or monarch – or, in *A Fistful of Dollars*, Clint Eastwood's character – who provides order and protection from roving bandits in exchange for some sort of a benefit – thought of as a tax. The key difference between a stationary bandit and a roving bandit is the consistency and predictability of the "theft" occurring. While a roving bandit steals as much as he desires whenever he desires, a stationary bandit standardizes what he takes and when he takes it. Instead of stealing randomly from the citizenry, he steals predictably through what we might call taxation. In exchange for paying tax to the stationary bandit, the local population purchases protection from roving bandits. In this sense, we can see that governance is also a competitive market in which individuals buy and sell security and other public goods in exchange for wealth and a set of freedoms.

When a roving bandit stops roving and fashions herself a ruler, her wealth and the wealth of the society she rules become intertwined. By regulating the transfer of wealth from the citizen to the bandit/ruler, the ruler provides predictability in the loss of wealth. This predictability gives the population incentives to invest and to produce, as the population will be able to enjoy the fruits of their additional labor without fear that their extra productivity will be robbed from them.

This virtuous cycle, however, will only take place if the ruler is able to displace other bandits who would threaten the population she seeks to tax. If the population is still targeted by other roving bandits to the point that the population does not gain from investing, they will not produce more and will be disinclined to support the ruler. The ruler must thus provide collective security for his population in exchange for some amount of wealth.

Once a bandit-cum-ruler has identified a population to steal from through taxes, he must determine the appropriate amount to steal. If he steals too much, he will dissuade the population from producing and jeopardize their loyalty; conversely, if he steals too little, he will not maximize his personal benefit. Let's call the tax *rate* the percentage that he appropriates from an individual, and the tax *level* the amount of money or goods yielded by the individual tax rate. For example, if an individual earns $100 a year and his tax rate is 20 percent, then his tax level would be $20. The revenue-maximizing tax rate is determined by individual preferences of the population, but it is the rate at which the tax level is maximized for the ruler. We can imagine a tax rate so high that people work less, decreasing the tax level or income for the ruler. So the optimum tax rate is one that is neither too high nor too low, keeping people incentivized to work and the ruler interested in protecting and providing other public goods.

The ruler's self-interest also encourages him to provide public goods based on two foundations. First, as discussed above, the ruler must provide collective security for the population in order for them to be willing to invest enough to advance beyond subsistence production and grow the economy. We examined this in terms of protection from other bandits, say through the recruiting, training, and paying of an army or police force. However, it also applies to security from natural disasters. A ruler might invest in irrigation to remedy the risk of drought if that risk discouraged investment and economic growth. Second, by investing in public goods, the ruler can increase the tax base and thus expand their wealth. For example, if a ruler builds a road between an area of production and an area of commerce, people will trade more freely. This investment by the ruler, therefore, grows the economy and the taxable wealth. While the ruler may have paid $100 for the road to be built, he may take in an additional $500 of tax revenue over 12 months because of this infrastructure investment. From this perspective, the provision of public goods is not merely a societal good or an act of altruism, but a utility-maximizing act.

However, the ruler will stop providing public goods when the last dollar spent on a public good yields less than a dollar of additional tax revenue. The people might benefit immensely from a bridge crossing a stream into town, but if the benefit does not yield enough tax revenue to more than offset the cost of building the bridge, the ruler will be disinclined to build the bridge. In a functioning free market, an entrepreneur could invest in the bridge, and charge a toll, if he believed he would make a profit that exceeded his opportunity cost. This is a crucial point: it is not enough for an investment to make a profit; the profit from the venture has to exceed the next best alternative investment. Even if the entrepreneur earned a profit from the bridge, it would be an economic loss if he would earn more money building a mill or opening a store.

Olson's concept of roving and stationary bandits challenges us to consider governance and how regime types manage the bargain between ruler and individual. Does the ruler have that "encompassing interest" in the well-being of the population? Is he incentivized to facilitate wealth creation and happiness? These questions determine outcomes more than the way in which the ruler comes to power. Augusto Pinochet stole power in 1973 but led Chile to increasing prosperity and freedom. Lee Kuan Yew of Singapore also ruled with a firm fist but is credited with bringing prosperity to Singapore. Both leaders ended up bringing wealth and prosperity to large segments of their populations, regardless of their motives. Even if one were to ascribe the motive of narcissistic greed to each, we see that the encompassing interest in the populations led to policies beneficial to many people.

Policymakers and analysts must exercise care when using the terms "government" and "governance." We will be dealing with governance, referring to the autocrat exercising the stationary bandit role and function. That person may be democratically elected in a hyper-local sense, or the beneficiary of superior skill in matters of coercion and wealth. Regardless of the form of selection, we want to look at population centers and identify the individuals and institutions of governance. Mullah Mohammed Omar governed the members of the Taliban as a so-called spiritual leader, but many individuals who self-identify as Taliban may have no idea who he is, what he stands for, or

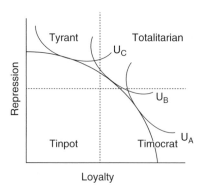

Figure 2 Typology of dictatorships.[27]

even care; they identify as Taliban because of local rulers far removed from Mullah Omar.

Goals and constraints dictate the behaviors of those who govern just as they do for other individuals. Not all rulers face the same constraints, have the same capabilities, or share the same preferences. Wintrobe outlines how state structure affects optimal choices, comparing four types of autocrats: the Tyrant, the Totalitarian, the Tinpot, and the Timocrat (Figure 2).[26] Each of these types of autocrats varies on two dimensions: loyalty and repression. Loyalty refers to the extent that the autocrat can ensure the support of those he rules over. Repression, conversely, refers to the ability of the autocrat to control those he rules over. Each type of autocrat must apply a mixture of loyalty and repression in the governed population in order to survive. No autocrat, for example, has sufficient material resources to ensure universal loyalty among all of his subjects. Likewise, no autocrat, however brutal, can rely on repression alone, since he must buy the loyalty of at least some of his subjects to ensure the repression of the rest. Therefore, an autocrat must rule with a mixture of repression and loyalty – and bases the choice on individual preferences and constraints.

Leaders of organized criminal networks, such as crime "families," or kinship groups, use this mixture of repression and loyalty to further their criminal activities. Organized crime groups appear across domains, regardless of the contraband being trafficked. Looking at individual behaviors and collective action through the economist's lens, we are able to understand why this occurs.

This phenomenon is well illustrated in the opening scene of *The Godfather*, as discussed in Chapter 1. When Bonasera comes to Vito asking him to murder the boys who attacked his daughter, the Don requests Bonasera's loyalty and a future service in exchange for violence. Vito, like any leader, governs through repression and loyalty. The exchange between him and Bonasera leaves the undertaker indebted to Vito – an opportunity for the Don to both earn his support as well as exercise some level of control over his actions. We also see Vito strike the chord of Bonasera's affiliative instinct, reminding him of their kinship ties. Bonasera has two choices: act within the legal system that he perceives as having failed him, or ally with someone with strong kinship ties offering him the good he seeks – justice. Kinship and created families, such as a crime network, encourage loyalty and trust as well as decrease transaction costs. As the ruler of a large group of criminals, one might want to employ the concept of family to expand loyalty. Of course, violence might be needed to punish defectors, enforce contracts, and deter further defections.

These issues are hardly unique to our fictional example, and we will see similar transactions in the upcoming discussions on organized crime, insurgency, and terrorism. Even in free societies with balanced powers, coercion is required to pay taxes, enforce contracts, and enforce speed limits and other laws. Governance of groups of people, regardless of the context, requires effective application of coercive powers as well as the provisioning of benefits. Douglass North's reference to "rents" and "coercion" and Ron Wintrobe's discussion of "loyalty" and "repression" really describe the same phenomena.[28]

I often talk to my students about how we might form a group to take over, by force if needed, a section of the city. As the leader, I would need to convince each of them, the group of 18 economic actors – rational and self-interested – that their best interests would be served in joining me. I could promise them a share of the wealth we would reap if successful. But given uncertainty, I would need to convince them of a high probability of success (I usually lose them here). I can also try to coerce them to join me, perhaps by giving a C to students who defect. Finally, I might appeal to our shared identity: how the Georgetown community has a common bond and we must certainly stick together given the perceived threat from the other universities in the area. If successful in this role as political entrepreneur, I can capitalize on the individual goals and constraints of each individual student to create collective action to engage in organized violence in order to achieve my interests – whether those interests are wealth, power, or revenge.

In the above example, it is easy to see how economic science gives us the ability to dissect and analyze individuals' actions. In this book, we use this approach to understand organized violence.

Having examined the role of governance, we must now return to the decisions of individuals, the first concept in our telling the story of human interaction. Often when scholars, policymakers, and practitioners discuss issues of governance or even competition between firms, they neglect or do not understand the foundations of human behavior. As Daniel Byman and Kenneth Pollack have argued, the tendency of scholars to ignore the role of individuals has limited the ability of political scientists to account for variation and accurately analyze political events.[29] Indeed, if Kalyvas is correct about the nature of conflict being an amalgam of individual, local, and national conflicts, little can be explained without moving between the macro-level of governance and competing firms and the individual level. In the end, these levels are inseparable. No theory of organized violence can have explanatory power without the behavioral and social science foundations. Without understanding human behavior in context, we do not understand violence. When we don't understand, we find cognitive ease associating action with identity and motivation, and sticking labels on the perpetrators.

We have now come full-circle, from the individual decision over how to divide resources, to the development of firms based on kinship, to the use of public goods and coercion to exercise governance, to the individual's decision to engage in acts of violence. In this chapter, we have discussed both the basics of economic theory as well as how economics contributes to the study of conflict. We have learned the elements of a market by looking at the simplest economy of one individual choosing between producing two goods. Furthermore, we have applied economic theory to explain how conflicts occur, how collective action takes place, and how governance arises from self-interested individuals. We have also described how rulers use loyalty and repression to bolster their leadership, or how they fail to do so and precipitate their own fall. In the next chapters, we will delve into the specific applications of these lessons to organized crime, insurgency, and terrorism, as well as draw out the lessons for policymakers and practitioners from the economic constants across forms of sub-state violence.

3 ORGANIZED CRIME

BONASERA: *I ask for justice.*
DON CORLEONE: *That is not justice. Your daughter is still alive.*
BONASERA: *Let them suffer then, as she suffers. How much
shall I pay you?*
DON CORLEONE: *Bonasera, Bonasera. What have I ever done to
make you treat me so disrespectfully? If you'd come to me in
friendship, then this scum that wounded your daughter would
be suffering this very day. And if by chance an honest man like
yourself should make enemies, then they would become my
enemies. And then they would fear you.*
BONASERA: *Be my friend – Godfather. [The Don shrugs. Bonasera
bows toward the Don and kisses the Don's hand.]*
DON CORLEONE: *Good. Someday, and that day may never come,
I'll call upon you to do a service for me. But until that day –
accept this justice as a gift on my daughter's wedding day.*
BONASERA: *Grazie, Godfather.*[1]

Don Corleone and Bonasera negotiate over the terms of an
agreement in the opening of *The Godfather*. The Don bargains
down from a murder to a beating. Bonasera gets revenge and pays
with loyalty to the Don.

In the previous two chapters we identified a problem with the tendency
of national security policymakers, practitioners, and scholars to divide
sub-state violence into several categories and we described a solution
in the form of a unifying trade-based approach to sub-state violence,

as highlighted above in the exchange between Don Corleone and Bonasera. In this book, however, we start with the identity-category typology, if only to see if it holds up to scrutiny. In this chapter, we examine chronologically the life of perhaps the most famous organized criminal of our time, Pablo Escobar, and the widely understood subfield of organized crime.

Pablo Escobar

Born into a middle-class family in Medellín, Colombia in 1949, Pablo Escobar's ambition from a young age led him to establish a firm, achieve wealth and fame, and become the world's "most wanted" drug trafficker. He served in the Colombian Congress, collected protection money, ran a crime "family," and governed. He also killed people. He bears responsibility for a bomb that took down an airliner in 1989, killing 110 people. Eventually, competing enterprises found and killed Pablo, ending his reign but perpetuating the market for violence.

This chapter describes Pablo Escobar as seen through the lens of economic activity – an entrepreneur and autocratic ruler seeking wealth and power in competitive marketplaces. We will review other illicit actors, including members of La Cosa Nostra, to show that Escobar is not a singular case but simply another instance of a universal pattern in which some rational decision-makers engage in violent activity due to incentives and market forces.

Until quite recently, crime was widely understood to be an expression of irrationality, an aberration from the normal interactions between humans in the marketplace. In 1968, economist Gary S. Becker made a proposal considered outrageous at the time: he argued that criminals are no different than everyone else. As Becker phrased it, most previous scholarship and approaches to crime relied upon "special theories of anomie, psychological inadequacies, or inheritance of special traits."[2] In other words, the general view was that individuals who committed crimes were fundamentally different from individuals who did not. Contrary to these views, Becker identified crime as a matter of individuals making thoughtful decisions regarding actions that maximized their preferred benefits:

> Theories about the determinants of the number of offenses differ greatly, from emphasis on skull types and biological

inheritance to family upbringing and disenchantment with society. Practically all the diverse theories agree, however, that when other variables are held constant, an increase in a person's probability of conviction or punishment if convicted would generally decrease, perhaps substantially, perhaps negligibly, the number of offenses he commits ... The approach taken here follows the economists' usual analysis of choice and assumes that a person commits an offense if the expected utility to him exceeds the utility he could get by using his time and other resources at other activities. Some persons become "criminals," therefore, not because their basic motivation differs from that of other persons, but because their benefits and costs differ.[3]

Like Robinson Crusoe in the last chapter, who was willing to resort to violence when Friday would not trade a good he needed for survival, the criminal engages in an economic exchange that cannot be conducted through licit trade channels, namely because the law forbids it.

Pablo Escobar fits the rational criminal-actor concept quite nicely. There are certainly aspects of his life that might be pointed to as strange or outrageous. Escobar was a heavy doper and was influenced by the *nadismo* movement sweeping Colombia in the wake of the 1950s, which Mark Bowden describes as a set of individuals who "lampooned their elders in song, dressed and behaved outrageously, and expressed their disdain for the established order in the established way of the sixties."[4] Yet it would be folly to ascribe Escobar's exceedingly violent criminal career to such activities. Escobar's participation in these activities was not special; large swaths of Colombia's youth exhibited similar behavior.

Escobar's home life and upbringing appear relatively normal with nothing to indicate a particular propensity for violence. He was born into an upper-middle-class family, not a poor one.[5] Nor did his family express a fundamental opposition to the existing social order. As Mark Bowden puts it, "The Escobars were not revolutionaries; they were staunchly middle class. To the extent that they had political leanings, they were allied with local Conservative landowners, which made them targets for the Liberal armies and insurrectionists who roamed the hills."[6]

Rather than describing Escobar's path toward criminality in outdated terms that suggest that criminals do not possess the same human nature as you and me, the type of analysis that Becker criticized, we must turn to the fundamental factors that, according to Adam Smith, facilitate the division of labor and wealth creation. That is, we must apply the story of trade, exchange, and competition to Pablo Escobar's pursuit of self-interest.

In what appears to reveal deep ambition and an impatience to achieve it, Escobar dropped out of school at the age of 17, telling his mother, "I want to be big."[7] Escobar sought wealth and power. Roberto Escobar, Pablo's brother and business partner, recalls that Pablo desired two things above all else: money and the Colombian presidency.[8] One of Escobar's favorite photos later in life was an image of him and his son standing in front of the White House as delegates for a Colombian–American advocacy group, illustrating his desire for membership in the political elite.[9] Roberto Escobar recalls a moment in which Pablo Escobar, while showing the photo to his cousin, Pelolindo, "told her that in the future he was going to go there and do business with the American president."[10]

As a teen in the 1960s, Escobar began his journey to power as a small-time confidence man, smuggling stereo equipment and stealing tombstones to resell, but he quickly set himself up to rise in the ranks of the gangsters controlling the drug smuggling enterprises he would later run.[11] He began stealing cars and led a small gang engaged in car theft by the age of 20 before discovering that he could sell protection from his own gang, developing a profitable protection racket.[12]

Escobar moved from simply forcibly taking property and selling it, akin to Crusoe's harvesting of bananas, to establishing a market for protection. He sold contracts promising protection to car owners who paid for that service – protection from Escobar's own thieves. He became a stationary bandit taxing the local population for "protection." Bowden writes that, "Pablo realized he had created an even more lucrative market. He started selling protection. People paid him to prevent their vehicles from being pinched – so Pablo began making money on cars he didn't steal as well as from those he did."[13]

Within this market, Escobar acted as an entrepreneur with employees and essentially ran a small firm. Some business activities, such as the actual provisioning of violence that occasionally accompanied stealing cars, were best kept within the tight bonds of Escobar's most loyal employees. Other activities could be acquired on the market-place for goods and services. Like any business, Escobar's engaged in trade with people outside of the firm when an external market exchange was cheaper than including the person within the group. For example, Bowden notes how "once he'd amassed sufficient capital, Pablo began simply bribing municipal officials to issue new papers for stolen vehicles, eliminating the need to disassemble the cars."[14] To include these officials as full-time gang members would have been unnecessarily risky and expensive, while the market exchange of cash for service, or a bribe, provided a cheap way to achieve the same end.

As Escobar's firm continued to expand, he required enhanced rules and enforcement to control his criminal enterprise. Escobar maintained internal rules of conduct for his employees and spelled out rules in contracts or agreements with those providing outsourced services and goods. Although rules need enforcement, illicit organizations cannot call the police or bring civil action against those who violate their obligations. Instead, Escobar hired people to coerce adherence to the rules. He used violence and the threat of violence to punish those who breached contracts and codes of conduct. For example, he would kidnap people who owed him money as a form of debt collection.[15] He would also kill debtors in order to send a message to others – increasing the likelihood that future contracts would be respected. These activities also taught him a lesson: that kidnapping itself could be a profitable business. Like many smart businesspeople before him and since, Escobar diversified his business portfolio into new markets.[16]

The Cosa Nostra

Rather than an anomaly in the competitive forces that dictated exchange and trade in the legitimate marketplace, Escobar's violence constituted the universal expression of competitive forces – but in the illicit marketplace. The division of labor requires exchange and therefore requires a system of rules and associated enforcement. When selling illegal goods or services, without recourse to police or courts, success must rely on the individual's ability to provide his own force. Let's look at a different place and time to test these ideas: the rise of the Sicilian Mafia, or Cosa Nostra. In Sicily in the mid-1800s, lemons, rather than cocaine, opened a market and created incentives for violent competition.

In 1860, Sicily's lemon groves held the honor of being Europe's most profitable agricultural land.[17] Individuals soon realized that the lemon groves were extremely vulnerable to destruction, making the establishment of protection rackets quite simple.[18] As expected, when an opportunity to develop wealth opened, individuals took advantage of it. For example, in 1872, a local doctor named Gaspare Galati began to manage a lemon farm that he had inherited from his brother-in-law, but soon discovered the lemon business to be deeply intertwined with Sicily's criminal activity.[19] His brother-in-law had been receiving threatening letters from the farm's warden, Benedetto Carollo.[20] Carollo would steal the lemons already promised for sale in order to tarnish the farm's reputation and forcing the grove's owners to sell him the product at a discount.[21] As Dr. Galati continued to investigate, he discovered that in the absence of cooperative law enforcement, Carollo's individual actions on his property were bolstered through his interaction with a larger network.[22] In short, Carollo was part of a criminal firm.

Like Escobar, Carollo chose individual violence as the best route to pursue his interests: when Dr. Galati attempted to stop the racket by firing Carollo, the replacement warden was shot in January 1875, supposedly at Carollo's hands.[23]

Carollo was far from unique in Sicily, and we have already seen similar dynamics in Escobar's story. Leopoldo Franchetti, a British liberal who encountered the violence of the Sicilian Mafia while traveling through Italy, wrote a history of the Mafia astutely identifying its violence as a form of capitalism.[24] A century before Becker's identification of the rational economic roots of criminal behavior, Franchetti wrote:

> [in the violence industry] the mafia boss ... acts as a capitalist, impresario and manager. He unifies the management of the crimes committed ... he regulates the way labour and duties are divided out, and controls discipline amongst the workers. (Discipline is indispensable in this as in any other industry if abundant and constant profits are to be obtained.) It is the mafia's boss's job to judge from the circumstances whether the acts of violence should be suspended for a while, or multiplied and made fiercer. He has to adapt to market conditions to choose which operations to carry out, which people to exploit, which form of violence to use.[25]

Though astute, Franchetti's propensity to view the Mafia as a peculiarly Sicilian form of capitalist development limited his analysis.[26] Instead, as John Dickie notes, "All capitalism has a bit of the bastard in it, particularly in the early stages. Even the English society that Franchetti so admired had had its violent entrepreneurs."[27] The violence was not an aberration from or warped mirror image of the dynamics identified by Adam Smith. The violence in Sicily, as well as in Colombia, stemmed from exactly the competitive dynamics identified by Smith and the Scottish Enlightenment writers of the mid-1700s.

Escobar's Competitive Market

Similarly, in a society wracked by banditry and the aftereffects of civil war, Escobar's early gangsterism was hardly out of the ordinary. Escobar's firm was only one among many regional organized criminal syndicates, and smuggling routes were already well established even though Escobar was not yet involved in the drug trade.[28] Escobar's criminal enterprise expanded, however, when the potential benefit available from criminal activity increased. As Bowden writes:

> A seismic shift in criminal opportunity presented itself in the mid-seventies: the pot generation discovered cocaine. The illicit pathways marijuana had carved from Colombia to North American cities and suburbs became expressways as coke became the fashionable drug of choice for adventurous young professionals.[29]

Based upon this perspective of the origins of Escobar's criminal enterprise, we see that he was not in his essence a drug dealer, but rather an ambitious entrepreneur who expected criminal activities to produce monetary and political profit. Focusing on the drugs in the kingpin story loses sight of the important drivers behind human behavior and reduces illicit and violent sub-state activities into categories that do not promote a proper understanding of Escobar and his choices.

For example, an informant known as "Bullet," the chief of transportation for a major Colombian cartel, told law enforcement officials that the cartel's leadership was made up of businessmen who did not care what they sold: that while at the time they were selling cocaine, before cocaine they sold marijuana, and they would be just as willing to sell dog shit if it would be more profitable.[30] Similarly, Roberto Escobar identified the key factor in Pablo Escobar's entry into drug trafficking in the mid-1970s as the incentivizing shift to the more profitable commodity when an increase in the cost of smuggling other contraband became too high. He described Escobar's decision to enter the cocaine trade, saying, "In fact, I don't think transporting cocaine was something he had carefully been planning for a long time or even gave much consideration ... I think the opportunity was there and Pablo recognized it. This was simply an easier way to make money than contraband."[31]

While Escobar took on the role of a criminal entrepreneur, many other Colombians took on different roles in the criminal industry for their own self-interested reasons. Mauricio Rubio has noted that the literature on crime in Colombia has to a large degree focused on theories of the lack of social capital such as the breakup of families or lack of social trust – or in other words, the type of social anomie theory that Becker criticized in 1968.[32] Rubio argues that these explanations fail to correspond with Escobar's often explicit commentary that he admired successful criminals.[33] Rather than stemming from a broken or dysfunctional family home, Escobar chose to enter the drug world to best serve his interests: a desire for fame, money, and power. Moving beyond Escobar, Rubio points out that while the formal legitimate economic sector remained relatively stagnant in the later 1980s, the informal sector grew by around 10 percent and remuneration for minor criminal activity tripled.[34]

Far from being a question of anomie or lack of social capital, crime in Colombia appears to have been the profitable choice for many rational individuals. The dominant drug traffickers in the 1970s were mostly older men, most of whom "were already well established, fairly well-to-do, and even respectable by the time they started to dabble in drugs."[35] The younger cohort who replaced them was similarly intelligent and ambitious.[36] As Rubio writes, "It is difficult to imagine that the country's most outstanding economic success stories – those that received the most attention in the media – have not affected the perception of the reward structure."[37]

Additionally, Escobar's firm competed with other legitimate firms for workers and often outcompeted them. When law enforcement agents asked the informant Bullet how Escobar recruited his pilots, he responded, "Half of Avianca wanted to fly for us."[38] The benefits were so good that the cartel preferred to hire young unmarried pilots because if a pilot with a family died on the job, the cartel was obligated to financially care for the family for a year.[39] Such benefits were far beyond what most Colombians could hope for. Roberto Escobar recalls paying one airport manager $500,000 for each flight on which the cargo was transported successfully.[40] Roberto writes, "Pilots mostly were paid by the kilo, at first about $2,500 per kilo but later as much as $6,000. For some flights a pilot could earn more than $1 million."[41] The men the Colombian cartels hired in the early 1980s to maintain the distribution network in New York made fortunes, and once they completed their tour would return to Colombia as "made men" able to buy property, horses, and other luxuries that would otherwise be beyond their reach.[42]

Like a billiards champion with no training in physics, the Escobars made trades in an active marketplace without necessarily having read Adam Smith. The pilots Roberto Escobar hired made salaries and benefits beyond what they could otherwise hope for, and in exchange the Escobars received the high-quality workforce needed to reliably transport their high-value product, cocaine. The workers in New York received money and the promise of riches once they returned to Colombia in return for their services protecting the distribution chain.

As Pablo succeeded as an individual and rose to lead a crime family, or what we now see as a "firm," he found himself competing against other businesses. To take advantage of the new criminal opportunity presented by the cocaine boom, Escobar's firm had to outcompete others that similarly sought to control the cocaine trade.

Initially the competition was small-scale. Amateurs dominated the cocaine market and Escobar, whose firm had already demonstrated its chops establishing protection markets, found it relatively easy to coerce those involved in the drug trade to pay.[43] As Bowden puts it, "He wasn't an entrepreneur, and he wasn't even an especially talented businessman. He was just ruthless. When he learned about a thriving cocaine-processing lab on his turf, he shouldered his way in. If someone developed a lucrative delivery route north, Pablo demanded a majority of the profits – for protection. No one dared refuse him."[44] The only thing Bowden gets wrong is that Escobar's ruthlessness did not prevent him from being an entrepreneur – it was instead a core characteristic of his entrepreneurship that enabled him to create a firm and expand his market share.

Escobar's violent methods, in the context of the exploding cocaine markets of that time, allowed him great success. In the 1970s,

Escobar worked for the established trafficker Fabio Restrepo, but saw an opportunity for expansion and decided to take a risk. Recruiting support from the prominent Ochoa brothers of Medellín: Jorge, Juan David, and Fabio, Escobar launched what would be considered a "hostile takeover" in the legitimate business world.[45] Restrepo had been a significant player in the market, selling 40 to 60 kilos at more than $40,000 each in Miami every year.[46] Escobar met with one of the Ochoa brothers to strike a small deal, but only two months later Restrepo was dead and Escobar took over what remained of his firm.[47] In the licit market, a company may similarly take over another even if the targeted management resists the deal. Although typically this does not lead to the other's extrajudicial killing, Escobar's competition with Restrepo reveals that the core market dynamics are the same even if the methods somewhat vary. Escobar's use of violence, rather than shareholders' votes, precludes us from making the connection between the two inherently similar motivations.

Over these years, Escobar realigned the Colombian drug scene through structured deals with the Ochoas, allowing him to control certain aspects of the industry while the brothers dominated others. As Guy Gugliotta and Jeff Leen put it, "Ochoa and Los Pablos were interested in sharing loads, dividing up the jobs and bringing a greater degree of control to the business. Escobar dominated cocaine production and enforcement. He ran labs, bought coca paste, paid necessary bribes, handled security, and, when expedient, killed whoever needed killing."[48] Through this arrangement, the Ochoas also dominated the drugs' transportation. The deal allowed tremendous growth in the size of the market, which relied upon the cooperation of the various criminal entrepreneurs in the market – the division of labor.

The growth of Escobar's firm and his partnership with the Ochoas brought him into further violent competition with firms run by other criminals. Many of the earlier traffickers left peacefully. As Gugliotta and Leen note, "The old-time smugglers had no place in the new scheme and for the most part gave ground gracefully ... Others evolved and adapted, content to take a subordinate position in the new order."[49] On the other hand, those who refused to go along with Pablo's new arrangement were violently forced out or killed.[50]

Eventually, these begrudged individuals and their firms retaliated against Escobar. Mark Bowden writes regarding an incident in 1976, "His [Escobar's] rapid rise had already earned him dangerous enemies.

One of them tipped off agents of the DAS (Departamento Administrativo de Seguridad), who arrested Pablo, his cousin Gustavo, and three other men."[51] After repeated failures to bribe the judge to drop the charges, Escobar tried a new strategy: murder. The arresting officers were killed and Escobar walked free. In general, this period was a time of substantial violence for all parties. Gugliotta and Leen write, "The realignment in Colombia, as in Miami, was a bloody, terrifying saga punctuated by kidnappings, torture, and murder. The eye of the storm was Medellín, and police could do nothing to stop the bloodshed."[52]

Escobar and his Medellín Firm

Escobar's expanding enterprise had to contend with another set of firms operating in the country – Colombia's guerrilla groups. Drug traffickers made appealing targets for guerrilla groups like M-19 who were engaged in kidnapping for ransom.[53] During the 1970s, M-19's leaders needed cash to finance their activities, leading to a series of strategies to obtain the needed capital, including bank robberies, kidnappings, and establishing legitimate firms.[54] As Escobar himself had learned through his use of kidnapping as a contract enforcement mechanism, kidnapping promised a particularly strong financial stream. In 1979, the group kidnapped Carlos Lehder, another drug trafficker, and demanded $5 million in exchange for his release.[55] Three years later, M-19 guerrillas kidnapped Martha Nieves Ochoa, the sister of Escobar's friends and business partners the Ochoas.[56] Kidnapping drug traffickers and their family members provided a particularly profitable opportunity because the criminal status of the targets reduced the costs associated with law enforcement involvement. Roberto Escobar stated that the guerrillas targeted the drug dealers and their families because "they were rich and could not go to the police for help."[57] The market grew in a simple and brilliant dimension.

Colombia's drug traffickers, however, could not allow the kidnappings to continue and sought to raise the costs to the guerrilla groups, previously kept artificially low by the lack of law enforcement action. They did this through the obvious method – violence. Following Lehder's kidnapping in 1979, an appeal for help reached Escobar, who organized a small team to rescue Lehder.[58] The rescue was merely a precursor to the reaction to the 1981 kidnapping of Martha Ochoa. Following Ochoa's kidnapping, Escobar and the

Ochoas, along with other drug traffickers, organized a militia called Muerte a Secuestradores (MAS), or "Death to Kidnappers," to impose serious costs upon the guerrillas.[59]

Violent response provided an immediate benefit – freeing the kidnapped person – and established long-term advantages by deterring future attempts. War between Colombia's guerrillas and drug traffickers arose out of the competition produced by M-19's kidnapping business. Roberto Escobar describes the war, writing, "Nothing was going to stop Pablo from dealing with the kidnappers. While Pablo had been working with some of the M-19 people, he told them that this was a war and he would destroy them."[60] The immediate campaign was brutal, but its brutality was a key part of its success in freeing Martha Ochoa and establishing the dominance of Escobar's firm. Roberto Escobar further wrote that, "Many of the M-19 were killed in the Colombian way of La Violencia, the most painful way imaginable, with limbs cut off. Within weeks, Martha Ochoa was let free without harm. The success of this effort made the drug traffickers realize how much stronger they were working together than independently."[61] Gugliotta and Leen concur with Roberto Escobar, writing:

> The formation of MAS marked the beginning of a new era in the history of Colombia's cocaine lords. Before MAS the bosses cooperated with each other in business; they had partied together; they had even taken the first steps toward building a common cocaine trafficking policy. But until MAS, they had never taken a joint public position on any matter in which they had an interest. MAS marked the consolidation of the Medellín cartel.[62]

The war also solidified and provided a set of rules for what would become an increasingly close and cooperative relationship between Escobar's firm and M-19. Pablo Escobar, like other drug traffickers, had long paid the guerrillas in exchange for protecting the drug production operations located in M-19-controlled territory. Roberto Escobar recalls, "If the guerrillas had wanted to destroy these laboratories they could have easily; instead they became the guards. All of the traffickers paid them."[63] However, the resolution of the Ochoa situation helped cement cooperative interactions between Escobar's firm and M-19, which he would utilize in his later war with the government. Escobar met with the rebel leader Ivan Marino Ospina to make an arrangement between MAS and M-19, forming a firm bond between the groups.[64]

The story of the war and its resolution between Escobar and M-19 tells us a lot about the economics of organized violence. Martha Ochoa's binds to Escobar through important social and fictive kinship ties ensured that her kidnapping would be treated differently. These kinship ties moved violence from the individual to intergroup level, leading to MAS' establishment and Escobar's subsequent increased control over other drug traffickers. This shift recalls Hirshleifer's economic explanation of war: we pick teams because it improves our chances of success. In both of these instances, individual relationships established during the war would shape the conduct of Colombia's drug traffickers in later years. Gugliotta and Leen suggest that the final ransom deal that Escobar and his aligned drug traffickers struck with M-19's leaders took place in Panama under the watch of Panamanian officials, including Panama's then chief of military intelligence, Manuel Noriega, establishing the first ties between Noriega and Escobar, which Escobar would later rely upon when he fled to Panama to avoid extradition.[65]

The story of the war between Escobar's firm and M-19 also illustrates the difficulty of separating types of sub-state violence into categories like organized crime, insurgency, and civil war. In many ways, it is difficult to differentiate the guerrilla group M-19 from the drug trafficking organization run by Escobar. Both ran protection rackets, kidnapped, and engaged in illegal armed violence. How is one to place the war between M-19 and Escobar's firm into a sub-category of violence? Is it a gang war? Such a designation fails to note M-19's politics. If we include them, is it then considered a civil war? That at least one of the participants was a criminal organization raises further difficulties given the tendency to exclude criminal violence from analysis of civil wars. When we pull the categories apart, we are left with the war's fundamental nature: inter-firm competition, collaboration, and collusion, with the use of violence when needed.

The Logic of Criminal Violence

Loyalty and Defection

As Escobar's firm grew, issues of organizational structure became increasingly acute. Each new person included in the firm increased the risk that a member would defect and provide intelligence and support to either law enforcement or competing organizations. Escobar sought to avoid this risk by tightening the kinship bonds between the members of his enterprise. Roberto Escobar notes the power of friendship and family in tying together the business: "Many of the friends we made as children would end up in the business with us, among them Jorge Ochoa, who with his brothers built his own organization, and Luis Carlos Maya."[66] Pablo Escobar himself expressed the role of friendship and fictive kinship bonds in maintaining his organization in a 1980 interview: "I am a great friend and I do everything possible so that people appreciate me,"[67] adding, "What is worth most in life are friends, of that I am sure."[68]

The value of friendship and kinship in organizing a firm is no surprise to the savvy businessperson, and, after all, that is what Escobar was. One only needs to read the *Harvard Business Review* to know that non-monetary rewards like benefits and team bonding can reduce the monetary cost of loyalty. In one piece, Sylvia Hewlett, the CEO and chairman of the Center for Talent Innovation, counseled, "With salaries frozen even as the scope of work expands, managers find it nearly impossible to lure A-players and compensate existing high performers without breaking the budget."[69] She continued that instead, "public recognition is also a powerful tool that doesn't cost money but can reap a huge return."[70] Illicit entrepreneurs use kinship ties to provide the recognition and status that come from being identified as part of a particular network. Similarly, just as a lawful business might offer vacation time or a holiday party, Escobar did the same, throwing wild and extravagant parties to show his appreciation for his employees.

As Coase discusses, some tasks are best kept within the firm rather than contracted out, thus requiring strong internal ties. Escobar cultivated a feeling of family throughout his cartel. This is clear in the case of the firm's accountants, a role that had to be kept within the firm because of the high costs of an accountant defecting to a competitor (either rival cartel or law enforcement) with knowledge of the organization's core workings. Regarding the biological and fictive kinship bonds that bound the accountants to the firm, Roberto Escobar writes, "Some of them were relatives; others were friends or strongly recommended professionals."[71] On top of the familial framing, these crucial employees were also paid handsomely to increase loyalty, as

Roberto Escobar states, "We didn't offer benefits, but we gave great salaries. All of our accountants, all of them, were millionaires. They had farms, their kids went to the best private schools."[72] Escobar did not rely solely on kinship, and provided other employees or ad hoc contractors cash in exchange for their services. For example, Roberto Escobar writes, "Pilots had to be hired for the trip; some of them were Vietnam veterans and they were paid by the kilos they carried."[73]

The story of Escobar's accountants reveals one organizational approach to costs imposed by law enforcement: decentralization. In different contexts, weighed costs and benefits reveal decentralization as a preferable strategy to reduce the risk of disruption by law enforcement.[74] For example, by the early 1980s Colombian cartel leaders generally found they could protect their distribution chain in New York by decentralizing it and adopting more networked structures. They replaced the old hierarchical and closely knit structures with people hired for a year of work who would only engage in one key job and whose only contact with the cartel's core was a phone number of a controller who would give them orders.[75] When these individuals were arrested, the investigation would hit a dead end as the only information they could provide would be a single Colombian email address or phone number.[76]

Another example of decentralization comes from a 1930s gang, termed – not irrelevantly – Murder, Inc. by the press, in which a Jewish gangster named Louis Buchalter found that he could sell the service of murdering the Italian Mafia's enemies for the mob, reducing their risk of prosecution.[77] Like the popular name for the group Murder, Inc., it is not a coincidence that such hits became known as contracts. Such a strategy of decentralizing the most violent parts of the Mafia business would reappear in the 1970s, and it makes perfect sense.[78]

For illicit firms, defection of key employees is often far costlier than it is for licit firms, and, as a result, kinship bonds, salaries, and changes in organizational structure are often insufficient to maintain organizational loyalty. To address this challenge, illicit firms use violence to increase the costs of defecting. Again, we see concepts such as loyalty and repression emerge as the keys to governance. In describing the aforementioned 1980 interview in which Escobar lauded the importance of friendship, Mark Bowden writes, "Of course, friendship also had its hazards ... unfortunately, along life's paths one also meets people who are disloyal.' "[79]

This is an application of the theory of contract enforcement discussed in Chapter 2, where an illicit firm does not have the option of enforcing a contract in a state court, through legal means. Such a firm then relies on the threat of violence to deter disloyal behaviors. But it only has to actually execute this violence against a select number of people in order to ensure loyalties in the others. This is similar to the music industry's lawsuits in the early 2000s against students downloading pirated music. The industry only had to sue a small number of students to scare others into abiding by the laws.

This double-sided nature of friendship – the promise of benefits to kin and the threat of violence against disloyal members – applies widely. On the eve of battle in Iraq, General Mattis told the Marine First Division, "Demonstrate to the world there is 'No Better Friend, No Worse Enemy' than a U.S. Marine."[80] In the formulation of "no better friend" we see fictive kinship ties, while the threatening "no worse enemy" emphasizes the importance of the offer of friendship. When President George W. Bush declared that "Every nation, in every region, now has a decision to make. Either you are with us, or you are with the terrorists" in the wake of the 9/11 attacks, he proposed a similar formulation. He offered the familial ties of the international community while threatening military action against those who stood aside. General Mattis' words, now commonly cited by and even tattooed on the arms of Marines, actually date back to the Roman general Lucius Sulla.[81] Understanding the quote's etymology and staying power reveals how ingrained and important kinship and its maintenance at times of insecurity remains to the human condition.

Often the threats and violence that criminals use to bind the group may appear irrational or cruel from an outside perspective – and it is possible that many criminals do exhibit sadistic tendencies – but sadism alone fails to explain the consistent replication of the violence. Instead, brutality and irrationality often serve their own role in cementing the organization's kinship bonds by putting into action the "no better friend, no worse enemy" concept. For example, Bowden recounts one such incident in which Escobar had a servant bound and, in front of horrified guests, kicked the man into his swimming pool to watch him drown, announcing, "This is what happens to those who steal from Pablo Escobar!"[82] Tempting as it is to call such an event irrationally cruel, Bowden notes the act's rational function, continuing, "The warning no doubt resonated among his guests, many of whom were in a position to steal far more from El Doctor than the unfortunate servant had."[83] Seemingly irrational acts of cruelty usually serve a rational function. Human nature has us seeking *our* team, *our* family, *our* people. When confronted with the display of power of a leader, possessing the ability to both reward and punish our actions, that power will certainly influence which team we choose.

Beyond the power of the leader, another way to limit defection is to require members of the crime family to demonstrate loyalty in action. The type of brutal violence committed in order to earn one's "bones" or establish a reputation was hardly unique to criminals in Escobar's cartel and predated his capture of Colombia's cocaine market. Take, for example, the rituals associated with Griselda Blanco de Trujillo's gang, one of the first cocaine trafficking groups to be targeted by American law enforcement in the mid-1970s, for which "full membership, it was said, was acquired by killing someone and cutting off a piece of the victim – an ear or a finger – as proof the deed was done." One pistolero earned renown by murdering Blanco's enemies with a machine pistol from the passenger seat of a speeding motorcycle. This technique was so admired that it became the trademark of Colombia's cocaine killers.[84]

Using acts of violence to deter defection does not define only the Latin American criminal structure. We find the same phenomena a century earlier among the lemon groves of Sicily and the difficulties facing Dr. Galati. As he investigated Carollo's ties, Dr. Galati found that a priest known as Father Rosario was running a religious co-fraternity, the Tertiaries of Saint Francis, which provided a front for criminal activity.[85] Father Rosario's religious status enabled him to connect imprisoned criminals with those still free. Later investigation would reveal that the organization bound its members through a blood oath and initiated members would engage in a coded dialogue, swear loyalty, and prick their arms in order to smear blood on a sacred image.[86] From afar these rituals appear to be strange relics of history or an expression of the peculiar Sicilian identity, but they were adopted and utilized by criminals for rational economic reasons. As John Dickie explains, "Creating a sinister ceremony and a constitution that had the punishment of traitors as its first article, helped create trust because it was a sensible way of putting up the price of betrayal among criminals who might normally betray each other without a second thought."[87] This is the central role of kinship in a market – to ease transaction costs and build trust.

Governing by Organizing Other Organizations

With a cohesive group established and defections deterred, the leader can then challenge other organizations, including the government. Escobar's firm had established itself and, as a result, Escobar now saw a path to the political greatness and status he claimed to have long wanted. As Bowden writes, "It wasn't enough anymore to have succeeded on the streets of Medellín or to dominate the international drug trade; somewhere along the way Pablo had begun to see himself as a great man."[88]

Groups above a certain size need formality in the form of rules and enforcement in order to survive and thrive. In social science, we call the system of rules and enforcement an institution: "the humanly devised constraints that structure human interaction. [Institutions] are made up of formal constraints (e.g., rules, laws, constitutions), informal constraints (e.g., norms of behavior, conventions, self-imposed codes of conduct), and their enforcement characteristics."[89]

Escobar invested in the Medellín population, providing order and public goods in return for the support of the people. He established rules of behavior and cultivated the means to enforce these rules, exercised near-monopoly control over the means of violence in large population centers, and rewarded compliance. In doing these things, his power grew. He governed more than a small group of thugs; he became a competitor in the marketplace for government services. Bowden describes a few of these goods and their effect:

> Pablo became one of Medellín's most generous employers, paying salaries to workers in his cocaine labs that enabled them to buy houses and cars ... he began spending millions on social improvements in the city, doing far more than the government ever had for the poor crammed into the city's expanding slums ... He would show up for ribbon cuttings and dedications, displaying a reluctance to accept applause or thanks, but always allowing himself to be drawn out eventually to center stage ... By the end of the decade, the people's don was not just the richest and most powerful man in Antioquia; he was also its most popular citizen.[90]

To govern, one must organize a group of people and establish institutional constraints; to increase one's political power, one must organize other group leaders. In 1978, Pablo Escobar entered the official political scene when he won election to a substitute city councilor position for Medellín. He did not stop at local politics, and in 1982 he ran for the Colombian Congress as a substitute representative.[91]

For Escobar, the decision to enter national politics placed him in competition with a new group of entrepreneurs: Colombian government officials. He pitted his cartel against Colombian government institutions, even though the political elite had not used state powers to go after rich drug traffickers. Bowden writes, "By then, much of the ruling class in Bogotá had made its peace with drug trafficking. Some saw cocaine simply as a new industry, one that had created a new, wealthy, young social class – and one highly fashionable at that."[92] Indeed, if Escobar had decided not to enter national politics, he could have continued to exercise substantial power; but as Bowden writes, he traded "a long fat lifetime" as a drug trafficker for a chance at getting the "limelight."[93] Although this decision may seem irrational to outsiders, Escobar was motivated by his own goals and self-interests – that of power and status. His lifelong dream to "do business with the American president" outweighed any risks associated with entering the political sphere.

Pablo Escobar considered the risks of entering national politics and weighed the expected gains and consequences. Roberto Escobar recalls raising the issue and warning him of the dangers. He writes, "The whole idea of getting involved in politics seemed very bad to both me and Gustavo. We were very much against it. In the business we were in, the last thing you want is attention; in politics, attention is first and necessary. I predicted it would cause us great problems."[94] However, Escobar disagreed, dismissing the arguments against entering national politics. "At no time," writes Roberto Escobar, "did he believe his business would prevent him from having a political career."[95] With elected political power, he could more freely achieve his goals. But as we will see, Escobar made a profoundly individual miscalculation with which other members of his organization vehemently disagreed, putting himself and his firm on the path toward a violent clash with political competitors and the Colombian state.

Rodrigo Lara, the newly appointed justice minister, led the Colombian state's attempts to counter Pablo Escobar. Lara, a member of the New Liberal Party, quickly took up the issue of drug traffickers' influence on politics.[96] As a political entrepreneur, the issue held many benefits for him, among them its potential as a means of competing with Pablo Escobar's Medellín Faction within the New Liberals. As Bowden writes, Lara saw Escobar as a rival: "Lara made the issue his own. His denunciations of hot money delighted the U.S. embassy and marked Lara as a man of principle, but his motives were not all selfless ... So Lara's attack on hot money was a way of protecting his own political base."[97]

At first the competition remained relatively contained. Belisario Betancur, Colombia's president, and other members of the governing elite kept their distance from Lara's campaign against the influence of drug money.[98] Gugliotta and Leen write, "Drug trafficking ... was a back-burner item, of concern largely because it bothered the gringos so much. Betancur was against drug trafficking when he thought about it, but he didn't think about it very often."[99] Lara himself avoided naming Pablo Escobar at first, contenting himself with vaguer criticisms of the Medellín Faction of the New Liberals.[100] The nature of the competition changed when Pablo Escobar entered Congress for the first time and when the Primary Representative, for whom Escobar was elected as an alternate, responded to the accusations by publicly displaying a check that Lara had accepted from another drug trafficker, in an attempt to tarnish the politician's image.[101] Lara, in turn, responded to the accusation that he had accepted dirty money by explicitly criticizing Escobar:

> [We have] a congressman who was born in a very poor area, himself very, very poor, and afterwards, through astute business deals in bicycles and other things, appears with a gigantic fortune, with nine planes, three hangars at the Medellín airport, and creates the movement "Death to Kidnappers," while on the other hand, mounts charitable organizations with which he tries to bribe a needy and unprotected people.[102]

This marked the first time that Pablo had been publicly accused of being a drug trafficker.[103] Gugliotta and Leen write that while Escobar's activities were well known, Lara had spoken out and "No Colombian politician had dared do this. With one speech he had forever forfeited any chance of peaceful coexistence with the Medellín cartel."[104] Pablo angrily responded by threatening to sue Lara.[105] Lara's allies responded by releasing the story of Pablo's 1976 arrest – where he had ordered the killing of police officers in order to avoid drug charges – triggering a new warrant for his arrest. Escobar raised the stakes by responding the way he was accustomed to: the judge who issued the warrant was murdered.[106]

Powerful allies in the Justice Ministry backed Lara in the conflict with Escobar: the Congress lifted his parliamentary immunity, the US Embassy revoked his visa, and the Church renounced support for Pablo's social programs in Medellín.[107] Escobar and Lehder threatened to use their coercive economic power if the government did not back down from its extradition plan, saying they would close their businesses and raise the unemployment rate.[108] Lara, in turn, used the state apparatus to place economic pressure on Escobar's firm. Lara authorized the US State Department to use herbicides against Escobar's coca fields.[109] On March 10, 1984, the police raided a cocaine processing plant known as Tranquilandia, conducting the largest cocaine bust in history, while several operations by the armed forces in the same month seized an additional more than $1 billion of cocaine.[110] Lara's campaign cut into Escobar's profits, and Roberto Escobar wrote, "No question he was making an impact. In Colombia, our secret had finally become public knowledge."[111] The raid on Tranquilandia was particularly devastating to Escobar's business, as the single plant had produced $12 billion worth of cocaine in only two years.[112]

At this point, with Escobar's attempt to use non-violent means of coercion appearing to have failed, he again turned to extra-legal violence. Escobar chose to escalate the conflict, and Lara was assassinated a little over a month after the Tranquilandia seizure.[113] According to the DAS, Colombia's security service, several drug traffickers planned the assassination, and, according to one informant, Escobar personally gave the order to kill Lara.[114] The assassination cost $521,000 and was contracted out to Los Quesitos, a murder gang that often worked for the Medellín cartel.[115] Some in Escobar's network, however, thought Lara's murder violated the rules of the game. Fernando Arenas, a personal pilot for Carlos Lehder, stated, "Jorge and the Ochoas they were not very happy with the operation. They thought that this is going to launch a huge, huge, huge operation against us, so this doesn't make any sense."[116]

Lara's death did not eliminate the competition. Instead, Escobar escalated the conflict from a personal one with Lara into Pablo Escobar versus the state itself – crossing a line and losing acquiescence of popular opinion. Lara's killing provided the political space, and the political necessity, for others in the Colombian state to either join in the fight against Escobar or risk losing political capital. Bowden writes, "Outrage in Colombia forced President Betancur to embrace both Lara's crusade and the American aid it required. He placed the entire country under a state of siege and authorized the national police to begin confiscating the narco kingpins' estates and other assets. He vowed at Lara's grave to enforce the extradition treaty with the United States."[117] Arenas, Lehder's pilot, confirms the fundamental shift that occurred following Lara's assassination: "With the assassination, it was a completely different environment. The picture changes completely."[118]

This shift demonstrates how a master cleavage, an overall narrative to a conflict, can emerge from individual decisions and further structure future individual action. We also see a great example of how even bad actors must live by rules. We might think that rules constrain us to behave within the law, but the criminals can act without constraint. The backlash to Escobar's decision proves that rules – albeit different ones from the social code you or I adhere to – still govern illicit actors' behavior. Putting this scenario into economic terms, we witness individuals making decisions consistent with their individual goals, most notably Escobar and Lara and, as we will see later, Betancur, while constrained by the institutions (rules and enforcement) in which they operate. Through their abilities to dictate the resource allocation of their respective firms, these entrepreneurs create significant levels of violence in the course of their competition for goods (for example, wealth, power, and revenge). Lara's assassination is also a strong example of the economic idea of operating under imperfect information. Had Escobar known that killing Lara would actually increase the threat to his organization, he would have had good reason to choose a different action. But, in marketplaces, people make decisions based on information available to them – decisions that, given that information, they believe are in their best interests.

As the conflict escalated, Betancur, who had kept his distance at the beginning of the competition between Lara and Escobar, now found himself compelled to lead the institutions of the Colombian government to further the assassinated politician's cause. The costs of the game continued to rise.

Terrain

Facing retaliation from Betancur's Colombian state, Escobar fled to Panama, where he sought to reestablish his operation while negotiating with the president.[119] In choosing Panama, he created a "safe space" away from the heightened competitive pressures in Colombia; but it was a safe haven with a critical flaw. Escobar had an ally in the chief of the Panama Defense Forces, General Manuel Antonio Noriega, considered to be "... the only friend an outsider needed in Panama."[120] The weakness in Panama was the risk that Noriega would defect. The rules governing the relationship between Noriega and Escobar might be thought of as a contract; contracts, like other institutions, have little meaning in the absence of enforcement. On the run, Escobar had little power of coercion over Noriega. And having gone from Colombia into Panama, whatever possible "us-against-them" story that might have been told (e.g., "it's us persecuted drug lords versus the world, and we're all in this together") appeared weak in the face of the risks continued allegiance would carry.

Like the pilots who transported Escobar's cocaine to the United States, Noriega was paid on an ad hoc basis. Between 1982 and 1983, Noriega received $100,000 per planeload of cocaine that moved through Panama, a number reached after Noriega rejected lower offers.[121] When Noriega's costs rose, he increased the price to $200,000.[122] Noriega also received a large payoff in the range of $4–5 million to allow the development of a new cocaine lab on Panamanian soil.[123] Fernando Arenas describes the lab, stating, "So basically this place in Panama would be like four or five times better than Tranquilandia, bigger than Tranquilandia, easier to handle than Tranquilandia. The operation would assign flights, hours, like any other airport in the world."[124]

Once in Panama, Escobar attempted to negotiate his safe return to Colombia. After meeting with his partner Jorge Ochoa, Escobar, claiming to represent the top 100 Colombian drug traffickers, offered to shutter the entire business operation in exchange for safe return, the promise that he would not be extradited, and the ability to keep the money he had already made. But the rift between elected government officials and drug bosses generated after the killing of Lara was too strong, and Betancur rejected the offer.[125]

Even as the effort to negotiate a return faltered, Manuel Noriega's ad hoc employee status began to threaten Escobar's safe haven in Panama. With a bond only as strong as the monetary payment was large, all knew that Noriega could be wooed to another side, possibly to the US Drug Enforcement Administration (DEA). Fernando Arenas describes this problem, stating, "Imagine if they hit that homerun of catching Escobar, the Ochoas, and the Mexican, Gacha, in Panama. [Noriega] would be like a saint for the American government, and for everybody every place. So he was playing both ends." Roberto Escobar recalls that Pablo paid individuals on Noriega's staff to inform on his activities as a form of protection.[126] Roberto Escobar writes that "it was one of these colonels who informed Pablo that Noriega had said that he was going to speak with the North American government, especially to the DEA" in an attempt to secure his own freedom in exchange for Escobar's.[127]

Escobar's weak control over Noriega soon produced a situation in which Escobar had to flee again, this time to Nicaragua.[128] Escobar's departure from Panama was precipitated by Panamanian forces raiding a cartel drug lab and arresting several of Ochoa's men.[129] Roberto Escobar recalls the raid: "Noriega ordered his military to capture 16,000 barrels of ether that were supposed to go to the new laboratory being built in Panama with his approval, organized by some of Pablo's associates."[130] Furthermore, "Pablo knew that there was nothing he could do as long as we were guests in Noriega's country. In secret he gave the order that everybody had to leave Panama right away."[131]

The collapse of the deal between Escobar and Noriega demonstrates the pervasiveness of the core rules of governance: repression and loyalty. The deal's pure cash basis without long-term contract enforcement, and no loyalty based upon shared identity or kinship, provided a weak bond in an otherwise competitive market. At a basic level, the deal's failure is analogous to a dispute between a contract employee and his employer in any other industry, licit or illicit. Voluntary trade benefits both parties, so when an exchange ceases to benefit both parties, the exchange will cease.

Violence

The failed deal in Panama played an important role in encouraging Escobar's eventual return to his home in Colombia. As Roberto Escobar writes, "Eventually Pablo decided that the safest place for him was Colombia, where he had control of the people around him. Things had cooled down enough for him to return, although no longer with a public profile."[132] Upon his arrival in Colombia, Escobar organized a meeting of important drug traffickers to develop a system of collective security.[133] Roberto Escobar recalls that the continued threat of extradition loomed large at the meeting and that Pablo Escobar stated, "... this extradition law is not only for me. It's going to be for all of you. That's why we have to be together to stop it now."[134] The meeting ended with a few traffickers agreeing to the plan, but most did not want to decide immediately.[135]

That same evening, Escobar would be reminded that even trusted relationships were exchanges conducted in the marketplace and therefore subject to loyalties for sale. Late that night, the police raided the meeting place.[136] Roberto Escobar recalls the betrayal:

> We learned two weeks later that a drug trafficker from Cali had gone from the meeting at the Circle and called someone in the government, believing he could win a guarantee that he would never be extradited by informing on Pablo. And Pablo also discovered that the raid had been directed by Colonel Casadiego Torrado, who Pablo had considered a friend and had been paying $50,000 a month for cooperation and information. But maybe this colonel figured that by capturing or killing Pablo Escobar he could ensure his career. Pablo sent him a message: "Now you are against me and you know what I think about that."[137]

Although established kinship networks lowered the dangers of betrayal in Colombia as compared to Panama, both Torrado's and Noriega's calculated decisions to betray Escobar demonstrate the utilitarian nature of relationships in competitive marketplaces.

During this time, Escobar continued to believe that he might be able to strike a deal with the government that would allow him to reemerge while avoiding extradition.[138] Yet with Betancur's ongoing refusal, Escobar increasingly turned to violence instead. Escobar established *plata o plomo*, silver or lead, as central to Medellín cartel business operations: take a bribe or take a bullet. By 1985, the cartel's apparatus for producing protective violence had been institutionalized and expanded. Gugliotta and Leen write:

> With the coming of the Medellín cartel, however, patterns of judicial intimidation, like patterns of everything else to do with cocaine trafficking, became institutionalized. By 1985 the cartel's bagmen were hanging around arraignment courts with

briefcases full of cash ... by 1985 the cartel had so many cops on the pad that judges could never tell if their court-ordered bodyguard was protecting them or following them.[139]

The increasing success of "silver or lead" provided a safe haven in Medellín and allowed Pablo to escalate his violent challenge to Betancur's regime. In July 1985 the judge investigating Lara's death was killed.[140] That same year, four officials involved in the lawsuit challenging Colombia's extradition law refused to accept bribes and were found murdered.[141]

Betancur, knowing Escobar feared extradition to the United States the most, chose to escalate as well. As Pablo Escobar and the other cartel leaders realized that they were not going to be able to negotiate their way out of the current war, they formed a new armed organization, Los Extraditables, just as a similar calculation had led Escobar to develop MAS to confront M-19's kidnapping spree. Roberto Escobar writes, "At the head was Pablo, but members were all of those who were indicted in the U.S. or might be charged there with crimes. Because our government had refused to negotiate, the leaders of the cartel had nothing to lose."[142]

At this point in the Escobar-as-drug-dealer narrative, ask yourself if his actions also fit the description of an insurgent. If we apply the identity-category approach to the discussion of these figures' stories, we begin to see the flaws with this approach. Is Escobar a drug dealer, an insurgent, or a terrorist? After all, the decision to form Los Extraditables gave rise to one of the most serious insurgent attacks in Colombian history. In November 1985, the Colombian guerrilla group M-19 held the Colombian Supreme Court hostage by barricading themselves inside the Palace of Justice and demanded an end to Colombia's 1979 extradition treaty.[143] It was widely reported that Escobar paid M-19 $1 million to conduct the operation.[144] The fighting between the M-19 guerrillas and government forces left 11 of Colombia's 24 Supreme Court justices dead as well as killing 39 other employees of the palace of justice, destroyed thousands of criminal files including that of Escobar himself, and threw the Colombian legal system into chaos.[145] Escobar's actions during this period again highlight the difficulty of categorizing him as only a drug dealer. In addition to clearly sponsoring terrorist attacks – the use of violence for political reasons against noncombatants – Escobar's violent campaign against the government could easily be conceived of as an insurgency.

As 1987 closed, violence reached such levels that it threatened the state's stability, and the Colombian government declared martial law.[146] During this period, the cartel's apparatus for producing violence – the ability to set rules and enforcement – and the government's increasing efforts to regain powers of governance – its own rules and enforcement – led to a large market for the murder of government officials. Pablo Escobar would buy the deaths of policemen, and he created the market, determining the payment based on the police officer's rank.[147]

The size of the market soon required Escobar and his cartel to establish regulations to guide the production of anti-government violence. Roberto Escobar writes, "It was a big business and sometimes different people made claims about the same shootings. So a system was set up that before the event the assassin would need to inform the head sicario where he would attack, and afterward he would have to present a newspaper story about the attack to receive his pay."[148] Even criminals need to exercise governance to regulate markets. As we know from Olson's story of the roving bandits, unregulated competition shrinks the market and available wealth. Indeed, the need for institutions regulating the killing of police officers should be familiar to Western counter-terrorism policymakers, who saw a similar process when the Bush administration increasingly began to offer rewards for the capture of Al Qaeda-affiliated individuals following the 9/11 attacks. The description of the practice by a 2005 International Crisis Group report sounds eerily similar to Roberto Escobar's description of the situation in Colombia, making the market dynamic quite explicit: "The scramble by Mogadishu faction leaders to nab al-Qaeda figures for American reward money has spawned a small industry in abductions. Like speculators on the stock market, faction leaders have taken to arresting foreigners – mainly, but not exclusively Arabs – in the hope they might be on a wanted list."[149]

Violent competition between the government of Colombia and a cartel of violent non-state actors continued to escalate as Luis Galán, a well-liked Liberal Party candidate who had vowed to take down the drug traffickers, appeared certain to win the 1990 presidential election, a victory that would threaten Escobar's progress in disrupting the judicial system.[150] On August 18, 1989, Escobar ordered a man to murder Galán with an uzi.[151]

However, the peak of Escobar's violent ascendance came three months later, when he attempted to have Galán's successor candidate killed.[152] On November 29, 1989, Escobar's men bombed Avianca Flight 203 when they believed Galán's successor to be on board, killing 110 people. US counter-terrorism officials now placed Escobar squarely in their sights. In the course of these pages, we have seen Pablo as a thug, a drug lord, an insurgent, and a terrorist. As a result, we begin to see the meaningless of the labels *criminal, insurgent,* and *terrorist* are, since one can be all three of these things, in succession or simultaneously.

The Negotiated End

In 1990, César Gaviria became president of Colombia, and Pablo Escobar shifted tactics in an attempt to coerce Gaviria into striking a deal. Escobar began to target Colombia's powerful upper class through kidnappings and other violence. At the same time, Gaviria signaled a potential willingness to negotiate. On August 30, 1990, Pablo Escobar had Diana Turbay, a journalist and daughter of a former president of Colombia, kidnapped as part of his new strategy. Bowden summarizes the thinking of Gaviria as he responded:

> Gaviria doubted at that point if the Colombian police and judicial system were capable of arresting, trying, and punishing Pablo anyway. The nation's best hopes were to keep the pressure on and to offer the drug boss a deal sweet enough to make him surrender. Just a week after Turbay was taken, Gaviria issued a decree offering Pablo and other indicted narcos immunity from extradition and reduced sentences if they would surrender and confess.[153]

Negotiations commenced, and on June 17, 1991, Pablo Escobar surrendered himself to the government. In exchange, the government ended the war, leading to the release of Escobar's remaining hostages. Escobar confessed to a single crime – taking part in a drug deal – and agreed to be held in a specially built prison.[154]

Pablo Escobar had sold Gaviria peace for the price of the president's refraining from extraditing him or pursuing further action against him. The deal did not, nor could it, bring an end to the market. As Jorge Ochoa explained regarding the previously rejected deal made from Panama, "We offered the government to stop the business. No one controls the business ... the business, exists because of supply and demand."[155] Moreover, the deal Gaviria made with Pablo did not even go as far as the offer made from Panama. The exchange was peace for a promise of non-extradition. The market still existed and Pablo continued to dominate it from a new location. The deal was just one more contract informing how Escobar could conduct his business.

It might seem absurd that Escobar was able to run his business from within prison. However, even prisons where one might expect the government's power to be absolute are not devoid of the economic exchanges of illicit and violent sub-state actors. Prison may at times increase the cost of illicit activity, but it would need to raise the costs above the benefits in order to eliminate it altogether. Rarely, if ever, do prisons fully succeed in doing this. Benjamin Lessing, who has examined this dynamic, explains, "The dirty little secret of prison life has long been that, more often and in more ways than not, inmates not guards run the show. Increasingly though, and across a variety of national contexts, well-organized prison gangs are leveraging that control to project power from within the prison walls out onto the street."[156]

The prison did not establish governmental authority over Escobar. Stephen Murphy, a Drug Enforcement Agency special agent in Medellín in the early 1990s, described Escobar's cell as more like a suite: "He had a living room, a kitchen in one room, and the other consisted of a master bedroom and an office combination. The bathroom had its own jacuzzi. The prison itself contained its own discotheque, its own bar. He was known to hold parties on a weekly basis at the prison. He was known to have visits from family."[157] Escobar continued to exercise control and run his business from within the prison. The police major who ran the unit tasked with listening to Escobar's communications within the prison called it "a grand business center."[158] Pablo Escobar even demanded pay from other traffickers for his agreement to surrender. Roberto Escobar writes, "He believed he was serving his sentence for all the traffickers who would be helped by the new laws. It was agreed that during his time in prison he was to be compensated by them from the business ... 'I am the price of peace,' he told them. 'I am making this sacrifice for you, so you should compensate me.' "[159]

Prison as Safe Haven

We cannot dismiss Pablo Escobar's continued business activity from prison in the 1990s as a peculiar quirk, given the conditions of his homemade prison within Colombia; Escobar simply benefited from universal economic dynamics. Another such story can be found in 1930s America, when Charles "Lucky" Luciano, one of the leading figures in the Italian-American Mafia, was imprisoned. As Selwyn Raab notes in his book on the American Mafia, "Just as on the outside, Lucky found a comfortable niche inside prison walls. In return for gifts of food and money and as homage to his godfather status, prisoners substituted for him in the laundry, cleaned his cell, and took care of all his odious prison chores."[160] The market continued inside prison walls for "Lucky" Luciano just as it later would for Escobar. Nor did Luciano's influence end with the inmates. "Guards," explains Raab, "aware of Luciano's criminal stature, never disturbed him ... 'He practically ran the place,' a guard observed. 'He used to stand there in the yard like he was the warden.' "[161] For Luciano, the threat of violence emanating from his stature within the Mafia served a similar purpose in structuring exchanges with guards as did Escobar's stature and monitoring of the laborers building the prison.

The ease with which a prison can become a safe haven for continued criminal enterprise has its roots in economic exchanges. These exchanges share a basic essence regardless of whether the individuals making the exchange are criminals, insurgents, or terrorists. It should come as no surprise that similar exchanges existed in the case of Osama bin Laden, who continued to operate his firm while living in a prison-like safe house. Like Pablo Escobar, bin Laden had his safe house specially constructed for the purpose, and it was located in what one would expect to have been a center of state authority – Abottabad, the city hosting Pakistan's premier military academy.

The concept of a safe haven is often discussed in terms of geography, with the popular narrative regarding bin Laden's whereabouts centered on Afghanistan's caves. This limited focus is not surprising, as geography often serves to raise the costs of asserting political authority by non-locals. It certainly did in Colombia, as Bowden explains in his story of the hunt for Escobar: "Colombia is a land that breeds outlaws. It has always been ungovernable, a nation of wild unsullied beauty ... from the white peaks of the three cordilleras that form its western spine to the triple-canopy equatorial jungle at sea level, it affords many good places to hide."[162]

However, geography is only one expression of the fundamental cause of safe havens – the cost of asserting political authority. If he had the funds and will, Colombia's president could search every square inch of the equatorial jungle, just as the United States could have checked every cave in Afghanistan for bin Laden. The key lesson here is that safe havens are a product of the market. That market does not simply disappear when an individual goes to prison or lives under the nose of agents of state power in a jungle hideout or cave. Under the right conditions, including for a time in Noriega's Panama, an entire country can be sold as a safe haven for the right price. But as Escobar learned, a location's safe status only exists as long as one's offer is better than the alternatives. To paraphrase Jeff Lebowski, "the market abides."[163]

Time Inconsistency

For Gaviria, the continued cocaine industry-fueled killings and the steady reports of Escobar's continued management of his network from within prison helped him mobilize the Colombian government to take action. Despite previous arrangements with Escobar, Gaviria chose to renege on his contract with Escobar, demonstrating "time inconsistency." This economic concept acknowledges that individuals' preferences, goals, and constraints vary and change over time. On July 21, 1992, Gaviria gave the order to seize Escobar and transfer him to a more secure prison.[164] Escobar's extensive power within his mini-state doomed the operation. The armed forces had surrounded the prison, but in a reminder of the falsehoods promoted by theories of unitary government, they did not follow the orders to seize and transfer Escobar.[165] One can read this as a moment of incompetence, or perhaps the pervasiveness of *plata o plomo* and the power of Pablo Escobar's influence.[166] The vice-minister of justice entered the prison to negotiate Escobar's transfer, yet Escobar – not the government – exercised control within the prison and took the vice-minister hostage.[167] Bowden writes, "When Mendoza looked to his armed guards, urging them to do something, the men drew up their weapons and pointed them ...

at him!"[168] Eventually the special operations forces raided the prison, freeing Mendoza, but by that time Escobar had fled.[169] While Escobar held Mendoza hostage, he told him something that emphasized the economic principles we have outlined in Escobar's story: "President Gaviria has betrayed me. You are going to pay for this and this country is going to pay for this, because I have an agreement and you are breaking the agreement."[170]

Gaviria and his supporters had broken the contract with Escobar, and Escobar, lacking a licit means of enforcement, intended to enforce the contract again through coercion. As discussed, all markets, even illicit markets, have rules. Yet in illicit markets, without access to legitimate (impartial, legal) courts, extra-judicial violence becomes a logical and reasonable tool of enforcement. This is not a natural aspect of crime but the result of its context. Governments also find themselves resorting to violence to enforce their rules. At the same time, illicit organizations can reduce the need for violence by establishing institutions of governance – moving from roving bandits to stationary bandits. In the end, the story is not at its core about illicit actors versus governments, but about the balance of rents and coercion that any institution, be it a government, an organized criminal enterprise, an insurgent army, or a terrorist network, can mobilize to ensure compliance with its rules.

Indeed, the factors shaping the dispute between Escobar and Gaviria were the same as those that shaped disputes between Escobar and his low-level employees when Escobar was merely a common gang leader. The exchange varied by degree with both Escobar and Gaviria running firms with immense capacity to enforce their wishes with violence, but the type remained the same – a disagreement perceived to be best resolved through the use of violence.

After his escape, Escobar reiterated his promise to make Gaviria and his government pay for violating their contract. He issued an offer to return to prison under the prior agreement, but when Gaviria rejected the offer, Los Extraditables followed up by threatening to kill government officials.[171] Los Extraditables also sent a fax to the United States embassy threatening to attack it if anything happened to Escobar.[172]

Escobar made good on his promise by initiating a car bomb campaign that would have familiar resonances decades later with Al Qaeda's similar actions in Iraq. A car bomb killed 23 people on January 30, 1993 in Colombia's capital Bogotá; another in December killed 13 people, including ten policemen; in another instance a 300-pound car bomb was discovered in front of the police headquarters in Antioquia.[173] The Coalition Forces would face a similar campaign as the insurgency took off in 2004 in Iraq. Yet, despite the similarities, any comparison between the two remains almost entirely excluded from key databases that focus on terrorism, including RAND's database and the University of Maryland's START Center's Global Terrorism Database.[174] These omissions represent a failure in which the current categorizations of sub-state violence divide fields and leave key cases under-analyzed.

During this period the Colombian police, with US support, were dismantling Pablo's firm, and 12 key Escobar figures had died by the end of 1992.[175] As the firm disintegrated, Escobar found himself more reliant on kinship ties and a small circle of closely trusted supporters. Roberto Escobar writes, "The most loyal of our sicarios fought back hard, but the circle of people around Pablo was getting smaller. It became safer for us to move around with very few people. Once I had thirty bodyguards, now I lived with only one. The main protection we had came from the people of Medellín, who believed in Pablo."[176] The cost of associating with Escobar rose, pushed upwards by the law enforcement and security service pressure and, as a result, Escobar had to increase payments to his remaining supporters.

The renewed and escalating competition between Gaviria and Escobar began to merge with the longstanding violence between Escobar and his competitors in the drug trade. Escobar's primary non-governmental competitors were the Orjuela brothers, the dominant figures in the Cali cartel. Like Pablo Escobar, Gilberto Rodriguez Orjuela was no product of societal anomie or cultural dysfunction, but an accomplished entrepreneur. He moved from kidnapping to running a business empire that included not only an illicit drug trafficking organization, but also pharmacies, banks, radio stations, and a variety of other legitimate businesses.[177] Miguel Orjuela, the family's other leading member, was educated abroad and traveled in top social circles.[178] The Orjuela brothers expanded along with other members of the Cali cartel, coming to dominate the New York market, with one DEA estimate putting four out of every five grams of cocaine sold in New York City as imported by the Cali cartel.[179]

At first, the Orjuela brothers and the Cali cartel cooperated with Pablo Escobar and his Medellín cartel. Gilberto Rodriguez

Orjuela had lived and conducted business with Jorge Ochoa while in Spain, and the two men had even been arrested together.[180] However, the forces of supply and demand soon drove cooperation into competition. Colombian cocaine had flooded the market, causing a global glut.[181] At the same time, the pool of potential customers was declining due to concerns over the drug's safety.[182] The Colombian cartels had overproduced at the same time that they found themselves losing customers due to a branding problem. Following the laws of supply and demand, the price for cocaine dropped precipitously. According to a 2003 Office of National Drug Control Policy report, the price fell by about 70 percent during the 1980s.[183]

The Size of the Market

Back in the wild, Escobar again chose to escalate the violence. In Colombia, with the available market on the decline, competition between the Cali cartel and the Medellín cartel, between the Orjuela brothers and Escobar, intensified. The Medellín cartel could no longer afford to stay clear of the Cali-dominated New York market.

As the competition heightened, so did the violence, and murders of Colombian nationals in the United States increased.[184] The Orjuela brothers sent at least ten professional killers to the United States in preparation for conflict.[185] Robert Stutman, the DEA agent in charge in New York, stated, "The reason this is coming to New York is that the profit per kilo they are making has dropped so significantly that the Medellín group cannot allow one of the largest and most lucrative markets, New York, to remain untouched."[186] Richard D. Gregorie, the Chief Assistant United States Attorney in the Southern District of Florida Office, noted the same competitive forces in Miami: "There was too much white powder and the price was too low in Miami, so they had to sell a larger amount ... What happened was the result of competition and a business decision. It ended up in a personal competition."[187]

The competition over the markets in the United States spilled over into Colombia and through the distribution lines. The cartels began to provide information on each other's shipments to law enforcement agencies.[188] Armed men attacked a radio station owned by Gilberto Rodriguez Orjuela.[189] As Gregorie noted, the economic competition began to implicate personal relations, a dynamic that doesn't separate the conflict from economic theory but demonstrates

Hirshleifer's analysis, highlighting the process of individual violence turning into war through the mobilization of kinship ties, the same dynamic as in the M-19–Escobar conflict. The Orjuela brothers and their firm, the Cali cartel, were going to war against Escobar and his firm, the Medellín cartel.

As with Escobar's offer of money for the killing of police officers, the violence between Escobar's Medellín cartel and the Orjuela brothers' Cali cartel opened new market opportunities. Into this market stepped Jorge Salceda. Salceda, like the other market participants whom we have already met, was no product of social anomie but an entrepreneur in the larger Colombian market for violence and security services. He was the son of a general who had been in contention for the role of chief of the Colombian armed forces.[190] He was part of the middle class who saw a business opportunity in working for a growth sector of the Colombian economy – the drug cartels. Having served in the Colombian reserves himself and with his family ties to help, Jorge Salceda had a number of business ventures in development in the defense and security sector, including with the Colombian government.[191] In one business deal, Salceda acted as liaison between David Tomkins, a British arms dealer, and a Colombian general to arrange a clandestine raid by British mercenaries on a FARC headquarters.[192]

FARC – or the Revolutionary Armed Forces of Colombia – emerged from the widespread violence and civil conflict in Colombia during the mid-twentieth century. Although its leaders espouse ideology rooted in Marxism and agrarianism, the group leaders behaved liked all leaders of organized violence that we've seen so far in Escobar's story and will see again throughout the book. As FARC waged their insurgency against the Colombian government, they increasingly relied on organized crime and drug trafficking to fund their operations, used terrorist tactics to increase competitive advantage, and eventually positioned themselves to politically and violently engage with the state.[193] FARC's involvement in drug trafficking challenged the Medellín cartels' dominance and forced Escobar to react. This market competition led to Salceda's attempted raid against the FARC headquarters, while funding for the operation came from a number of sources, including Pablo Escobar's business partner José Rodríguez-Gacha.[194] The operation fell through after the military men involved had second thoughts, but the mercenaries left happily after informing Salceda that they were interested in future jobs.[195]

Given the fluidity of the labor markets for violence that we have already seen, it should come as no surprise that the Cali cartel found itself cooperating with Colombian law enforcement and security services to hunt down Escobar following his escape from prison, ending the contract that allowed Escobar to continue his business in exchange for peace. An exchange of intelligence with Escobar's violent sub-state rivals, including the violent anti-Escobar paramilitary group Los Pepes, promised to enrich both parties. Joe Toft, the DEA's country attaché in Colombia, explained to CNN, "Unofficially, when I first heard of the Los Pepes, you know, I felt that it was about time. That this would happen and I actually applauded this effort."[196]

Eventually, on December 2, 1993, Colombian security services located Pablo Escobar after a 16-month search when they intercepted a call coming from a barrio in Medellín. Escobar was shot in the head and killed as he ran across the rooftops. For some in the Colombian security services, the potential benefit of trading intelligence and perhaps other support with the Cali cartel and Los Pepes was more than a matter of initial unofficial applause. According to Salceda, Miguel Orjuela received the news of Escobar's death from a source inside the government task force, hunting him down only minutes after he was killed.[197] In December 1993, after Escobar's death, the *New York Times* quoted an anonymous mid-level member of the Cali cartel as saying, "Hey, we helped the Government with intelligence," and stated that the cartel sent $5 million every two months to Fidel Castaño's anti-Escobar death squad, Los Pepes.[198] The US government appeared aware of the possibility of cooperation on the part of some employed by the Colombian security services. One CIA document released under the Freedom of Information Act reported that the Colombian Defense Minister "is concerned that the police are providing intelligence to Los Pepes."[199]

Far from being a war between different unitary actors – on the one side the Medellín Cartel, on another the Colombian government, and yet on another the Cali cartel – the violence following Escobar's escape was a fluctuating mix of individuals whose economic interests at times allowed for exchanges of mutual benefit. While the extent and nature of the sharing of intelligence between members of the security services, the Cali cartel, and Los Pepes is debated – Hugo Martinez, who led Colombia's search, and Morris Busby, the US ambassador to Colombia at the time, both strongly deny any formal cooperation between the security services and Cali or Los Pepes – the larger exchange is clear.[200] The Cali cartel conducted a war on Escobar that aided the government's immediate security objectives, and the security services killed Escobar, removing the Cali cartel's greatest competitor. During that exchange, the Cali cartel was treated with relative impunity – essentially being offered the deal of continued business in exchange for support for the state's security objectives.[201] To hunt for a handshake between key figures in the security services and Cali or Los Pepes misses the point and reasserts the fallible focus on unitary actors. As individuals, members of all three groups existed in the same markets. As Joe Toft told Burt Ruiz, the author of a history of Colombia's civil war,

> Escobar's death sentence was orchestrated by the Cali Cartel ... They financed the deadly behind the scenes illegal operations to limit Escobar's reach and pulled the strings for the destruction of Escobar's powerful infrastructure. The Cali Cartel was well organized, they knew what they were doing ... We wanted Escobar so bad we actually rooted for them. They didn't have the constraints we had ... Without a doubt, the Cali Cartel was responsible for the destruction of Escobar ... We killed him ... but they set it up.[202]

With Escobar dead and his firm in ruins after years of war and sustained pressure from law enforcement, his competitors, specifically the Cali cartel, began to sweep up the market share that had been freed up.[203] Escobar was dead, but the market remained. The Cali cartel now dominated the market through their established connections with government officials and newfound control over Colombia's drug trade. Demand persisted, so individuals and firms continued to fill it while competition continued both with other traffickers and with the state.

Knowing the Escobar story and the outcome to this point, let us pause to consider Pablo Escobar's uniqueness, or at least dissimilarity to an insurgent like Mullah Omar of the Taliban in Afghanistan or Joseph Kony of the Lord's Resistance Army in Uganda. We have already seen evidence in Escobar's story that the distinction is flawed. If Escobar's organized crime led to car-bomb campaigns similar to those in Iraq, the bombing of an airliner killing innocents for political purposes in the most substantial terrorist attack in Colombian history, and also involved wars with guerrilla groups and the Colombian government, how can Escobar's acts be meaningfully distinguished from insurgency and terrorism? The answer cannot lie in reversion to the rhetoric of narco-insurgency or narco-terror – after all, drugs were just a particularly desirable commodity. The Sicilian Mafia has a similar history sparked by lemons, of all things, and as the drug traffickers colorfully put it, they would have been just as willing to sell dog shit.

Instead, Escobar's story was shaped by universal economic forces and created by fundamental human tendencies. Throughout the development and fall of Escobar's firm, we saw the crucial role of individuals making rational trades. Whether it was Noriega trading a safe haven for money with Escobar, Gaviria trading Escobar's continued operation of his business in security for peace, or Salcedo selling his security services, the story of trade remains the same, as does the competition, often violent, that comes with such trades.

In the next chapter, we will more fully explore the foundational similarities that undermine the separation between organized crime and insurgency by tracing the story of Joseph Kony and the Lord's Resistance Army. The context might be different – central Africa rather than the Americas, Christian guerrillas rather than non-religious drug traffickers – but as we will see, the story is still about individuals making rational economic exchanges, the firms' entrepreneurs develop, the kinship networks that facilitate these firms, the rents and coercion that allow for governance, and the ability of competition to turn into violence.

While it is true that Pablo Escobar earned the moniker "drug kingpin," that label overly simplifies his story. As his actions demonstrated, Escobar also deserves the titles "insurgent" and "terrorist." Escobar engaged in a struggle for political power over the state and, in the process of that struggle, used violence and the threat of violence against innocent civilians. Some might argue that these facts complicate our approach to combating violent actors; instead, the labels themselves are what complicate our understanding of the actors and, thereby, policy decisions regarding them. From the economist's perspective, Escobar's criminal, terrorist, and insurgent violence appears rational and rooted in market dynamics: goals and constraints.

4 INSURGENCY

A new surge of violence from the Christian fundamentalist rebels,
who have been fighting the Government on and off since 1987,
threatens to disrupt the first presidential elections to be held in this
country in more than 10 years. ... Despite having more than 18,000
troops in the region, President Museveni's Government has been
unable to quell the rebellion or to capture the rebels' enigmatic
leader, Joseph Kony, a former faith healer who often wears white
robes and claims to talk directly to God.

New York Times, April 1, 1996[1]

In the last chapter, we saw how certain circumstances enable
actors to logically choose violence. The previous chapter used the
example of Pablo Escobar to demonstrate the need to consider tearing
down the walls created by misleading labels and unnecessary institutional divisions between the terms terrorist, insurgent, or criminal,
allowing us to see the unity of organized violence. In this chapter
we apply the same economic lens, shifting our focus to the character of someone typically acknowledged as an insurgent engaged
in a civil war. Focusing on Joseph Kony, while weaving in stories of
other insurgents, we will examine whether Kony, like Escobar, fits
the description of an economic actor making exchanges in a marketplace. As we see common empirical phenomena across the Escobar
and Kony stories, we will find that the lines between the so-called
fields of crime and insurgency blur. Neither individual can be solely
classified as either a criminal or an insurgent; rather, both are rational,

economic actors who, given the right circumstances, might engage in acts of crime, insurgency, or even terrorism. As we move through this book, it becomes increasingly clear that an analysis of the economic origins of violence will transform our understanding of and approach to countering organized violence.

Our protagonist in this chapter, Joseph Kony, has led the Lord's Resistance Army (LRA) in an insurgency challenging Yoweri Museveni since the latter seized the Ugandan presidency in 1986. As leader of the LRA, Kony resorts to brutal tactics to recruit soldiers and provide support for his personnel, including the forced conscription of children and the mass murder of villagers who refuse to supply and house LRA members.

Joseph Kony

Joseph Kony may seem like an unusual case from which to further the investigation of the unity of organized violence. Journalists covering the LRA insurgency often focus on issues of identity, most notably ethnicity and religion.[2] News sources make it a point to emphasize Kony's mysticism – that he was a quiet, timid child who enjoyed prayer, avoided fighting, and served as an altar boy in the local Catholic church.[3] His uncle, S.J. Okello, claims that Kony was "a very polite boy. He joked a lot and was the leader of the Lakaraka group (Acholi traditional dance). He could not even fight and was mentally sound, and liked praying at church."[4] Yet Okello also remembers the day when his nephew changed, claiming that Kony left Odek and ran away to the nearby Awere Hills. His family was unable to locate the boy for four weeks. Okello recalls that Kony "was then 18 years old and we looked for him in vain. He came back wearing white clothes. We asked where he had been but he could not answer. [Later] he said he was with God." His claims of religious sanctity remained consistent in his rhetoric, and this mysticism seemingly differentiates him from a profit-seeking drug trafficker such as Pablo Escobar.

His tactics also appear unique and unapologetically brutal, and at the surface narrative Kony's violent strategies may appear to set him and his firm apart from other illicit actors. Under Kony's leadership the LRA abducted approximately 66,000 children from Uganda, South Sudan, and the Democratic Republic of the Congo between 1989 and 2004.[5] The LRA's fighters have also relied upon the abduction and sale of young women. The religious rhetoric and child-soldier tactics form an all-too-easy narrative of a psychotic, religious zealot. In this chapter, however, we will see in Kony what we saw in Escobar: fundamental human nature manifesting understandable and predictable behaviors in competitive markets.

Just as Gary Becker suggested that the causes of crime were not animus but market-based, we need to understand that warfare happens when it is economically viable, regardless of the religion, ethnicity, or mental health of the actors. Interpreting Kony as irrational, psychotic, or motivated by a religious zeal unrelated to the market insufficiently explains his actions. This simplistic analysis, as Adam Smith recognized in the *Wealth of Nations*, ignores the forces of specialization and division of labor and falsely portrays human differences as natural and intrinsic, rather than as the product of market dynamics.

Joseph Kony's childhood, like Pablo Escobar's, appears ordinary. His parents were not radical ideologues nor particularly excluded from the local society. Like many of his peers, Kony's father, Ocen Lunyi, was a retired British Army soldier who fought in the King's African Rifles (KAR) during World War II and in Kenya to suppress the Mau-Mau rebellion.[6] After his military service, he worked as a catechist in the village and demonstrated more of an interest in church affairs than Ugandan politics.[7] Kony's mother, Nora Oting, was Lunyi's third wife; family members claim that prior to her death in 2009, her last wish was for Kony to reconcile with Museveni and desist his attempts to overthrow the Ugandan government.[8] This book does not argue that Kony's childhood was marked by exclusion or radical politics, as this would be overly simplistic, and perhaps clichéd. Rather, it is important to note how sweeping, generalized explanations that hone in on radical ideology overlook market factors and therefore fail to explain why individuals with common backgrounds find themselves engaged in insurgency.

If Kony does have a sincere reverence for the mystical, it would not negate or supersede the more fundamental economic forces that underlie violence as well as all other human interactions. We would consider preposterous the proposition that all mystics are inclined toward violent insurgencies or would make successful insurgents. Just as we tend not to ascribe any individual's success or failure in the market to religious belief, Kony's mysticism alone is not sufficient to explain his use and means of violence. Unless Kony received comprehensive guidance on insurgency from "on high," we must challenge ourselves to find other explanations for his actions.

Kony's actions were not rooted in his unique essence as an individual but, rather, in the forces that shaped human interactions and exchanges in Uganda at the time, namely, a competitive market for authority. Uganda's history of contested politics and power struggles characterized the country and shaped marketplace dynamics. Great Britain granted Uganda independence in 1962 and, in 1971, Idi Amin overthrew the nascent country's first president, Milton Obote. Amin, a Muslim from the northwest, notoriously murdered all Langi and Acholi soldiers in the Ugandan army immediately after rising to power in order to quell any potential domestic opposition.[9] In 1979, following a disputed election, a Tanzanian invasion removed Amin from power and installed Obote as president yet again. However, Museveni, Obote's opponent in the 1980 Ugandan elections, opposed the election results and waged a guerilla war against Obote's government in the early 1980s.[10] Large populations of Acholi were caught in the fighting between Obote's Uganda National Liberation Army (UNLA) and Museveni's National Resistance Army (NRA).[11] While Acholi civilians bore the brunt of wartime violence, Acholi soldiers made up a significant portion of the national army and claimed that they were more likely to be deployed to dangerous locations in comparison to Langi soldiers.[12] Consequently, rebel leaders of the aggrieved Acholi people seized power from Obote in 1985 following an army coup led by Tito Okello, who later became president. Despite Okello's attempts to broker peace with Museveni and the NRA, Museveni marched on Kampala, installed himself as president, and has maintained a monopoly on power ever since.[13] Defeated Acholi soldiers retreated back to the north and into Sudan where, faced with high levels of unemployment, many disenfranchised Acholi men joined the secular Uganda People's Democratic Army (UPDA) in 1986 to continue a rebellion against government forces.[14] The UPDA's campaign to overthrow Museveni only lasted three years, and internal power struggles between Latek and his deputy, Angelo Okello, eventually divided UPDA combatants and led to the organization's dissolution in 1989.[15]

When Joseph Kony established his insurgency in 1986, the Holy Spirit Mobile Forces (HSMF) was the predominant Acholi insurgent group within Uganda, the most organized rebel firm, and the organization most able to direct attacks outside of Acholiland.[16] Another savvy entrepreneur, Alice Auma, built the HSMF on a mix of principles from Pentecostal Christianity and an Acholi understanding of the metaphysical spirit world. Alice Auma was born around 1957 and lived in Opit, a railway town near Gulu in Northern Uganda. Before she led a spiritual militant movement, however, Alice sold flour, fish, and tomatoes – humble origins that few imagine when thinking about violent insurgents.[17] Her father, Severino Lukoya, was at one point an Anglican catechist, although Alice later converted to Catholicism.[18] By some accounts, Lukoya was also an uncle to Kony, making the competing militant leaders cousins.[19]

Around 1986, Auma claimed she was guided by a spirit known as "Lakwena," and consequently adopted the spirit's name as her own surname when she became a self-proclaimed healer and spirit medium. Although Lakwena's story is steeped in symbolism and spiritual images, her story hardly requires a scholarly background in the intricacies of Acholi theology to understand. Instead, her evolution from vegetable merchant to spiritual leader to militant leader can be understood within the context of market forces and the basic human instinct to seek survival and improvement amidst those forces. She evolved from selling foodstuff, to selling stories of the supernatural, to selling visions of a political future, and the market allowed her to use organized violence to further her goals.

After observing the abduction of several of her neighbors by the NRA on August 20, 1986, Lakwena claimed that she and the 150 soldiers she had recruited had liberated the prisoners without killing anyone.[20] Her claims were not unique, but mirror the universal story of a threat incentivizing the provision of public security. By the end of 1986, the HSMF had grown to over 18,000 members, and Lakwena subsequently commenced a campaign to overthrow President Museveni's government. She mobilized a march to Kampala in October 1987, overwhelming the opposition on the way south.[21] Similar to other leaders, both illicit and licit, Lakwena balanced loyalty and repression to manage her constituents. By defining herself using the imagery of a spiritual leader with a divine order to lead, she engendered support from many of her followers. For example, Lakwena instituted the "Holy Spirit Safety Precautions," a series of prohibitions against any "sinful" activity, such as lying, killing, sexual activity, or drinking, to "reconstitute the moral order and to control violence."[22] She used the power of her position in coercive ways, such as asserting that soldiers who were killed in battle had broken these "precautions," making their deaths a just punishment. This was another way of asserting that those who challenged her would lose – a key to survival and success of any autocrat.[23]

The strength of Lakwena's Holy Spirit Mobile Forces and its competitive advantages constrained Kony's ability to lead his own insurgency. Instead, he modeled his inchoate organization after HSMF and initially emulated its leader's tactics. As Heike Behrend's work *Alice Lakwena and the Holy Spirits* makes clear, like Lakwena, Kony claimed that spirits possessed him and provided him with instructions to form his own branch of the HSMF in order to overthrow Museveni and eradicate Uganda from sin and evil forces.[24] Initially, Kony recruited soldiers from the Gulu region of Uganda, many of whom were former soldiers of the struggling UPDA, a weaker competing firm that lacked strong leadership. Kony refrained from conducting operations in the Kitgum area where Lakwena's forces operated. Without sufficient resources or personnel to launch a successful attack on government infrastructure, Kony's forces predominantly attacked UPDA forces near Gulu, where he faced the lowest expected battle costs. Targeting UPDA enabled Kony to gather additional supplies and forcefully con-script former UPDA soldiers to fight for him instead.

In February of 1987, Kony approached Alice Lakwena to form an alliance with her branch of the HSMF and expand his own operations while avoiding competition with her stronger organization. Kony informed her that he was Lakwena's distant cousin, had started his own Holy Spirit Movement, and sought Lakwena's support to combat the NRA. Kony's appeal to Lakwena reflected the human con-dition and the affiliative instinct, attempting to call on shared kinship bonds to form the basis of a contract. We've seen this same dynamic in organized-crime families and drug trafficking organizations of the previous chapter.

Despite Kony's appeal, however, Lakwena was fiercely pro-tective of her monopoly on local instruments of violence – additional insurgent movements meant increased competition for resources, funds, and personnel – and viewed Kony's organization as a threat. Subsequently, she rejected Kony's offer of partnership and informed him that even though he was possessed by a spirit, it was his purpose to be a healer rather than a rebel leader. She also admonished Kony, telling him that he was incapable of leading his own forces, should stop his campaign against the government, and should purify himself and join the HSMF as her subordinate instead. Lakwena reported that Kony departed in silence.

Placed into direct competition for authority within the rebel movement, Kony vowed that he would exact his revenge and destroy the HSMF. He and his followers later attacked and killed several HSMF members and terrorized villagers outside of Opit, where the HSMF based their operations, significantly weakening HSMF forces in the area.[25] Just as Pablo Escobar engaged in violent conflict with the entrepreneurs who dominated the smuggling market in Colombia prior to his rise, Kony engaged in violent competition with Lakwena's firm. Kony's decision again recalls the motto of being either "with us or against us," choosing violence as the appropriate response to Lakwena's rejection of an alliance.

Eventually another competing firm eliminated the HSMF as Kony's most immediate competitor for dominance in Uganda's market for insurgency. On October 30, 1987, the NRA defeated Lakwena, who had mobilized her forces to march on Kampala, 80 miles east of the capital in Iganga. Lakwena, however, managed to escape to Kenya, where she resided, defeated, in a refugee camp until her death in 2007.[26]

Kony, with his entrepreneurial spirit, took the initiative to realize his rise to power as the leader of the sole Acholi rebel faction. He took over former HSMF territory and resources following Lakwena's defeat, expanding his market share. Kony also aggressively recruited former UPDA soldiers after the firm dissolved. He coerced former UPDA combatants to reject government-offered amnesty and rewarded those who chose to join his forces.[27] In essence, Kony played the same "kinship" game that Escobar did, which, as discussed in the previous chapter, has universal economic roots. Kony grew his power and influence from within his tribe, the Acholi people. He augmented his forces with trained, veteran soldiers in addition to the civilians he abducted from villages, increasing the number and quality of combatants within his organization. This blended workforce addresses the classic "dictator's dilemma": the need for coercion to stay in power, but the need for a loyal workforce to do the coercing.[28]

The dictator must simultaneously use repression and loyalty to limit future challenges and remain in power: *If you challenge me, I will win and you will pay a price for the failed attempt. However, to convincingly threaten any and all challenges, I require people loyal to me;*

someone must support and carry out my acts of repression. Therefore, I must also rely on the loyalty of some people; otherwise, I cannot maintain power. While Kony's Acholi membership provided him with loyalty based on their shared kinship ties, he repressed other demographics in order to maintain his control over them.

Kony's movement initially assumed many different names, such as the Holy Spirit Movement, the United Holy Salvation Front, and the People's Democratic Christian Army.[29] Most significantly, his adoption of the Lord's Resistance Army name at the end of 1989 corresponded with his decision to merge his forces with those of former UPDA commander Odong Latek and appoint Latek as his second-in-command.[30] As Kony's chief military advisor, Latek helped Kony train his forces in guerrilla warfare tactics and heavily influenced Kony's preference for attacking civilian targets and raiding villages to replenish lost supplies.[31]

Kony's employment of Latek reveals much regarding the market forces behind his insurgency. It demonstrates a fluid labor market between insurgent groups in which key leaders, like Latek, as well as low-level foot soldiers could switch loyalties between various groups depending on circumstances. It also reveals how individual exchanges, such as Kony granting Latek a leadership position in exchange for his expertise, can have critical effects on the way insurgent groups use violence – in this case through improving Kony's capabilities and encouraging the targeting of civilians.

However, Kony's affiliation with Latek, although productive, would eventually impose a cost: specifically forcing the LRA out of Uganda, just as Escobar's embrace of violence to resist Colombian law enforcement imposed costs on his business empire. Kony's large-scale attacks on civilians – including raids on elementary schools and clinics – lost him the sympathy of the Acholi and Northern Ugandan people.[32] This loss of support brought weakness and provoked increased pressure from the Ugandan People's Defense Force (UPDF). Museveni deployed additional UPDF personnel to Northern Uganda in response to increased LRA attacks on civilians and concomitant public demands for Kony's eradication. Without adjusting Latek's tactics, Kony further expanded his conquest of villages throughout Northern Uganda and into Sudan to sustain his insurgency efforts and compensate for the supplies and personnel he no longer received voluntarily.[33] By 1995, the LRA successfully occupied territory in southern Sudan,

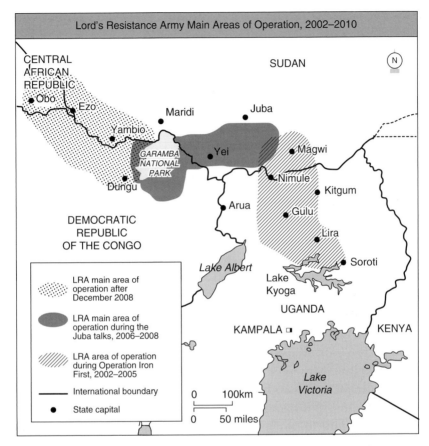

Figure 3 Map of Kony and the LRA's control throughout Uganda, Kenya, and the Sudan (2002–2010).[35]

and Kony and Latek used the cross-border safe haven to their advantage, developing a system for training soldiers and abductees.[34]

Crime ≈ Insurgency

Throughout the 1990s and early 2000s, when Kony was gaining power, those of us in the national security policy and academic fields missed the explanatory power of the market. Instead, we focused our academic discourse on grievance and the role of greed. Some scholars argued that greed was the key motivating factor behind civil wars, believing that rebellions were primarily motivated by the acquisition of power or material goods. Other scholars opposed this view; they argued instead that real or perceived grievances led people to take up arms against their governments. Even today, the popular justifications for civil wars include religious or ethnic persecution, income inequality, and lack of political participation.

One might distinguish between Escobar and Kony, or between crime and insurgency, by claiming that the former was motivated by greed and the latter by grievance. As we have seen, this simplistic explanation would be wrong. Like Escobar, Kony also acquired power and wealth, although he focused his rhetoric on grievance and identity politics.

Recent scholarship on civil war has pointed to the near-ubiquity of both greed and grievance, and proposed that the real determinant of civil violence is the *feasibility* of initiating civil violence. Former World Bank economist Paul Collier and colleagues best capture this argument, proposing that civil war will occur where leaders can overcome the barriers to entry to insurgency.[36] It is evident that greed, power, and grievance remain legitimate and valid motivations for human behavior. However, these motivations fail to explain the actual onset of civil violence, since they also exist in societies without war. Instead, civil wars erupt when it is feasible for violent entrepreneurs to launch them.[37] Certain barriers exist, however, that limit when this feasibility emerges: resource constraints, for example, limit insurgents' ability to enter into a conflict without convincing others of their ability to succeed. More specifically, "the occurrence of war depends on the product of the rebel and the government labor force exceeding a certain threshold – a rebel leader will only establish an organization if it can survive in the face of government forces and make a profit."[38] This threshold is what we see limiting some groups from expanding from a covert terrorist organization to a full insurgency with territorial control and popular mobilization, for example. This dynamic highlights a central view presented in this book: what separates a criminal from using terrorism, or a terrorist from becoming an insurgent, has less to do with the motivations for violence and more to do with the entrepreneur's goals and constraints within a marketplace.

If Kony's actions still seem fundamentally different from Escobar's, look beyond the common narrative and examine *why* Kony focused his narrative around grievances and identity politics. These issues simply allowed Kony to surpass the threshold to conflict. By relying on the affiliative instinct and kinship ties, Kony was able to recruit soldiers to fight for him, supporters to provide him with funds and arms, and support bases from which to launch attacks. Similarly, his ability to call on religious and spiritual imagery further buttressed a sense of duty among his firm's employees that proved hard to resist. Rather than the motivating reasons for violence, Kony's reliance on ethnic ties and religious imagery served as tools to enable his firm to operate in the market for organized violence.

Kony's Lord's Resistance Army and Child Soldiers

If not unique in his motivations, what of his tactics? Kony's LRA has received worldwide attention for the use of child soldiers and sexual violence. What drives those violent practices? Can we find a market-based explanation?

The media's popular narrative might lead one to imagine that Kony's recruitment of children derives from religious fanaticism. Kony's rhetoric uses religion to justify his actions, claiming religious guidance. Kony has stated, for example, "We are fighting for the Ten Commandments. Is it bad? It is not against human rights. And that commandment was not given by Joseph. It was not given by the LRA. No, that commandment was given by God."[39] While Kony's commentary on his actions lends itself initially to such a religion-as-motivation explanation, looking at behaviors and beyond rhetoric we see economic foundations for his use of child soldiers. We also see these tactics in use outside of Kony's unique specific environment, but always where the market enables them. Armed groups in various other contexts and adherent to different ideologies have resorted to similar tactics, suggesting that the root of his violence lies in something beyond Kony the individual.

If religion does not motivate the violence, then when religious rhetoric occurs together with violence, then the rhetoric is used by the violent leader to enable and support the violence. This should sound familiar. We saw religious rituals functioning in a similar way in our examination of the Sicilian Mafia and its blood oath, where the religion and ritual functioned to raise the cost of the defection.

Al Shabaab in Somalia, like the Lord's Resistance Army, employs child soldiers and uses religion among the levers of influence in the market. Al Shabaab recruited and used child soldiers under the leadership of another violent entrepreneur, Ahmed Abdi Godane.[40] Human

Rights Watch reports a complex set of market relations governing Al Shabaab's use of child soldiers that combine simple cash payments, coercion, violence in the case of non-compliance, and religious indoctrination.[41] One 16-year-old boy related the mix of coercion and indoctrination: "I was a student and al-Shabaab forced me to fight against the TFG ... They came to the mosque when we went for prayers. They pretend they are an imam [preacher] and use Islamic teaching to try and make you join. If you refuse to join they will kill you."[42] Another interviewed individual, Baashi M., explained Al Shabaab's use of a mix of material incentives and non-material incentives to recruit his 12-year-old brother: "They gave him $100 and convinced him at school that if he became a martyr he would go to paradise. They also bought him clothes. He never told my parents he was going, he just disappeared. He wanted to be a driver and Al Shabaab said they would send him to driving school."[43] A 15-year-old recalled how children were paid to recruit other children: "Many of my friends were given incentives – money to enroll others. Depending on how many you enroll you would be given more or less money. Many boys enrolled. If you refused to enroll you were forced to."[44]

These interviews demonstrate that Al Shabaab curates a labor market for child soldiers. The market is structured by violent coercion and payment, similar to Escobar's *plata o plomo*. Children receive money, religious group affiliation, other non-material benefits, and often, most importantly, protection from coercive violence that would otherwise be applied. In exchange, the children provide a cheap labor base vulnerable to Al Shabaab's recruitment and with little ability to challenge the firm's demands. As a 14-year-old boy told Human Rights Watch, "I tried to refuse but I couldn't. I just had to go with them [Al Shabaab]. If you refuse, maybe sometimes they come and kill you or harm you, so I just went with them. One of my friends who was older than me, they came and started with him the same as they did to me and he refused, and they left him but another day they found him on the street and shot him."[45]

Moving across the globe to the Americas, we see similar market dynamics driving child recruitment into cartels and organized criminal networks. As the *Washington Post* noted, one cartel, La Familia, "inculcates the youngsters with a radical religious doctrine that demands loyalty, a promise to respect women and children – and a commitment to kill rivals."[46] Recruiting children made economic sense. As Joe Garcia, an Immigration and Customs Enforcement supervisory agent, told the *Washington Post*: "They'll risk their futures for an iPod," adding, "and there is almost an endless supply of teenagers."[47] In other words, their labor was cheap and available – two factors that would incentivize any firm, licit or illicit. As Martin Barron Cruz, a researcher at the National Institute of Criminal Science in Mexico, put it, "It is a question of the market. A kid of 15 ends up doing the same job as a 20-year-old, but for half the money."[48]

The use of child labor is not merely the province of illicit violent actors. The forces enumerated above comprise, in part, the market and occur in non-violent contexts. Child labor was once widespread in the United States and other developed countries.[49] Where child labor is cost-efficient and feasible, it will be used in the absence of imposed regulations or social norms that change the incentive structure, whether in pursuit of illicit violent ends or not.

For Kony and his firm, abducting and recruiting children provided an economically rational means of reducing costs and finding inefficiencies in the management of his labor force. Kony deliberately targeted males between the ages of 12 and 16 in order to capitalize on this demographic's physical capability and malleability. Ugandan children within this age range were 50 percent more likely to be abducted than children or young adults in any other age group.[50] The cost of abduction was low, but, more importantly, child soldiers offered the highest expected benefit.[51] Adolescents in this age range were old enough to carry a weapon and engage in military tasks. Compared to older fighters, adolescents are more easily indoctrinated and controlled.[52] Maria Micaela Sviatschi's research has argued that exposing children to illegal labor markets predicts a greater participation in crime as adults.[53] Children who are abducted into the LRA at a young age have social capital invested, in the form of kinship bonds, that keep them in the social network of the group. Furthermore, they do not develop skills for working outside of the LRA in a licit marketplace.

The Economy of the Rebellion

Kony's abduction and use of sexual violence against children also derives from economic roots. Kony abducts adolescent girls, often distributing them as "wives" to select LRA commanders. This is not an issue purely of sexual violence as sadism or brutality disconnected from the marketplace. Instead, Kony's abuse and enslavement of adolescent girls as wives serves four distinct yet strategic purposes: 1) to reward senior officers for their loyalty and incentivize younger soldiers to continue their faithful service; 2) to reinforce bonds of kinship amongst LRA officers; 3) to fulfill Kony's perverse vision of a pure Acholi nation; and 4) to demonstrate his absolute authority over his soldiers' and commanders' lives. By keeping women enslaved and suppressed through institutions such as forced marriage, Kony reinforces his firm's patriarchal structure and strengthens bonds of loyalty among the men under his command in order to achieve his own goals.

First, Kony rewards his top commanders with wives in exchange for their continued loyalty and sustained performance as soldiers. Escaped LRA "wives" interviewed between 2006 and 2011 reported that they all were married to senior LRA officials with at least ten years of service. In fact, these officers typically had more than one wife at a time, typically including several junior wives (*ting ting*). Young girls between the ages of 9 and 12 serving as LRA combatants would assist senior wives, acting as a sort of apprentice wife for their future husband; once they reached the age of 12 or 13, they left their role as soldiers and became *ting ting*.[54] While junior soldiers are not permitted to marry, the promise that they can one day possess several wives can serve as a powerful incentive to remain in service.

Second, Kony seeks to form a new family for abducted children by recreating the family unit within the LRA command structure. To achieve this end, young male soldiers are placed with LRA commanders and instructed to treat them as their surrogate fathers. Similarly, forced marriage further recreates the family dynamic within the LRA command structure. Former LRA wives often report that they initially viewed marriage and pregnancy as a way to escape life as a soldier; many even saw maternity as a means to survive since they would be looked upon favorably and would be better cared for if they provided their husband with children. Furthermore, most former wives interviewed reported that they were less inclined to attempt to escape after they gave birth, feeling compelled to remain with their husband in order to care for their newborn children.[55]

Third, part of Kony's professed mission is the establishment of the *manyen*, or the "new Acholi."[56] His violence against local populations is part of his proclaimed spiritual and political mission to cleanse the Acholi and develop a new generation of purified, battle-hardened *manyen* who will successfully overthrow Museveni and the Ugandan government. Children play an integral part of this process; Kony not only employs them as soldiers, but he attempts to cultivate a new generation indoctrinated into the LRA from birth. Between 1988 and 2004, an estimated 10,000 girls abducted by the LRA became forced child mothers.[57] Typically between 15 and 21 years of age, at the time of their escape, most had given birth to at least two children.[58] Through the sexual abuse and rape of young girls, Kony tries to maximize the number of children born during the course of a girl's forced union with an LRA leader, ultimately maximizing the number of potential *manyen*. Kony exploits and capitalizes on sexual violence in order to build political capital and bolster his organization.

Finally, forced marriage regulates sexual activity within the LRA, reinforcing the LRA's internal governance, perpetuating the LRA's value structure, and promoting Kony's own power. According to LRA rules, soldiers accused of rape (in this case sexual assault against someone other than one's wife) or sexual promiscuity are beaten or, in some cases, put to death.[59] By providing wives for LRA commanders, Kony attempts to confine sexual activity within the bonds of marriage, even if forced, and to dissuade soldiers from sexual activity and unregulated acts of sexual violence. These rules are enforced throughout the LRA command structure. One escaped wife reported that when one of Kony's most senior commanders, Charles Tabuley, married her without Kony's permission, Tabuley was demoted, publicly beaten, and removed from high command.[60] By imposing this regulation on his subordinates, Kony succeeds in regulating his combatants' behaviors on and off the battlefield, asserting his authority over all of his personnel regardless of their rank and position, and promoting his core governing tenants of moral purity.

Sexual Violence as a Political Tool

Dara Cohen's research notes that in many cases the logic of gratification does not explain wartime rape and sexual violence. Rather, in many cases, sexual violence is used as a tool for establishing unit cohesion. Just as those under Pablo Escobar committed acts of violence to show their level of commitment to the group, so too can rape during wartime serve a similar purpose.[61]

This dynamic is not unique to Kony or his brand of local African Christian traditions. Even the radical leftist Weather Underground, whose ideology is as distant from Kony's as possible, sought to regulate the sexuality of its members to ensure security. Though the Weather Underground did not embrace the particular tactic of abduction, there are certainly similarities between the groups' efforts to distribute sexual activity according to regulations that are similar to Kony's use of wives to incentivize and ensure loyalty from his soldiers. Jacob Shapiro writes:

> Weather Underground leaders also tried to control operatives' personal lives to prevent emotional attachments they felt could weaken the group's security, going so far as to try to regulate the sexual activities of members. For example, the group's Seattle collective, or cell, ordered one couple to break up and set up a "sleeping schedule" that determined which members would have sex with which other members. At one point members from the national organization, the "Weather Bureau," traveled to different collectives to reorganize individuals and break up monogamous relationships.[62]

Other groups have adopted Kony's tactics of forced marriage. Al Shabaab has similarly abducted adolescent girls and forced them to marry its fighters.[63] As Human Rights Watch states, "Both girls who were targeted and other eyewitnesses consistently described a more organized practice in which al-Shabaab preached marriage with fighters to girls still in school, and abducted and detained girls under the group's auspices for this purpose."[64] The Cosa Nostra enforced strict rules of fidelity, and the Islamic State employs the assignment of wives to reward loyal soldiers. The organized character of the practice belies the notion that it represented the gratification of sadistic urges outside of market exchanges. Instead, the capitalization on sexual violence highlights that rape and other forms of sexual assault are grounded in power and control, and that entrepreneurial individuals can find ways to use sexual assault as part of a business strategy. Where there is organized exchange of a commodity, there is a market and, hence, market forces – even if that commodity is human beings.

Tara Maller and Akhi Peretz, who both worked as CIA analysts focused on the Iraqi insurgency, have noted widespread use of sexual violence in Iraq, including the forced sexual slavery of adolescent girls as a war tactic practiced by insurgent groups.[65] According to Maller and Peretz, the use of sexual violence acts as a deterrent for those considering rebellion and serves as another tool of coercion. Yet despite the clear tactical use of sexual violence and its expression in a market, discussion of the practice was sidelined. Maller and Peretz state, "We don't recall reading internal or external intelligence products that exclusively focused upon the sexual violence that occurred in Iraq during that time, despite evidence that it was rampant as an instrument of war during the vicious sectarian reprisals of the mid-2000s." Among several possible explanations for the lack of focus upon sexual violence, Maller and Peretz point to the separation of security topics from other fields of study, writing, "Many policymakers and intelligence analysts have studied political science and war studies at top universities. That might also be part of the problem. Sexual violence is too often academically walled off in gender studies or feminism classes." Because of this lack of understanding of the motivations and reasoning behind sexual violence, coupled with all too often a lack of willpower to critically examine and address issues impacting women, analysts may have failed to fully examine the issue. Sexual exploitation and human trafficking presents another example of how field-specific analyses that reject a unity between crime, insurgency, terrorism, legitimate business, and other human interactions hinder our understanding of national security threats and responses.

An obituary for Gary Becker, written by Kathleen Geier, helps illustrate the radical potential of economic theory in such a context.[66] Though critical of Becker's specific theories, Geier notes the importance of his popularization of the use of economic analysis to examine subjects previously considered non-economic – whether crime, as we saw in the previous chapter, or gender relations, as he did in *Treatise on the Family*. Geier writes:

> But marital relationships, parent-child relationships, decisions to marry and divorce, etc., are *also* profoundly economic acts. That can sometimes be hard to see, given the pervasiveness of sentimental claptrap about the family throughout American society. But Becker blasted through the Victorian detritus of all that bourgeois romantic ideology to analyze the ways in which marital and reproductive behaviors are fundamentally rooted

in a utilitarian economic calculus. You could appreciate his general approach without necessarily buying into the details of his argument. That was a real contribution, and even a radical one, after a fashion.[67]

Security studies and many of its sub-fields also tend to ignore the relevance and motives of certain experiences and behaviors. The specifics of the Iraqi predecessors to ISIS' sexual violence disappeared from the analysis of many security practitioners, just as the Colombian narco-car bomb campaigns disappeared from datasets on terrorism. Such acts do not fit the traditional views of the counterinsurgency and counter-terrorism fields. Applying economic theory, however, provides the opportunity to see through the established dogma of criminology versus counterinsurgency versus counter-terrorism, and enhances our understanding of and approach to many forms of violence.

Other-Than-Monetary Rewards

These particular cases of child soldiers and sexual violence are part of the larger market for labor and loyalty that defines much of insurgent activity. Kony's story also illustrates how the market functions in other cases that evoke less moral outrage. Similar to the cases of child soldiers and sexual violence, general insurgent recruitment combines monetary reward, non-monetary reward, and coercive violence to establish a loyal workforce.

Developing a loyal workforce is a challenging problem for a rebel entrepreneur. A rebel leader can promise public goods in the event of success, but in doing so confronts the problem of collective action: that these goods are generally not exclusive to the rebellion's participants and so pose little incentive for joining the firm, and that goods only result if the rebellion succeeds. For example, if an individual chooses to sit out the rebellion, he may receive all the benefits of rebellion success while avoiding the consequences of rebellion failure. To overcome this problem, rebel entrepreneurs provide various forms of payment to their employees depending on their circumstances. As Jeremy Weinstein writes in his book on how the choice of payment shapes rebel behavior, "Rebel leaders may draw on two types of endowments: economic endowments, which come from diverse sources, including natural resource extraction, taxation, criminal activity, or external patronage; and social endowments, including shared beliefs, expectations, and norms that may exist in (or be mobilized from within) certain ethnic, religious, cultural, or ideological groups."[68] In other words, the exchanges that are made in the rebel labor market can be monetary or non-monetary.

Kony is far from unique among insurgents in using non-monetary rewards alongside other forms of payment in this way. Let us again look at the example of Al Qaeda's Somali affiliate, Al Shabaab. Interviews between a small sample of former Al Shabaab fighters and Muhsin Hassan reveal a range of motivations for joining, including a $50–$150 monthly salary.[69] Like the Colombian pilots who ferried Escobar's drugs, these individuals found the pay for being an insurgent to be a competitive offer compared to the alternatives. As one former fighter told Hassan, "It was an easy job compared to other jobs such as construction work."[70] This is easily recognizable as an economic exchange.

However, Al Shabaab also recruited members using other forms of value. Some former militants cited their provision of protection from bombardment by the African Union's operations in the country, and others cited fear of victimization by Al Shabaab if they did not join.[71] Both of these, though not exchanges of cash, are still exchanges in a labor market where protection is traded for labor. Others cited a desire for revenge; although that may at first appear to be outside of the market, revenge and the feeling of accomplishing it is merely another good provided by Al Shabaab to those who want it. Revenge can also function as a means of sending a deterrent message to those who might do one harm. In other words, rather than being outside the market, revenge may be in large part a restatement of the protection-for-labor exchange.

The use of non-monetary rewards is not the province only of insurgents or terrorists, who we often associate with images of rewards such as a religious cause, ethnic aggrandizement, or revenge. We saw in the previous chapter how Pablo Escobar used kinship and non-monetary rewards to help maintain his firm. We also saw that such practices stem from an economic reasoning and that one might find articles in *Harvard Business Review* instructing entrepreneurs in the licit economy on their importance.

Some entrepreneurs may actually prefer the utilization of non-monetary rewards as a way of structuring their labor force. One study by Benjamin Bahney, Radha Iyengar, Patrick Johnston, Danielle Jung, Jacob Shapiro, and Howard Shatz found, for example, that Al Qaeda in Iraq (AQI) paid lower wages than other work and did not increase wages for participation in combat as one might expect.[72] The report noted, however, "One possibility is that wages in AQI were used as a kind of screening mechanism in an environment where any uncommitted individual posed huge security risks for the group as a whole. For wages to screen effectively while still allowing the group to operate, AQI would have to set them just high enough that committed types could survive and support their families if they joined, but low enough that only sufficiently committed individuals would accept." Though only a hypothesis in need of further testing, this study illustrates how an economic lens can help analysts understand phenomena within a violent market that might initially appear irrational.

The hypothesized measures potentially taken by Al Qaeda in Iraq are merely one response to a more universal economic problem of regulating the workforce. Though the costs of defection may be less severe than for an insurgent or terrorist organization, licit companies also face costs when their employees leave and have at times adopted wage-screening measures to shape their workforces to reduce such costs.[73]

Rebel entrepreneurs may also use non-monetary rewards and ideological kinship networks in order to reduce the monetary cost of recruitment and salaries – in essence ensuring a higher profit for themselves. In the previous chapter, we saw how Pablo Escobar would appeal to friendship, anti-Americanism, and class-consciousness along with, and at times instead of, monetary payoffs, to gain support for his criminal activity. Gretchen Peters reports a somewhat similar circumstance in Afghanistan and Central Asia, where Haji Juma Khan embraced Al Qaeda and the Taliban's ideological efforts to further his drug trafficking:

> Similar to Pablo Escobar … HJK, fifty-four, was notorious for his colossal drug shipments and his extravagant lifestyle. For a man who embedded himself with the Taliban and al Qaeda, HJK hardly behaved like his fundamentalist compatriots. "He has many sheep, but even more women," a Kabul police official said. "Juma Khan keeps three wives and so many girlfriends," reported an Afghan diplomat, unable to be more specific. "He

loves music and dancing." HJK owns palatial residences in at least six different countries, and it is reported that alcohol-drenched parties hosted by Russian and Turkish prostitutes extended late into the night whenever he was in residence.[74]

Peters reports that Khan often helped move Al Qaeda and Taliban members, provided the insurgency with weapons, and used his contacts to provide intelligence to insurgents to help plan attacks on the Afghan government and coalition forces. In exchange for his support of their ideological objectives, Khan received the insurgents' support of his criminal enterprise and protection from Taliban troops. Peters quotes a CIA report saying, "Haji Juma Khan supported the Taliban because his business was more lucrative under the former Taliban regime."[75] Of course, the division between ideological insurgents and the criminally motivated Khan was not perfectly clean. Peters notes that Afghan officials often argued and that little distinguished Khan's thugs from the Taliban soldiers. She continues to quote one Afghan police official as saying, "They pretend to be Taliban ... but they are just Juma Khan's thugs."

The choices rebel entrepreneurs make regarding what type of rewards to use in order to acquire labor profoundly shape the character of their activities. As a result, theoretical explanations that avoid economic analysis of the insurgent labor market miss factors that are often decisive in determining overall political results. Weinstein, for example, argues that the use of violence by rebels is related to the type of endowments they have available for paying their labor force.[76] According to Weinstein's theory, "Groups with access to economic resources are able to translate those endowments into selective incentives, or payoffs, in order to motivate individuals to join the rebellion. Resource-constrained groups must develop alternative strategies," such as reliance on kinship or ideology.[77] Weinstein then argues that reliance on these alternative forms of payment can restrain violence:

> Opportunistic groups have more difficulty identifying potential defectors and are prone to make mistakes. A constant demand for short-term rewards also drives combatants to loot, destroy property, and attack indiscriminately. A group's early missteps then initiate a cycle of civilian resistance and retribution by group members that spirals quickly out of control.

> The indiscriminate character of insurgent behavior results in higher aggregate levels of violence as civilian resistance makes it increasingly difficult for opportunistic insurgencies to operate.[78]

While Weinstein emphasizes the structuring influence of initial endowments rather than the agency of the rebel entrepreneur, one can also see how an individual might decide between various forms of payment with similar consequences.

If these market forces are ignored, it is easy to fall into a simple analysis that leads one to believe that people act in certain ways because behavior is the essence of their identity. But, as economic science suggests, people's identities and differences emerge from forces at play in markets. We have already noted how Kony's use of child soldiers and sexual violence is not simply the result of an evil essence or religious zealotry. In the previous chapter, we saw how the Mafia's actions were interpreted in religious terms when their rituals actually had economic foundations – something liberal economists noted at the time. Even models of rational, strategic decision-making can fall into this trap of overlooking market dynamics and the structure of the firm. Weinstein, for example, argues "that groups commit high levels of abuse not because of ethnic hatred or because it benefits them strategically but instead because their membership renders group leaders unable to discipline and restrain the use of force – and membership is determined in important ways by the endowments leaders have at their disposal at the start of a rebellion."[79] Per this argument, advocates of primordialist and essentialist theories of ethnic conflict are not the only ones who are prone to missing the market dynamics that produce or restrain violence and atrocity in civil wars.

Unsurprisingly we see dynamics similar to those Weinstein notes in contexts other than insurgencies with clear ethnic or religious dynamics. For example, in the last chapter, we saw that when Escobar began to offer monetary rewards for killing police officers, he incentivized a wave of unproductive violence, forcing him to institute regulations. The economic incentives and markets created by the actions of entrepreneurs and their firms prove far more important to explaining the character of violence, making almost unimportant the question of whether the entrepreneur is best categorized as a criminal, insurgent, terrorist, Muslim, Jew, Christian, Hindu, Buddhist, a legitimate businessman, or a head of state.

Having read the story of Joseph Kony's rise to power, his innovation, risk taking, and allocation of scarce resources to support his ambitions across the political marketplace, we easily see that the insurgent-cum-religious-extremist leader responds to the same market forces as do organized criminals and licit businesses. We may find anecdotes of an insurgent who appears to fail the test of rational economic exchange, but such insurgents will likely fail to pose sustained challenges in a competitive marketplace. Like successful businesses, successful insurgencies cannot escape basic economic laws. Like the truly psychopathic criminal, such an insurgent's violence is the exception rather than the rule – as such, it ought not be the focus of security practitioners and policymakers.

Having noted this, we must return to a point raised at the beginning of this chapter: if the foundational forces shaping the decisions of ideological insurgents are the same as those that shape the decisions of organized criminals, which are the same as those that shape the decisions of legitimate business leaders and the elected officials of the democratic state, how can there be a fundamental difference between the categories? At their roots, licit business leaders, organized criminals, and insurgents share an ontological foundation. They may exhibit different behaviors due to division of labor within the particular markets they inhabit – but that is a matter of context, not essence. Given the different circumstances, behaviors could change and, more importantly, the distinctions likely blur.

Some counterinsurgency practitioners and scholars of civil wars and insurgencies are realizing the false distinctions. The work of John Nagl, one of the foremost proponents of counterinsurgency theory, provides a powerful perspective consistent with economic ideas, and specifically how the focus on counterinsurgency as a separate entity continues to limit the field's analysis. In his book *Learning to Eat Soup with a Knife*, Nagl criticized how "black box theories of international relations suggest that states act only in order to increase their power in the international system; any state placed in the same situation would react in exactly the same way."[80] His thesis utilized and promoted analysis based in organizational theory – a foundational part of economic analysis – and argued, "The organizational culture of military forces is a decisive determinant in their effectiveness and hence helps to determine the course of international politics."[81] His comparison of the US military's strategy against insurgency in Vietnam with the British strategy against insurgency in Malaya draws out the influence of individuals, most notably British Field Marshal Gerald Templer, and of organizational structure.

Interestingly, Nagl's own professional life, as well as those of many of the other central figures in the counterinsurgency field, as they moved their theories into mainstream military doctrine, reveals the importance of individual exchange and organizational structure to armed organizations. Nagl speaks to this in his memoir *Knife Fights*, and it has also been chronicled in other books, including Fred Kaplan's *The Insurgents* and Tom Ricks' *The Gamble*.[82]

On the other hand, Nagl's work also reveals the limitations of the counterinsurgency field when juxtaposed against a fuller economic analysis. In *Learning to Eat Soup with a Knife*, Nagl speaks of "essential features of guerrilla warfare."[83] Statements like this promote essential views of insurgent behavior rather than an analysis of the market forces and incentive structures that give rise to specific behaviors. This is the case even though Nagl himself writes, just prior to stating an essential character of guerrilla warfare, "Until recently, however, those who took up arms against the state were referred to as bandits or criminals rather than as combatants in irregular warfare."[84] In these cases, governments can also purposefully create divisions between insurgents and criminals to delegitimize any political movement and dismiss potentially legitimate grievances. Drawing these artificial lines hinders thorough analysis and effective responses.

Nagl also draws upon Mao's famous statement regarding insurgents being like fish in the sea of the people, suggesting that separating the insurgent fish from that sea is the core of counterinsurgency.[85] The counterinsurgency field manual, of which Nagl helped write the first draft, mirrors this view, arguing, "The struggle for legitimacy with the population is typically a central issue of an insurgency. The insurgency will attack the legitimacy of the host-nation government while attempting to develop its own credibility with the population."[86] Yet this view poses problems for counterinsurgency theory. For example, such a perspective focuses on the political ambitions of insurgent leaders, thus downplaying that insurgency rests upon and combines other often decisive roots, including local grievance, organizational structure, monetary gain, and other processes within a larger market. Examining the economic roots and unity of organized violence reveals that insurgent groups, like other firms, provide a way for individuals to maximize value and achieve goals. Moreover, the typical COIN perspective enacts a theoretical separation between warring parties and the insurgents, the counterinsurgents, and the population over which they fight, although in practice these groups are not fully separable because they rest upon fluid labor markets. As Robert Taber points out in *War of the Flea*, revolutions need to be understood as a part of the historical or social process. He writes, "… it will not do to consider guerrillas, terrorists, or political assassins as deviants or agents somehow apart from social fabric … Guerrillas are of the people, or they cannot survive, they cannot come into being."[87]

We have already discussed in the Introduction Kilcullen's case of the sheikh who acted as an insurgent based on the failure of a contract deal. As Kilcullen noted, this example demonstrates counterinsurgency theory's limitations, because applying efforts to separate the sheikh from the people cannot work. The sheikh is of the people. Kilcullen is far from the only one noting these linkages and the inability to fully divide insurgency as an ideological construct from other fields, such as organized crime or legitimate business activity, and his sheikh is not a lone anecdote. Scholars who have conducted interviews with Taliban figures in Afghanistan argue that many cite financial rather than ideological reasons for joining the insurgency, including the opportunity to profit from criminal activity.[88] We have also already touched upon Gretchen Peters' work on how the separation of law enforcement, specifically the separation of counternarcotics efforts from counterinsurgency and counter-terrorism in Afghanistan, allowed insurgents who sat upon drug trafficking routes or controlled production to mobilize those resources to continue war efforts. In Iraq, crime not only provided funding for insurgent organizations but often motivated many of the insurgents.[89] One senior military official argued, "[The insurgency] has a great deal more to do with the economy than with ideology."[90] The large numbers of insurgents seeking merely monetary rewards, and thus susceptible to having their loyalty bought by American forces, is part of the reason that Al Qaeda in Iraq found it necessary to use non-monetary rather than monetary payment for participation in the insurgency, according to the study by Bahney et al.[91]

While for Nagl the importance of organizational theory in analyzing the militaries of counterinsurgents is enough to upend "blackbox" theories of international relations, the role of organizational and other economic theories located at the individual level do not appear to fully upend his discourse of an essential character of "insurgency," or the structured identity of "the counterinsurgent," "the insurgent," and "the people."

Nagl recognizes some of these challenges with counterinsurgency theory in his memoir. He recalls arriving in Iraq and having to organize a joint patrol with an Iraqi police unit only to find that the police did not want to conduct a joint patrol and would flee when approached because the insurgents in the area exercised greater coercive power over the policemen's lives.[92] Nagl wrote, "All the things I'd read about that were required to succeed in counterinsurgency were a lot harder than they'd seemed in the books, including the one I'd written."[93] In the end, Nagl had to rely on shifting the policemen's understanding of the costs of noncompliance, actually having his men force the police to patrol with guns at their backs.[94] Nagl recalls another negotiation with Iraqi security forces in which he explains the exchange of weapons and technology for intelligence he made with the Iraq commander, Colonel Suleiman.[95] When insurgents in Fallujah killed Suleiman, however, many of the men under his control joined the insurgents, taking the weapons with them.

The fluidity of the market for labor and difficulty of distinguishing between insurgents and security forces should not be surprising. We saw the same dynamic occur in the Colombian case, where Escobar and his cartel both relied upon buying the loyalty of government officials, including their prison guards, to enable Escobar's escape from La Catedral, as well as in the challenges of Escobar's own men often leaving his organization for other cartels or the government.

During the so-called "surge" of US forces in Iraq in 2007, American money and military capability – at least for a time – shifted much of the previously insurgent-friendly Sunni areas of northern Iraq against Al Qaeda in Iraq, again demonstrating the power of market forces to drive behaviors. The action in many ways parallels American consideration of buying Noriega's willingness to expel Escobar from his safe haven in Panama, which in the end forced him to leave due to the risk that he would be handed over to the DEA. Market forces act on humans, whether in the case of the insurgency in Iraq or of organized crime in Latin America.

Crime ≈ Insurgency ≈ Terrorism

With this theoretical basis, let us return to the story of Joseph Kony. We have envisioned Kony as an insurgent, but we could just as well envision him as an organized criminal or terrorist. When the economic calculations encouraged the use of crime or terror, Kony acted accordingly. Just as when Pablo Escobar perceived that his criminal firm was threatened by the government, he did not hesitate to bomb an airliner or wage a terror campaign of car bombs against the government while developing parallel lines of authority. In his attacks on civilian populations, Kony employs many of the same tactics as terrorists, such as kidnapping, mass murder, and widespread destruction with the intent to intimidate, coerce, and spread fear amongst a population.

For example, in the early 2000s Kony initiated an increasingly violent campaign against civilians in villages, deliberately deciding to use mutilation as a tactic of terror, as well as using the attacks to coerce government forces to defend larger areas at a lower cost, rather than accomplishing the same goal by targeting military forces.[96] Isador Bashima, a survivor of one such massacre, recalls, "The LRA had guns, but they did not use them … they used machetes and swords."[97] According to Colonel Joseph Ngere, the deputy governor of the South Sudanese state of Western Equatoria, Kony used such tactics to pressure the South Sudanese government into negotiations, a seemingly classic case of terrorism as traditionally understood.[98] Ngere asserts, "He has much to gain from this strategy. During the talks Kony gets free food and money. His wives and children are transported from Uganda to come and see him. He gets recognition. That is what he wants."[99] That the same violent acts serve both a terrorist and insurgent purpose suggests that there is no requirement for a motivational division between who becomes an insurgent or terrorist. In essence, the motivations for a terrorist or insurgent – be it greed, power, or grievance – can be the same, or different, but each choose tactics based on standard business terms: feasibility and return on investment. An organized violent group may aspire to launch an insurgency, but without the funds or recruits necessary to cross the entry threshold into conflict, may only be able to accomplish sporadic acts of terrorism. Kony's terrorist tactics include a 1998 threat to non-governmental organizations supporting Ugandan government aid efforts, and the 1996 kidnapping of schoolgirls, after which a released prisoner delivered a letter stating Kony's political goals.[100]

Kony's campaign throughout Uganda has earned him international recognition as a terrorist. For example, the US State Department has included Kony and the LRA on the "Terror Exclusion List" since 2001. In 2005, the International Criminal Court issued an arrest warrant for Joseph Kony and his senior leaders, including LRA vice chairman Vincent Otti, LRA deputy commander Okot Okhiambo, and LRA brigade commander Dominic Ongwen, for war crimes and crimes against humanity.[101] In 2008, the US Department of Treasury passed Executive Order 13324, designating Kony as a "Specially Designated Global Terrorist."[102] Additionally, the African Union formally designated the LRA as a terrorist group in 2011.

Despite the differences between various definitions of terrorism, the majority of organizations and terrorism scholars agree that terrorism is "the deliberate creation and exploitation of fear through violence or the threat of violence in the pursuit of political change."[103] Furthermore, scholars contend that acts of terrorism have five distinct characteristics: 1) they involve violence, or the threat of violence; 2) they include goals or objectives that are "ineluctably political"; 3) they entail attacks that have "far-reaching psychological repercussions beyond the immediate victim or target"; 4) they are conducted by a coherent organization with an identifiable chain of command; and 5) they involve a sub-national or non-state entity.[104] Kony's actions appear to fit this multi-faceted definition.

Kony and the Lord's Resistance Army have also engaged in organized crime to help fund and sustain their militant organization. For example, Kony ordered the LRA to engage in elephant poaching to help raise funds.[105] The LRA's elephant poaching does not emerge out of any particular essential characteristic of the LRA, but out of the market forces that incentivize poaching – specifically, high prices for elephant tusks.[106] That the LRA was far from the only armed group to enter the poaching market demonstrates its roots in market forces. Indeed, state-sponsored militias like the Janjaweed in Sudan and members of multiple states' armed forces are also believed to have entered the market.[107] As Robert Hormats, a senior State Department official, told the *New York Times*, "Without the demand from China, this would all but dry up."[108] Hormat's statement closely resembles Stuttman's comments on how supply-and-demand dynamics drove the violence between the Medellín and Cali cartels.

Poaching is also not clearly separable from insurgent violence. The reserves where the elephants live have become battlegrounds for well-armed poachers fighting against rangers using assault rifles and rocket-propelled grenades to counter criminal networks.[109] One chief ranger told the *New York Times*, "Most poachers are conservative with their ammo, but these guys were shooting like they were in Iraq. All of a sudden, we were outgunned and outnumbered."[110]

The criminal market for poached elephant tusks has also generated armed opposition to groups engaged in poaching that exhibits an eerie similarity to the Sunni awakening against Al Qaeda in Iraq. A *New York Times* report, for example, profiles a former Kenyan poacher, who bowed to community pressure and took up arms against poachers.[111] The report notes that the behavior of poachers fueled a backlash: "Villagers are also turning against poachers because the illegal wildlife trade fuels crime, corruption, instability and intercommunal fighting."[112] As with the surge that took advantage of the awakening movement in Iraq, the United States stepped in to help fund the militias fight poaching by providing salaries, and, as with the surge, raised the risk that the funds would support groups that would themselves become predatory.[113] The similarities between the surge in Iraq and anti-poaching efforts in East Africa reveal the continuity between counterinsurgency and counter-organized-crime efforts.

To attempt an analysis that divides a militant group like the Lord's Resistance Army, which uses organized crime, from an organized criminal group that uses violence against the state, ignores the multi-faceted ontology of civil wars and conflict. The causal pathways are rarely unidirectional, with pure insurgents who only use crime to feed their political goals and pure criminals who do not engage in politics except as a way to further their crime. For example, one *New York Times* report noted evidence that Sierra Leonean rebel leader Foday Sankoh and his rebel firm was well integrated in the international diamond trade both to enrich himself and further his rebellion.[114] As described in the report, Sankoh's forces kidnapped almost 500 United Nations peacekeepers, partially because the peacekeepers were deployed in key diamond producing areas and threatened his control. One senior Sierra

Leonean government official told the *New York Times*: "As soon as Sankoh saw that the U.N. was serious about deploying in Kono [the major diamond producing region], then he declared war on the U.N." Sankoh went to war when his profit was threatened, just as Escobar went to war when Lara's counternarcotic efforts threatened his profits. Indeed, it is even difficult not to view Sankoh as a legitimate businessman. His diamond production was well regulated and organized. The *New York Times* noted that captured documents included "handwritten lists identifying every courier who brought stones to Mr. Sankoh, with notes about their color and size." The report indicated that he was also trading with legitimate diamond markets in the West.

It might be tempting to dismiss Sankoh as merely a criminal out to enrich himself. It's a storyline that is often heard, for example, in the claims that a formerly ideological group like Colombia's FARC has transitioned from being an ideological insurgency to a criminal cartel because of drug revenues. However, such a story misses the point – that there was never such a foundational division to begin with. Indeed, the *New York Times* report ends by stating, "Sierra Leone officials say that Mr. Sankoh may have been doing more than merely enriching himself and buying weapons for his rebel troops in the field. There is some evidence emerging, they say, that he may have been planning to accumulate enough resources to attempt to overthrow the government." Greed, power, or grievance – we often do not know the true motivations of a violent entrepreneur, but we often know a lot about the way they behave.

We have now deconstructed crime and insurgency to find that they share an economic essence that undercuts their study as separate phenomena. But surely the kind of terrorism conducted by Al Qaeda or Hamas represents something different – an irrational desire to kill civilians for other-worldly ends? In the next chapter, we examine terrorism and terrorist organizations, in particular using the story of Osama bin Laden, to ask if terrorism represents an escape from the economic logic of violence presented thus far, or a continuation of the same market forces discussion of violence.

Thought Experiment: Revisiting the Cosa Nostra Narrative

Similar to an experiment conducted in my classes at Georgetown University in Washington, DC, we will conduct a thought experiment on the nature of organized violence. We conclude with an historic case study, and return to the Sicilian Mafia in Sicily, la Cosa Nostra, which "pursues power and money by cultivating the art of killing people and getting away with it, and by organizing itself in a unique way that combines the attributes of a shadow state, an illegal business, and a sworn secret society."[115]

The Mafia's origins stretch back to 1812, when the feudal system in Italy began breaking down during the Napoleonic Wars.[116] Without the state available to protect personal property, individuals emerged to take advantage of the resulting violence to create a new industry collecting money in exchange for protection. On the outskirts of Palermo, the Mafia cultivated its burgeoning operations with the growth of the citrus industry. As lemon groves proved both vulnerable and valuable, the Mafia preyed on the citrus industry through protection rackets and physical intimidation. In the mid-nineteenth century, revolution in Palermo allowed Mafia leaders to expand their power of governance – setting rules and expanding their abilities to provide violence in a sustained manner, as a firm would produce goods. As revolutions swept through Palermo in the mid-nineteenth century, the Mafia began selling protection to threatened political party leaders.[117]

The corrupted Italian political system allowed the Mafia to thrive in its nascent years. During the late 1860s, the Mafia deepened its ties with the local government, helping to obtain votes and to police the streets in exchange for the local government's assistance in keeping the Mafiosi's rivals at bay.[118] During the late 1870s and early 1880s, Rome began to accept the inevitability of cooperating with Sicilian politicians with ties to the Mafia, normalizing the Mafia's political positioning. While the Mafia continued to collect from protection rackets, political alliances became central to the organization's success and complimented the illicit activities taking place simultaneously.[119]

The Mafia continued to adapt its behavior to stay relevant and powerful through Italy's next century of political evolution and churn. In the fall of 1892, peasants in western and central Sicily began to form Fasci groups, demanding new contracts to give the peasants who worked the land a share equal to the proprietors.[120] The fight for land ownership consumed Sicily a second time, in 1919 and 1920, when soldiers returned from World War I and wanted land in exchange for their service, sometimes attempting to take it by force from land-owners. The Mafia at times supported the Fasci, and at other times supported the landowners. But regardless of who held the political power, the Mafia managed to remain relevant and operated with consistent methods through the years: it "infiltrated, cajoled, corrupted" and, when necessary, "terrorized and murdered."[121]

The Mafia's intense demand for loyalty, shrouded by ritual, bolstered the firm's success: families mandated vows of secrecy and blood-oath bonds during each individual's initiation ceremony, demanding trust, silence, and loyalty. Further strengthening these ties, the Mafia maintained governance and controlled its membership through clear rules and strict enforcement. In 1898 General Luigi Pellox became prime minister of Italy and, in his determination to combat crime in Sicily, positioned Ermanno Sangiorgi as the new chief of police in Palermo to defeat the Mafia. Sangiorgi noted that, even during a war, the Mafia abided by a set of internal laws and legal proceedings, allowing them to evade destruction by the emboldened police force.[122]

Where new economic opportunities emerged for the Sicilian diaspora, organized violence followed. As Sicilians began immigrating to distant shores in search of new opportunities, the Mafia adapted and spread. From 1901 to 1913, approximately 800,000 Sicilians immigrated to the United States, including Mafiosi.[123] The Mafia as an institution successfully expanded into the United States through the time-tested approach of adapting to markets – markets for business, politics, and violence. In addition to spreading its influence within specific industries, such as ongoing citrus exports and the drug trade, the Mafia required and built a solid foundation to expand governance (rules and enforcement) outside normal networks of western Sicily. This foundation relied on continued protection rackets; new alliances with politicians, law enforcement, the press, and local citizens; and agreements with other crime organizations and families.

After World War II, the Mafia used these alliances to secure its continued influence in a shaken Italy. As the Allied troops invaded Sicily and dismissed Fascist mayors, many Mafiosi found themselves postured to fill the resulting power vacuum. They protected territory for the landowners within the evolving political landscape of the newly forming separatist movement, and later switched their loyalty to a new national party, the Christian Democracy.[124]

In the West, the Sicilian Mafia became more closely entangled with the United States' drug smuggling industry during the late 1950s, increasing wealth but also internal competition. The Mafia families eventually established "the Commission" to settle disputes and prevent Mafia wars. This Commission served as a representative assembly with strict rules and associated enforcement.[125]

Back in Sicily, however, Mafia families did go to war for a short time. After a car bomb attributed to the Sicilian Mafia killed seven police officers in June 1963 in Ciaculli, public pressure mounted on politicians to crack down on the criminal network until the "men of honor" were beaten into submission. The resulting law enforcement campaign essentially ended the violence that raged between 1962 and 1963, a period that witnessed regular bloodshed as warring families brought their violent disputes to the streets.[126] This conflict, dubbed the First Mafia War, traces its origins to disputes over a drug deal that stretched from Egypt to Sicily and finally to Brooklyn. When it was discovered that the delivered packages were short on the expected heroin load, suspicions flared. After the Consortium ruled that the suspected thief, Calcedonio Di Pisa, was innocent, the Mafiosi he had partnered with on the drug deal took matters into their own hands. Di Pisa's killing in December 1962 set off a chain of retribution killings.

Complicating the matter were the power struggles that followed the assassinations of family leaders. Ultimately the First Mafia War was a "giant game of murder in the dark," as the complex political moves and thirst for vengeance began spiraling out of control.[127] The culmination of the First Mafia War with the Ciaculli car bomb alienated the public so much that Italy's parliament was forced to take action. A parliamentary inquiry was formed and became known as the "Antimafia" – eventually making recommendations for specific criminal legislation targeting the Mafia for the first time in Italy's history.[128]

Despite this initial effort, fading public outrage as violence cooled, ineffective policy recommendations, and high turnover among members of the commission all served to weaken the Antimafia's ability to confront the mob head-on. Alongside the disappointing political response was a weak judicial system that acquitted or handed out reduced sentences to Mafiosi facing charges related to the Mafia War.[129] Part of the difficulty in shutting down the Mafia stemmed from its ability to bribe politicians and intimidate witnesses, thereby weakening any case against it. At the same time, Italy's government continued to fail to fully understand the threat it was facing. Instead of recognizing that "Cosa Nostra can be organized without being a rigid bureaucracy of crime," judges dismissed the possibility of shared norms or criteria between members.[130] This inability to recognize the fundamental nature and strengths of the Mafia allowed the group to continue operations and thrive.

With more success, however, came more inter-family competition. Increased violence between rival factions of the Cosa Nostra escalated in the 1970s and 1980s, culminating in a conflict known as the Second Mafia War. This bloodshed stemmed from the rising influence of the Corleonesi faction that grew to dominate the Sicilian Mafia. Although the Corleonesi eventually achieved near-hegemonic control over the sprawling criminal organization, their enforcement of rules through *mattanza* (slaughter) proved so destructive that it resulted in a massive crackdown against the mob, de-escalating violence and weakening the organization overall.

Tensions had been mounting between the Mafia's factions for years in the 1970s, and the war's outbreak in 1981 did not come as a surprise to either the Mafia members or Italy's law enforcement communities. In 1978, a mob boss and police informant named Giuseppe di Cristini called a meeting with the captain of the carabinieri (Italy's military police) to discuss the splitting political divisions within the Cosa Nostra.[131] Di Cristini recognized that the Corleonesi, led by Luciano Leggio, had been implementing a clear strategy to eliminate rival factions by stealing their support bases and the associated use of brute force violence. Di Cristini was killed a few weeks after this meeting, though his last meeting led the carabinieri to eventually recognize that the Cosa Nostra worked "parallel to the authority of the state" as a "more incisive and efficient power that acts, moves, makes money, kills, and even makes judgments – all behind the backs of the authorities."[132]

With violence clearly on the horizon, the Corleonesi's primary rivals began fleeing Italy – Tommaso Buscetta to Brazil and Tano Badalamenti to the United States – providing an opportunity to strike. Corleonesi assassins swiftly began a killing spree that targeted both the remaining bosses as well as hundreds of supporters in rival groups. The slaughter spread to New York, as anyone whose loyalty was uncertain was targeted, including friends or relatives who may have offered shelter. While violence yielded short-term political victories for the Corleonesi who established complete authority over the

Cosa Nostra, the bloodshed provoked a counter-response finally capable of weakening the Mafia.[133]

Violence was aimed not only at rival Mafia members and their supporters, but anyone who attempted to bring an end to the *mattanza*. Seemingly endless coverage of state funerals for murdered politicians and police officers dominated the news, creating a heightened public demand for the Italian government to finally confront the Mafia. Eventually, under the leadership of Antonino Caponnetto, a group of investigators and magistrates began collecting evidence and intelligence to build a more accurate picture of the Cosa Nostra threat. This culminated in Caponnetto's decision to place the Mafia on trial as a singular, cohesive unit – a massive prosecution that became known as the "maxi-trial."

In 1987, the maxi-trial convicted 360 individuals of the 474 accused, sharing 2,665 years of jail between them.[134] While the verdict was subject to a long appeals process, it was upheld in 1992 and the Mafia was legally viewed as a singular unit. In response, the Mafia, led by Toto Riina, attempted to reassert its power by carrying out a campaign of violence from 1992 to 1993.

The violent campaign was undermined, however, by mass defections, as Mafia members began turning themselves over to the Italian authorities in large numbers, subsequently leading to more arrests and further weakening the organization.[135] Riina's arrest in 1993 left the Mafia disjointed, and Bernardo Provenzano's rise to power in 1995 was marked by a new strategic vision for the Cosa Nostra's operations. Provenzano slightly decentralized the organization, compartmentalized information, removed the Mafia from the public eye, abated the wave of Mafiosi turning to the authorities, and refocused on protection racketeering, moves he saw as essential to the group's survival.[136]

In my class of graduate students at Georgetown University, we do a group exercise in the classroom – a case study on the Cosa Nostra to deeply understand the attributes of and surrounding a successful criminal organization. The students study the Cosa Nostra for a week, reviewing the history recounted here in greater depth. Then we meet in the classroom, and I ask the students three questions. Having just reviewed the history of the Cosa Nostra, although abbreviated for the purpose of this book's thought experiment, consider the students' answers over several years summarized below to these three questions: 1) What enabled the creation of the Cosa Nostra? 2) How did the organization survive and grow as an institution – a firm – for over 150 years? 3) What caused the firm to weaken in the 1990s?

1. **What enabled their creation?**
   - valuable and vulnerable crop/commodity
   - a market for protection/justice
   - weak central government; inability of state to provide for security; scarcity of security
   - provision of security by entrepreneurs in violence
   - development of protection rackets and extortion markets
   - co-opting of local government officials
   - cooperation of central government with the group
   - effective use of violence
2. **How did they succeed over time?**
   - fragile state institutions
   - corrupt local institutions
   - cooperation with rivals, when necessary; political "flexibility"
   - managed perceptions – internally and externally
   - use of religion by institutions and local religious leaders
   - use of religion to constrain behaviors not conducive to loyalty (adultery, prostitution, etc.)
   - maintenance of an "honor code"
   - secretive nature of membership, organizational structure
   - geographical remoteness; difficult terrain
   - intense ritualism – to create bonding, family, loyalty, legitimacy
   - punishment of disloyalty; high price for defection
   - effective use of violence as a tool of enforcement; not random; institutionalized
   - diversified networks/power base (e.g., police, politicians, judiciary, clergy, and beyond)
   - use of support network for families of members in prison, killed, etc., in service to the group
   - patronage – web of reciprocal obligation
   - building of bridges from the licit to the illicit world
3. **How did they weaken?**
   - increase of violence
   - change of public image
   - increase in local demand for state law enforcement
   - loss of support from local politicians and religious leaders
   - increase of political infighting; decrease of cohesion and loyalty and bonds of "family"
   - provision of comparably theatrical counter-narrative by media
   - increase in defection

Satisfied with a good list of attributes of the history of the Sicilian Mafia in Sicily (we call the list above the Cosa Nostra list), I now suggest a twist in the thought experiment. Now think instead of a violent group other than the Cosa Nostra; for example, think of Al Qaeda, the Medellín cartel, the Lord's Resistance Army, ISIS, or any other you happen to know or find compelling. Now, review the list above and ask yourself if that Cosa Nostra list comes close to also describing your other violent group. Now think of another, and another. Year after year, students react with a mix of shock and smiles as they quickly sense that they've pierced some veil, or seen behind some curtain: a list compiled while thinking about a crime family on a remote island in Western Europe and started approximately 200 years ago also describes almost any organized violent group.

The experiment highlights something profound: groups engaged in the persistent provision of violence tend to have a lot in common, even though the motives ascribed to the group differ. It appears that specific religious, ethnic, or other identity attributes do not matter in the way the news and the foreign policy elite commonly portray them. Stated another way, perhaps the use of identity matters a great deal, but not the specific traits of that identity. Religion can play an important role in the success of a violent group, but perhaps the specific elements of the religion do not. When a group kills under the banner of Islam, it is not the Islamic religion that need concern us, only the fact that the leadership of the group successfully uses religion as a means of branding: creating loyalty to enhance recruitment and retention, and to deter defection.

Perhaps this Cosa Nostra list illuminates the landscape beyond short-term policies, headlines, and political punditry, so we can see a more persistent and consistent view of violence. If it does not emerge from identity-category, where does violence come from?

Violence or the threat of violence can improve one's well-being, given the institutions in which one lives. Institutions, their rules and associated enforcement, influence the behaviors of individuals, firms, and entrepreneurs acting in competitive markets. People face scarcity, and so have almost constant need for others; we need to know the "us" and the "them" so we know who to look out for and who will look out for us when matters of survival and growth arise. Issues such as "radical Islam" matter only in the way that branding and marketing matter for a firm. These identity terms help with recruitment, retention, fundraising, and branding in general. So "radical Islam" matters in the same way "Cali," "Medellín," "Sicilian," and "Corleonese" matter. To restate this: it is not the tenets of Islam that matter to Islamic terrorism, just as it is not the racial makeup of Sicilians that matters to Sicilian organized criminal violence. The institutions that frame human behavior make all the difference, and the identity categories help us determine the "us" from the "them."

We now know that violent groups throughout the world, such as ISIS, the Sinaloa cartel in Mexico, and MS-13 in the United States, have a lot in common – and these common traits seems important to understanding in defeating these sources of violence. Each group operates like a firm. And each is led by entrepreneurs. And each leader has a lot to worry about – most notably external competition from competing firms, and internal competition from rival factions and ambitious peers and underlings. Each operates in a marketplace, or multiple marketplaces, which contribute to the feasibility of the sustained provision of violence. Each manages to provide some level of degree of governance, to the exclusion of others, including the provision of violence. In the absence of that specific firm with that brand, for example Al Qaeda, some other firm will arise under the leadership of an entrepreneur, because the market allows or even demands a firm to fill some need.

The questions we must ask today relate not to the nature of radical Islam, but to the scarcities among the population centers where these violent groups operate and the rules of the marketplaces that allow entrepreneurs to engage in sustained acts of coercion and violence. How did Abu Bakr al Baghdadi rise to power and assume the leadership role left by the departure of Osama bin Laden? What competition exists in his market? What scarcities? These seem to be better questions to ask when we seek to counter a violent organization.

5 TERRORISM

Tyler Durden: I see in the fight club the strongest and smartest men who've ever lived. I see all this potential and I see squandering. God damn it, an entire generation pumping gas, waiting tables, slaves with white collars, advertising has us chasing cars and clothes, working jobs we hate so we can buy shit we don't need. We're the middle children of history man, no purpose or place, we have no Great War, no Great Depression, our Great War is a spiritual war, our Great Depression is our lives, we've been all raised by television to believe that one day we'd all be millionaires and movie gods and rock stars, but we won't and we're slowly learning that fact. And we're very very pissed off.

Chuck Palahniuk, *Fight Club*

MOSS: *What's your name?*

BLAKE: *Fuck you, that's my name! You know why, mister? Because you drove a Hyundai to get here tonight, I drove an $80,000 BMW. That's my name.*

[...]

MOSS: *You're such a hero, you're so rich. Why you coming down here and waste your time on a bunch of bums?*

BLAKE: *You see this watch? That watch cost more than your car. I made $970,000 last year. How much you make? You see, pal, that's who I am, and you're nothing.*

David Mamet, *Glengarry Glen Ross*

The Damage of Definition

In the script for the film *Glengarry Glen Ross*, David Mamet powerfully captures the role of the market's oppressive forces in shaping human identity and behavior; you've got to make sales so you can purchase nice things; otherwise, you don't exist. Blake's words tell us that our behavior is linked to our identity, and his speech bullies Moss into behaving in the interest of the firm by making sales. Perhaps this scene reminds the audience of similar pressure felt or observed in their lives.[1] Contrasting this famous Mamet scene with Chuck Palahniuk's cult classic *Fight Club* shows how violence emerges from these market dynamics.[2] Palahniuk's Tyler Durden uses Mamet-style oppression and the grievance it creates to form a terrorist group; Durden encourages disgruntled men to join his "fight club." A subset of members under Durden's leadership later comprise "project mayhem," a domestic terrorist group, bound by shared grievances that create kinship-like bonds. Together they bring down some city skyscrapers.

Comparing dialogue from Mamet and Palahniuk shows us two types of behavior in response to common challenges in the market-place of human interaction. In *Fight Club*, Tyler Durden taps into the market's soul-sucking pressure to create a terrorist group. In *Glengarry Glen Ross*, Moss inspires a robbery. Understanding that terrorism and crime share origins in human behavior and the marketplace, we need to look at other factors to understand when and how violence occurs. Why do individuals sometimes choose crime, insurgency, or terrorism? What causes an individual to choose one violent tool over another?

On September 11, 2001, 19 people associated with Osama bin Laden and his Al Qaeda group conducted the deadliest terrorist attack ever on American soil. The magnitude of evil stunned people around the world, most of whom had never heard of the group before they killed nearly 3,000 unsuspecting people. People watched helplessly as New York City's skyscrapers collapsed and the Pentagon burned. The specter of radical Islam gone global raised a sudden, deep fear: if they can get to them, they can get to me. Security professionals and scholars now had a new enemy and paradigm to study in radical Islam and violent radical extremism.

Speaking before a joint session of Congress on September 20, 2001, President George W. Bush gave voice to the widely held view that hatred drove 9/11's perpetrators, stating, "They hate our freedoms: our freedom of religion, our freedom of speech, our freedom to vote and assemble and disagree with each other ..." He also attributed power as a primary motive, continuing, "By sacrificing human life to serve their radical visions, by abandoning every value except the will to power, they follow in the path of fascism, Nazism and totalitarianism."[3]

In the years since the 9/11 attacks, we've witnessed competing radical Islamic terrorist groups and Al Qaeda affiliates, such as Boko Haram and the Islamic State (also known as Daesh, ISIS, or ISIL), vie for power, leading to three major perspectives that dominate security and policy discussions of how to address the ongoing challenge.

One predominant outlook framed discussions of violence around radical Islamic thought. In 2015, France's prime minister called for a war on radical Islam following Al Qaeda's deadly attack on the French satirical magazine *Charlie Hebdo*.[4] Former senator and vice-presidential candidate Joseph Lieberman echoed the French prime minister, writing, "The U.S., along with the world's other great powers, should form and lead a global alliance against radical Islam."[5] Some commentators have also focused on Islamic theology to explain suicide terrorism.[6]

While both President Bush and these individuals cited above took pains to distinguish between "radical Islam" and "Islam," defining the former as the ideology driving the 9/11 attackers, others peddled a more toxic view that portrayed the attacks as an extension of core Islamic doctrine. The controversy over the so-called "Ground Zero mosque," in which commentators portrayed a Muslim community center as tied to a broader Islamic threat, revealed a strong political current that saw terrorism as intrinsically linked to Muslims and their faith.[7] Political figures have increasingly used Islamophobic rhetoric that ties the actions of known terrorist groups to the beliefs of over 1 billion people, rooting the argument in a religious narrative.[8]

A second perspective suggested that the 9/11 violence was an issue of terrorism at large rather than centering on the ideology driving the attackers. The "War on Terror" narrative broadens the issue to threats beyond radical Islamic terror. President Bush, for example, stated in his speech, "Our war on terror begins with al Qaeda, but it does not end there. It will not end until every terrorist group of global reach has been found, stopped and defeated."[9] He continued, "These measures are essential. But the only way to defeat terrorism as a threat to our way of life is to stop it, eliminate it, and destroy it where it grows."[10]

A third framework focused neither on radical Islam nor on terrorism generally but specifically on Al Qaeda, the organization responsible for the 9/11 attacks. President Obama's Chief of Staff Denis McDonough, for example, expressed this perspective when he articulated how President Obama differed from President Bush on CBS' Face the Nation: "Well, we say we're in a war against al Qaeda. We have just never said we have been in a war against terrorism, which is a tactic. It's an unusual thing to say that we're at war against a tactic."[11]

Each of these three frames at once grasps part of the challenge while distracting us from a full understanding. Blaming violence on a particular religion, religious sect, or ethnicity is like blaming violence on an abundance of young men or an absence of women. We confuse correlation with causation. The scholarly and policy community has largely produced distractions in the past decade, not solutions. The common refrain in the halls of power places this issue within discussions of marginalization, arguing that people engage in violence because they feel marginalized due to their ethnicity, religion, or lack of job prospects. This theory distracts from essential knowledge because violence does not stem from marginalization, real or perceived. Instead, marginalization facilitates entrepreneurs of organized violence. We saw this in *Fight Club* when Tyler Durden harnessed marginalization to create "Project Mayhem." In the absence of Durden, we would need a substitute leader to create a similar institution of organized violence. Approaching terrorism from an economic perspective focuses on both the institution providing violence as well as the leaders controlling the organization. In this chapter, we will focus on Osama bin Laden as an entrepreneur acting in the marketplace for power.

Osama bin Laden

By examining Osama bin Laden as a political entrepreneur who behaved consistently within the logic of the marketplace for violence, we can recognize parallels with the actions of other violent leaders in contexts beyond radical Islam, including Pablo Escobar and Joseph Kony. We will not say there is no religious story, but instead see that the influence of radical Islam proves secondary – important and perhaps necessary to understand, of course, but insufficient as the primary point of analysis or used without integrating into a market-based explanation. To see the Osama bin Laden narrative merely as a story of terrorism would ignore the other activities – whether crime, insurgency, or legal businesses – that enabled bin Laden and his followers to carry out the 9/11 attacks and develop the networked firm that became Al Qaeda. Throughout this chapter we will also note how bin Laden's story is not atypical, but one that recurs in context after context, helping to explain the behavior of violent entrepreneurs, including Abu Bakr al Baghdadi, the leader of ISIS.

Osama bin Laden was raised in an environment that would shape his religion, political views, and behavior. Like Escobar and Kony, bin Laden was not born into circumstances defined by radical antipathy or marginalization. Instead, when bin Laden was born in Saudi Arabia on March 10, 1957, his family was at the center of the country's economic development. In the early 1970s, bin Laden became involved with Islamist politics and religious activism outside his home and school.[12] The Palestinian struggle resonated strongly for him. His mother recalled: "He thought Muslim youths were too busy having fun to care about what they should do to propagate Islam and bring back the old glories of the Muslim nation. He wanted Muslims to unite and fight to liberate Palestine."[13] She continued, "He had been a devoted Muslim all his life but he was a moderate one, according to those who knew him. He played football. Went to picnics, rode horses and socialized. He never caused me to worry about him in his teenage years."[14] Bin Laden's early views were neither unique nor even particularly extreme. While they certainly were a factor in his life path, focusing on them fails to distinguish between him and the millions of other Muslims with similar views or upbringings.

Another aspect of bin Laden's early life, however, holds more analytical importance. The family business and its work ethic both strongly influenced bin Laden's goals and opportunities. As Michael Scheuer, the former head of the CIA's bin Laden unit, puts it, "Osama was born into a large, wealthy, and prominent family of Yemeni origin whose males rose to positions of business and family leadership via unrelenting hard work, perseverance, stubbornness, genuine religious faith, self-reliance, and risk-taking. This shaped the man bin Laden would become."[15] Bin Laden's high-school teacher would reflect that his student began working hard to "prove himself within the company," and noted, "there is a law in the bin Laden family that if you prove yourself as a man, you can inherit."[16] As part of his work for his father's construction business, bin Laden managed a multi-ethnic labor force and began developing skills that likely influenced his management of Al Qaeda's workforce.[17] In 1978, Bin Laden enrolled in King Abdul Aziz University to study economics and business management.[18] We will see throughout this chapter that these skills and the entrepreneurial spirit instilled in bin Laden hold far more explanatory power than his early religiosity or political views.

Bin Laden further revealed his entrepreneurial drive when he left Saudi Arabia to fight with the Mujahideen in Afghanistan following the 1979 Soviet Union invasion.[19] Although bin Laden's mother pointed out his early fixation on "defending Muslim lands against invaders," this political ambition, steeped in a religious context, was likely pervasive at the time and hardly unique to bin Laden. Religiosity, politicized Islam, and anti-Western and anti-American views were not rare, and bin Laden's beliefs did little to distinguish him from the many others who fought in Afghanistan. At the same time, many individuals with similar views or backgrounds did *not* join the Mujahideen, demonstrating that fixating on religious views holds little salience when understanding bin Laden's choice to engage in organized violence. Indeed, Saudi prince and director general of Saudi Arabia's intelligence service, Turki al Faisal, met bin Laden during the war against the Soviets in Afghanistan and considered him ordinary. Faisal told the deputy editor-in-chief of *Arab News* during an interview, "His behavior at the time left no impression that he would become what he has become. As you know at that time there were many volunteers, Saudis and non-Saudis, and he was one of them. He did not enjoy special status that made us focus on him."[20] This same pattern is reflected in bin Laden's later decision to form Al Qaeda and eventually direct the 9/11 attacks. Focusing solely on bin Laden's religion fails to explain why he, and not one of the many other bin Laden family members, let alone one of the millions of Middle Eastern Muslims with vaguely anti-American views, would embark on the path to 9/11. Instead, a clear behavioral economic explanation distinguishes bin Laden from others.

Stated directly, bin Laden's decisions to engage in organized violence followed his recognition that there was little room for advancement in the Saudi arena: the market was too crowded, and he lacked the skills to pursue any available opportunities. Bin Laden lacked sufficient academic credentials to pursue a position in the Saudi upper class outside of work in the family business, and he lacked the religious training to become a member of the clergy.[21] Despite the opportunity to obtain a position in the family business, this path did not necessarily promise a life of advancement. As Lawrence Wright notes, "His obvious future was to remain in the family company, far down the list in seniority, respected within his family ambit but never able to really make a mark."[22] As with Pablo Escobar, who from a young age sought greatness beyond what was available to a man of his social class and familial lineage, Osama bin Laden was not content with the fate of being a mid-level figure in the family business and once declared, "I want to be like my father. I will work day and night with no rest."[23] In such a situation, it is hardly surprising that bin Laden would depart to make his mark in the way young men – whether Muslim, Christian, Jewish, atheist, or of any other background – have for ages. He went to war.[24] He chose violence.

Bin Laden's entrepreneurial spirit and his business management and organizing skills quickly distinguished him in the Afghan jihad and its aftermath. Ahmad Zaidan, who reported on the Afghan jihad, recalls that bin Laden's personality resembled that of a businessman, stating, "He was very much organized and very much calculating things."[25] Upon his arrival in Pakistan, where much of the fight against the Soviets was based, bin Laden took up a role handling the war effort's financial aspects.[26] This placed him directly within the market where he used his personal connections and business training to raise funds for the Mujahideen. Scheuer writes, "That he moved easily among the Gulf's royal and business elite is not a surprise; he had grown up among them and studied and played with their sons."[27]

In 1984, bin Laden met with Abdullah Azzam, a Palestinian teacher who joined the Muslim Brotherhood and supported the armed struggle in Afghanistan. Together, Azzam and bin Laden established a group to help conduct the war against the Soviets – the Makhtab al-Khadamat, or Services Bureau.[28] Azzam served as the official leader, but bin Laden provided the start-up capital in the form of $300,000 per year to cover operating costs.[29] This proved to be the key moment that established the organizational structure that would later become Al Qaeda. As a result, it is worth examining the context in which Azzam and bin Laden were able to establish a violent sub-state firm.

The Services Bureau engaged in civil war, to use lexicon familiar to the national security reader. We saw in the previous chapter that feasibility, rather than the existence of greed or grievance, is the critical factor in determining when a rebel movement can take hold. The conditions facing Azzam and bin Laden provided a favorable route to overcome threshold barriers to entering the market for civil violence. Bin Laden brought his family wealth; the Soviet invasion created a grievance narrative and a way to recruit supporters; and Pakistan's commitment to the war against the Soviets in Afghanistan provided a geographic safe haven from which the firm could run business operations. If the conditions had been unfavorable for the development for the Services Bureau, Azzam and bin Laden would have failed, and Al Qaeda as we know it may never have happened – no matter how aggrieved and ideologically motivated the leaders. In other words, without the economic story of markets for violence, the religious-ideological story of Al Qaeda would have no practical impact.

The Services Bureau

The Services Bureau ran in a way similar to any other firm: the leaders required revenues to exceed costs, otherwise they would fail. The Bureau used its funds to develop guesthouses and support systems for Arab fighters and others supporting the war against the Soviets. In exchange, Azzam and bin Laden gained the loyalty and knowledge of those conducting the fighting.[30] Like many firms in an era of globalization, the bureau built a multinational network of offices that raised funds and sent recruits to the headquarters in Pakistan.[31]

Buoyed with start-up capital from bin Laden, the Services Bureau published *Al-Jihad* magazine.[32] The magazine was constrained and shaped by the same market forces that shape any other business, licit or illicit. Jamal Ismail, who worked as a journalist with the magazine, recalls, "I think after the issue 25 of maybe 30 [*Jihad* magazine] was printed in Lahore. After that we shifted printing to Karachi for commercial reasons, because instead of bringing it from Lahore by truck we were sending it abroad from Karachi directly."[33]

In addition to revealing another instance of universal market forces, the story of *Jihad* magazine also demonstrates how individuals within the jihadist movement used appeals to kinship and ideology as a form of non-monetary payment. Ismail states, "We were in need to recruit more people. Sheikh Abdullah Azzam started campaigning for the magazine among the Arabs, saying that if you work for the magazine inside Afghanistan, maybe in the eyes of the Almighty Allah, your achievements will be more important than carrying a Kalashnikov."[34]

This promise teased religious affirmation as payment in exchange for labor. Hardly unique from other forms of payment we have seen, Ismail's recollections show us that bin Laden and Azzam used religion as the context for marketplace exchanges. This is a starkly different perspective from a focus on the religious theology behind the promise.

Of course, in addition to the everlasting promises, Azzam also provided traditional monetary payments. This mixture of monetary and non-monetary payment should be familiar from the previous chapters. Although these wages were considerably low, as Jacob Shapiro and others noted in their examination of Al Qaeda in Iraq's wage structure, this may have stemmed from the need to institute a screening system in the firm. By developing a workforce tied to the firm by non-monetary rewards, violent organization leaders made it more difficult for American and coalition forces to supplant their control.[35]

Likewise, the jihadist marketplace was not devoid of competition. There were many disputes within the market, and as Lawrence Wright writes, "at the root of these quarrels was the usual culprit – money. Peshawar was the funnel through which cash poured into the jihad and the vast relief effort to help the refugees." He continues, "Scarcity only fed the frenzy over what remained: the international aid agencies, private charities, and bin Laden's pockets."[36] Azzam, for example, once complained that "the Saudi authorities are not pleased that I am leading the Arabs in Afghanistan," continuing, "All the money that comes for orphans and widows and schools comes from Saudi Arabia. They are unhappy to see the young Saudis being organized under my leadership. They fear they will become a part of the Muslim Brotherhood."[37]

Indeed, the collaboration between bin Laden and Azzam came under great pressure as each sought decision-making power over resources. In 1986, bin Laden began to distance himself from Azzam in a dispute centered on organizational practice. Bin Laden opposed providing funds to Ahmed Shah Massoud, preferring to support the Pashtun commanders he was closest to, and resisted distributing Arab volunteers to Afghan command, wanting to centralize Arab forces under his leadership.[38] Azzam held the opposite views. The entrepreneurial Azzam–bin Laden split is revealed by a comment of Azzam's, playing down bin Laden's threat to his firm: "Osama is limited [...] What can Osama do to organize people? Nobody knows him! Don't worry."[39] Azzam was right to flag the ability to organize people and make exchanges as the determinant of who would lead within the jihadist market – but he vastly underestimated bin Laden's capacity to do so. We have seen that disagreement and competition do not preclude some cooperation – for example, Escobar's cooperation with the Cali cartel and M-19 amidst wars with those two firms. Similarly, bin Laden kept funding Azzam's Services Bureau until 1988.[40]

The disagreement between Azzam and bin Laden shows us another instance where, if the economic and organizational structure had formed differently, the bin Laden story would have radically shifted. If bin Laden had acquiesced to Azzam's organizational preference for dispersing Arab fighters among the Afghans, it is unlikely that a globalized, centrally controlled terrorist organization capable of the 9/11 attacks could have emerged. After the split, Azzam's Services Bureau became an increasingly non-violent, non-governmental organization, devoting substantial effort to charity and schooling and less effort to direct armed conflict.[41]

Building a Firm

Bin Laden's Arab Unit was structured and constrained by the same market forces as legitimate business activity, and its development was not entirely separate from licit international markets. When bin Laden broke away from Azzam and formed his own group, he brought his business training and family wealth to the market of Salafi jihadists, flowering in the permissive environment of 1980s Afghanistan and Pakistan. No matter how wealthy or skilled, however, he still needed to assemble a trusted team. Bin Laden launched his centralized firm of Arab fighters and turned to his network for assistance. For his headquarters, he struck a deal with Abdul Rasul Sayyaf. As Scheuer notes, "Before he could start an Arab-only unit, bin Laden needed a place inside Afghanistan to use as a base for training, for caching ordnance and other supplies, and for launching operations".[42] In exchange for Sayyaf's assistance, bin Laden helped build Sayyaf's training facilities.[43] Through this transaction, Bin Laden and 11 others moved into what would become known as the Lion's Den. He borrowed an engineer from his father's company, Abdullah Saadi, to oversee its construction and importing materials from Saudi Arabia.[44] Bin Laden moved in on October 24, 1986, and by 1987 the base had grown significantly.

Religion, Terrorism, and Economics

Up to this point, the discussion of terrorism and bin Laden's story resembles our discussions on insurgent and criminal groups in previous chapters. Despite the dominant perspective that religion distinguishes Al Qaeda or other terrorist groups from insurgents or criminals, religion serves as an element in a marketplace. Religion provides goods, branding and marketing, recruiting, and rules and enforcement to individuals. When seen this way, terrorism falls neatly into the logic of organized violence. Empirical proof of this lies in the observable use of religious rhetoric by insurgents and criminals, not just terrorists.

It is important to ask here why Islamic terrorism only emerged in the 1990s. The answer is economic for the most part. The rise of so-called Islamic terrorism occurred during a moment in history when leftwing terrorism supported by communism and the Soviet Union was on the decline. The Soviet Union was a cheap source of capital for revolutionary movements during the Cold War, but once the Soviet Union was no longer a participant in the market, revolutionaries of leftwing and nationalist movements began shifting to Islamic-backed terrorism.

Sayyid Qutb and the rise of the Muslim Brotherhood started an anti-American theme in the Arab world as early as the 1950s, but the strength of today's anti-Americanism would have been hard to predict. It gained power during and after the Islamic Revolution of 1979, when religious leaders of Iran used anti-US rhetoric to defeat the moderate domestic Iranian opposition. Interestingly, however, through the mid-1980s it was the communists, not Islamic fundamentalists, whose policies were most hostile to the US.[45] The end of the Cold War provided for the right market structure to allow for and encourage the growing movement of anti-Americanism; this is why the 1990s collapse of the Soviet Union marks the 1990s rise of the so-called era of Islamic Terrorism.

Today, this terrorism has morphed into a fundamentalist movement. But is important to note that this "Islamic Terrorism" differs from jihad in traditional Islamic thought. Khaleel Mohammed, in his work *Islam and Violence*, argues that it is an error to equate the scriptural use of jihad with "holy war." In fact, he says, there has never been any single Islamic creed about jihad; the Koran actually has other words, like *harb* and *qitāl*, that are used to describe war and fighting.

The concept of jihad is one that has instead evolved over time with changing interpretations of the Koran and scripturally has nothing to do with terrorism. Its literal and earliest meaning in the Koran is "struggle," not, as many have argued, "to wage war."[46]

Evidence from the study of religious movements suggests that the logic of organized violence rests comfortably within the rules and norms of the religious institution.[47] In fact, demand for the supernatural proves almost universal among societies around the world, and many individuals willingly offer to sacrifice themselves in exchange for supernatural fulfillment.[48] As such, religious entrepreneurs emerge to create sects – firms that provide supernatural goods.[49]

Radicalization, violence, and the relationship between the two concepts vary greatly over time, suggesting they do not derive from the language of a sacred text but from markets and competition.[50] For example, Hamas, for many years a largely non-violent group, changed when the first Palestinian intifada stirred competitors, forcing the leaders to move toward violence to maintain political relevance in the market.[51] In the shift from non-violence to violence, the market conditions changed, not the Koran. Therefore, we must approach with skepticism any analysis that, seeking to determine the causes or levels of violence used by religious groups, focuses on the religious texts and dogma rather than on the market conditions.

Although not the cause of radical violence, religious rhetoric plays an important part in the markets for power, wealth, and revenge. For example, using religious rhetoric helped bin Laden manage, recruit, and retain workers and form organizational partnerships during Al Qaeda's early and formative days. Think of religion as a technology, a way to recruit and retain employees, and to increase sales by marketing the group to potential members, donors, and supporters.[52] As Laurence Iannaccone notes, religion's promise of an afterlife can motivate people to risk or even sacrifice their lives.[53] Additionally, the high costs of fulfilling religious duties can act as a screening mechanism to weed out free-riders – individuals who benefit from the group without providing anything in exchange.[54] Wrapping organizational goals in religious language also benefits an entrepreneur by providing a ready-made social network for members; the leader gets the incredible ability to incentivize membership and loyalty by providing friendship and belonging. By framing violence as part of a religious conflict, the entrepreneur can benefit from the distaste for and even hatred of "others" that the leader may weave into the religious-based narrative he sells to his group.[55] The key point is that, far from being sacred-text specific, religion can serve important purposes for entrepreneurs, especially entrepreneurs of violence.

Managing Radicalism

Like grabbing a tiger by the tail, inspiring zealotry requires the ability to manage. Although bin Laden used the exposition of religious views to recruit and manage his organization – just as we have seen other organized violent actors do – he needed to balance his rhetoric to avoid extremism that might weaken his control. Michael Scheuer notes that individuals seeking martyrdom posed a management challenge for bin Laden: unwilling to lose his workforce to overzealousness, bin Laden would encourage his men to remain patient.[56] Jamal Ismail, a journalist with *Jihad* magazine at the time, recalls one instance of bin Laden reining in religious zeal. Saudi King Fahd was being criticized in the Afghan-Arab jihadist circles for having accepted an award from Queen Elizabeth II that had a cross on it, and, according to Ismail, "Some people [in Peshawar] they were saying it is a cross which represents the British ideas about Christianity and therefore [King Fahd] is not Muslim. [Osama] asked all of them, 'For God's sake, don't discuss this subject. Concentrate on your mission. I don't permit anyone to discuss this issue here.'"[57] The organizational management challenge also manifested itself in bin Laden's relations with Afghan commanders. Scheuer writes, "Bin Laden and his lieutenants were constantly engaged in negotiating with or mollifying local Afghan commanders, some of whom did not like Arabs, seeing them as reckless would-be martyrs with whom they could not communicate."[58]

Bin Laden's efforts to counsel restraint among his subordinates provides another example of a leader instituting rules and constraints within his firm. Bin Laden recognized the necessity in governing the behaviors of the workforce, underscoring the paucity of analytical rigor in accounts that focus solely on bin Laden's religiosity. When a firm fails to govern its workforce, it fails; bin Laden received no free pass from this rule. Lawrence Wright recounts another story of bin Laden restraining religious zeal in response to market pressures. The story involves Sheikh Tameem al Adnani, who according to Wright "was consistently pushing bin Laden to throw the men into battle, giving voice to the bold and heedless elements in the camp who were lusting for death. Bin Laden managed to put him off, citing the men's lack of training and the pressing need to finish construction, but Tameem never let up."[59] At one point, when bin Laden was visiting Saudi Arabia, Tameem attempted an operation that would have surely failed if bin Laden had not returned in time to stop him.[60] While the story illustrates that religious zeal was subordinated to economic necessity by bin Laden, it also reveals that some leaders face incentives to allow religious zeal to run its course. In exchange for Tameem's compliance, bin Laden eventually "allowed the sheikh to climb a peak and fire mortars and machine guns toward the enemy."[61] Indeed, bin Laden would explain his choices in quite practical terms, admitting, "I was afraid that some of the brothers might return to their countries and tell their people that they had stayed here for six months without ever shooting a gun," adding, "People might conclude that we don't need their support."[62] The economic context and incentives that enabled bin Laden as an entrepreneur to create an armed sub-state group required him to manage religious zealotry by channeling it to serve his interests.

Similar to religious extremism cutting both ways, the presence of foreign fighters in bin Laden's camp, creating a multi-ethnic workforce, posed both benefits and challenges. Although his labor base shared a Salafi jihadist ideology, their diverse backgrounds, cultures, and languages complicated bin Laden's efforts to effectively control his firm. Scheuer explains the managerial issues that these diverse preferences and skills presented:

> Besides channeling this religious zeal, bin Laden, Abu Ubaydah, and Abu Hafs also had to learn how to manage young men of various nationalities and ethnic groups. While Saudis and Yemenis dominated the group, there also were North Africans, Kurds, Egyptians, and Sudanese. The men also differed in educational levels – some had attended college, others high school, and some were semi-literate – and work experience. The volunteers included businessmen, soldiers, policemen, laborers, and dilettante sons of the wealthy. Their degree of commitment and dedication to jihad also varied. There were those who joined for the duration – and are with al-Qaeda or other Islamist groups today – those who came on a lark, and those who wanted to go home as soon as winter started. On

top of such variables, each volunteer reacted in a different way to living in a foreign country, many for the first time.[63]

That the diverse labor market in terrorism would create a managerial problem should not surprise us. We have seen in earlier chapters that organized criminals and insurgents are also limited by the labor markets they draw upon and do not represent unitary actors but, instead, groups of individuals that need to be organized. For example, Escobar found himself regulating the production of violence against Colombian police officers because it did not serve his interests. Jacob Shapiro studied 108 memoirs and autobiographies of terrorists spanning multiple ideologies, regions, and time periods, and found that disputes within groups as well as organizational management issues were pervasive.[64] From Al Qaeda in Iraq, to the Red Army Faction, the IRA, and Mau-Mau insurgents, terrorist organizations reported disunity in the ranks, requiring their leaders to undertake certain procedures to limit disorder.[65]

Thought Experiment: Voodoo Donuts

To understand this phenomenon further, let's imagine how it may relate to a licit business. Picture a small, remote town with one intersection. In that town, "Allen" opens the first ever donut shop, A's Donuts. The town responds with great enthusiasm; we witness a line out the door over the first months and Allen, the owner, makes a great profit. Seeing this, another member of the town, Bert, opens a second donut shop across the street, B's Donuts, and cuts into Allen's profits by selling similar donuts at a lower price. They each face the same cost curve for costs of good sold; they purchase flour, sugar, pay rent, hire employees, etc. Over time, Allen decreases prices in order to compete against Bert, lowering Bert's profits. Bert responds in kind. At some point, Allen and Bert reach a price that they cannot lower any further since neither would make any money and so hit a price equilibrium. But the story does not end there.

Unable to compete any more on price, Bert decides to compete on quality. Bert starts selling organic coffee and uses organic whole-wheat flour. She also raises her prices and therefore increases her profits and market share. Allen responds by mimicking *Voodoo Donut*, the famous Portland, Oregon shop, with unusual flavors and fancy packaging. Now that they're selling different products, they can each continue to raise prices and regain some profit. This story of Allen and Bert essentially describes markets and competition for almost anything, although greatly simplified.

Now picture these same two businesses, competing on price and quality, but instead of bakers, Allen and Bert lead houses of worship; they preach as clergy. They use the same sacred texts and need to compete in this small town for members. Instead of pastries, think how the story changes if we talk about religion. Allen and Bert still compete for the time, attention, and resources of the town's people, but instead of selling a tangible product with immediate rewards – sugar and fried dough – they now sell a supernatural product. They might still compete on price, or the expected contribution that a worshiper needs to provide (e.g., tithe, zakat, tzedakah). They might also compete qualitatively – offering a qualitatively different product, in this case, supernatural rewards, blessings, or the afterlife.

Like any market, where a demand for the supernatural exists, suppliers will appear; however, marketing the supernatural presents a challenge for potential suppliers: they require high levels of credibility. This is where religion becomes complicated. If Allen and Bert sell me different stories of the supernatural, how do I know who is more likely to get me a better deal? Who is more likely to deliver on promises in the afterlife? I cannot walk out of a service and be sure of what I've purchased like I can with a donut. Instead, I need to trust the person doing the selling; I must have faith that the religious leader speaks the truth. Once earned, the leaders also need to compete to maintain their constituents' loyalty. To do this, religious institutions diversify and cater to the here-and-now. They do not merely sell a version of the supernatural; they address the needs of the population today by running soup kitchens, feeding and clothing the poor among the town, or maybe building hospitals and schools.

In effect, the religious institution sells several goods: a narrative about life and the afterlife; fellowship and a sense of community for people to belong; and mutual aid, providing social and physical benefits to members. Through membership in a church, synagogue, temple, mosque, etc., I certainly see tangible benefits: friendship, belonging, and community support during hard times, such as food brought to the house during periods of mourning. Regardless of the credibility of the supernatural story, individual members of religious communities benefit in the present moment. This gives Allen and Bert the opportunity to compete in multiple dimensions. Bert can open a daycare, for example, while Allen can organize affinity groups for singles or teens. In this way, just like the bakers, Allen and Bert as religious leaders behave like entrepreneurs in a competitive market. In many ways, the story remains exactly the same. But in the market for the supernatural, some differences pose serious implications.

In a compelling body of literature, Eli Berman builds on Iannaccone's work and applies what economists would call a "Club Goods" model to terrorist organizations.[66] In this work, Berman demonstrates empirically that the most lethal groups also tend to be radical religious sects. For example, Hezbollah, founded by a group of former seminary students, later becomes a comparatively "successful" group at killing innocents. Seminary students also created the Taliban. Prior to its success at violence, Hamas was a benign group for many years, a non-violent religious organization with a network to provide social services and support charities. Many other would-be violent terrorist groups failed while these three succeeded, and Berman attributes the failure to their secular nature. Although these examples represent radical Islam, Berman points out that it is not the particular theology of the group that determines success or failure in terrorism, but rather the organizational design.

Returning to our town, leaders Allen and Bert are competing for membership among the community, are believed to have credibility with regard to the afterlife, offer community and camaraderie, and begin to compete in the provision of goods. Once established, Allen also has the ability to increase the cost of membership. If you join his congregation and receive significant social benefits, then he can raise the price of membership. This in essence is the Club Goods model: Allen's religious community is a club that provides services and benefits to its members. If you defect, you lose the benefits – both immediate and everlasting. In this way, religious sects that provide large amounts of mutual aid have solved the defection problem.

All radical religious groups share a common organizational design in the supply of mutual aid, or social services and charitable goods provided by the community.[67] In order to become a full member of one of these groups, one must follow the rules. For some select subsections of religious groups, an effective means to obtain longevity involves sacrifice: high-cost behaviors such as strict rules regarding dress, means of prayer, sex, diet, and social relations. We saw Alice Lakwena and Joseph Kony use similar control measures to moderate their insurgent groups' behaviors in Chapter 4. These "fundamentalist" or "extremist" behaviors may seem irrational to the outsider, but for the in-group they provide a means of ensuring competitive advantage in a crowded market as well as avoiding free-riders.[68]

The more prohibitions one accepts, the more mutual aid opportunities one receives. These opportunities are mutual in the sense that members who contribute will also receive, necessitating a sacrifice from individuals in order to be fully included with the group. Sacrifice demonstrates commitment, and members who have contributed are less likely to defect from the cause given their investments and attachment to benefits. The greater the subsidies received by the members, the greater the amount and degree of prohibitions will be accepted. This process of sacrifice and prohibition weeds out members who might cheat – those who attempt to benefit from aid provision without giving in exchange.

This prohibition system enables radical religious sects to deter defection. This is critically important for the success of terrorist cells since lower defection odds enable higher-risk and higher-value attacks. As we saw with Pablo Escobar's story, deterring defection is critical for any business, but more so for illicit businesses given their associated operating constraints and potential losses if a member turns to law enforcement. Without risk of betrayal, a violent or criminal group can plan and execute complex operations successfully.

Not all radical religious sects engage in acts of terrorism, and in fact the large majority of sects provide value to their members and communities without doing harm to outsiders. However, the organizational design that deters defection from religious groups also deters defection from violent groups. So it is the organizational design that correlates violence with radical religious sects, and not the religious text. This Club Goods approach applied to terrorist groups by Berman and Iannaccone nicely clarifies this perspective: organizations that supply high levels of mutual aid can deter defection and therefore have greater ability and manpower to engage in complex acts of terrorist violence.

Think about the implications for those engaged in countering organized violence; if we appreciate the entire organizational design, rather than focusing on the ideology, we get a higher return on investment from combating the organization itself rather than its adherents. Religious beliefs are complex and widespread, and individuals join groups for many reasons. The challenge of countering radical religious rhetoric and stopping individuals from joining extremist groups seems daunting; people willingly fight and die for many causes. To think we can stop this is foolish. Further, terrorist entrepreneurs only need to select a small number of recruits to engage in substitution strategies that challenge supply-side solutions.[69] For example, United States and Coalition forces' counter-messaging strategies may decrease the likelihood of a certain demographic within a certain population to join a violent movement, but the entrepreneur can switch messaging and target different populations in response. Counter-messaging provides utility in the fight against organized violence when the messaging increases the violent entrepreneur's costs of doing business.

In noting how these economic forces structured bin Laden's development of the Arab Unit, it is important not to separate this knowledge from violence defined by other fields. Bin Laden's terrorist organization was affected by the same universal market dynamics. As this discussion has demonstrated, bin Laden's religious beliefs do not preclude his experience from these economic forces. We have seen similar patterns in Joseph Kony's use of Christian ideology, and in the Italian mafia's Catholic rituals. Indeed, what bin Laden personally believed is in many ways less of an interesting story than how the market shaped his actions. If bin Laden did not have the economic acumen to work amidst those market incentives – regardless of whether or not he believed in martyrdom and in the religiosity surrounding him – he might have remained a marginalized worker stuck in a mid-level position in his family's business. Stated another way, we could imagine many other people with radical religious views and aspirations similar to Osama bin Laden, but without his success. Like any business, terrorism is difficult to sustain – perhaps even more so than other opportunities.

Building a religious firm is a complex process, and terrorist leaders are unable to simply latch wholesale onto religious zealotry without engaging in management and exchange to organize the belief system, as illustrated by bin Laden's difficulties with the Afghan Arab jihadists' zealotry preventing battlefield success. Moreover, as Thomas Hegghammer notes in his study of Al Qaeda's post-9/11 campaign of violence in Saudi Arabia, violent entrepreneurs face a trust dilemma, and apparent religious belief on its own is often an insufficient signal of loyalty.[70] Relying on the outward claims of religiosity in the absence of good managerial tactics makes disloyalty lower costs and opens an organization up to spies and infiltrators. Benefits in the here-and-now increase the costs of defection, and make supernatural payments comparatively risky and less efficient.[71]

Bin Laden's Bonds and the Firm within the Firm: Al Qaeda

In 1988, bin Laden formed a firm within the Arab Unit, a group of closely bound individuals known as *Al Qaeda*, or "The Base."[72] Minutes from an August 11, 1988 meeting between bin Laden and Abu Rida, another founding member, illustrate the roots of the deliberate, calculated decision to develop Al Qaeda as a close-knit and organized group. The account records bin Laden describing the rationally and deliberately organized economic activity he engaged in prior to Al Qaeda's formation: "I am one person. We have not started an organization or an Islamic group. It was a period of one year and a half, it was a period of education, building energy, and testing the brothers who came. Starting all these matters, in the darkest of circumstances, and the period is very short, we took very huge gains from the people in Saudi Arabia. We were able to give political power to the Mujahedeen; gathering donations in very large amounts."[73] The minutes also reveal the leaders' discussion on future training and goals, stating, "Initial estimate, within 6 months of al Qaeda (the Base), 314 brothers will be trained and ready."[74]

Notes from a second meeting made the division even clearer, drawing a distinction between those who would be trained for a "limited duration" and "distributed on Afghan fronts" and those in the category "Open [ended] duration: They enter a testing camp and the best brothers of them are chosen to enter al Qaeda Al Askariya (the military base)."[75] The decision to form Al Qaeda also followed a desire to form what Prince Turki called a "brotherhood of experienced mujahedeen from the Arab World, to take care of one another," or, in economic terms, creating kinship ties to solidify the firm's internal cohesion.[76]

Two events in 1989 enabled bin Laden to strengthen his organizational control and expand his nascent Al Qaeda firm: the assassination of Azzam, bin Laden's former partner and the competing entrepreneur posing the greatest challenge to the new group, and the Soviet withdrawal from Afghanistan.[77] Azzam's killer remains unknown, but the Palestinian had drawn criticism from both Egyptian and Saudi leaders in jihadist circles, and was seen as a competitor and obstacle to their own goals.[78] Azzam's death enabled Ayman al-Zawahiri, who had spread rumors that Azzam worked for the Americans the week prior to his assassination, to solidify his influence with bin Laden.[79] Wright describes the reciprocal benefits of their cooperation: "Each man fulfilled a need in the other. Zawahiri wanted money and contacts, which bin Laden had in abundance. Bin laden, an idealist given causes, sought direction; Zawahiri, a seasoned propagandist, supplied it."[80]

al-Zawahiri's role also facilitated increased Egyptian jihadist participation in bin Laden's group. Bin Laden's wealth posed an opportunity for al-Zawahiri. Hassan Adu-Rabbuh al Surayhi, a Saudi involved in the Afghan jihad, recalls this exchange, stating:

> Bin Laden's finances were not a secret to anyone and I think the Egyptians wanted to exploit this angle. After the end of the jihad, the Egyptians began to gather and meet in bin Laden's residence in Peshawar. They began to invite journalists and the representatives of relief agencies to bin Laden's residence in order to put him in the spotlight because they began to operate under his umbrella.[81]

Surayhi recalls Abu Ubaidah al Banjshiri, one of the central founders of Al Qaeda, telling him, following one such meeting at bin Laden's home:

> You are aware of brother Osama bin Laden's generosity. He has spent a lot of money to buy arms for the young mujahedeen as well as in training them and paying for their travel tickets. Now that the jihad has ended, we should not waste this. We should invest in these young men and we should mobilize them under his umbrella.[82]

By investing in bin Laden's firm early on, the Egyptian jihadist leaders secured their influence and subsequently used the group to further their own aims.

This story also highlights the challenge of funding that followed the second pivotal event: the Soviet withdrawal from Afghanistan. As the Soviet threat diminished, United States and Saudi funding that once flowed through Peshawar and into Afghanistan began to dry up, creating conditions of scarcity that increased competition over the remaining funding sources: "international aid agencies, private charities, and bin Laden's pockets."[83] Prince Turki stated that "once the Soviet withdrew from Afghanistan … the U.S. particularly turned its back on the situation and let things develop without much attention or care."[84] Bin Laden's wealthy background and access to capital positioned him well in these conditions of scarcity – he had money when others did not – enabling him to emerge as a particularly powerful individual. As *Time* magazine put it in a 2009 piece, "the Arab Afghans argued about where the jihad should go next and squabbled over shrinking resources. Bin Laden, with his deep pockets, was the prize."[85] Osama bin Laden had achieved prominence and power.

While the markets of the late 1980s increased the comparative advantage of bin Laden, they also posed challenges to his new firm. The Soviet withdrawal did not fully end the war, and the Arab and Afghan militants continued to fight the communist Afghan government that remained in control. As an influx of Arab militants entered the country to take advantage of the waning conflict and "boast … of adventure," bin Laden's group faced chaos and increased competition.[86] Following a disastrous defeat at Jalalabad and observing Afghanistan's collapse into prolonged civil war, bin Laden increasingly disengaged from the country. He returned to Saudi Arabia a celebrity and resumed an active role in the family business engaging with Western engineers and helping coordinate construction projects.[87]

Bin Laden's return to Saudi Arabia illustrates the relationship and blurred boundaries between terrorism and licit business. Individuals engaged in organized crime and terrorism do not possess essential violent identities from which their actions spring. Instead, they *choose* to participate in particular forms of violence based on economic calculations and the division of labor at specific moments. Although bin Laden increased his participation in licit business activities in Saudi Arabia, he continued to support insurgency and terrorism in the international jihadist market. For example, in 1991, bin Laden provided funding and support to Tariq al-Fadhli and Jamal al-Hadhi, two veterans of the Afghan war, in order to foment insurgency in Yemen.[88] The line between the licit and the illicit again blurred. Bin Laden had even approached Prince Turki al Faisal to urge him to back him in an effort to fight the Marxist regime in South Yemen.[89] Faisal rejected the plan, considering it "a bad idea."[90] However, that bin Laden actually approached the Saudi government reveals the lack of essential separation between Al Qaeda and the licit, and even governmental, spheres. Al Qaeda's existence as a non-state entity was not an essential characteristic, but the product of particular choices and exchanges. Nor was bin Laden's offer an exceptional instance – he would again suggest cooperation with the Saudi government during the Gulf War when he offered to use his men to fight Saddam Hussein's army, an offer again rejected by Prince Turki al Faisal. Prince Turki noted this rejection as a defining moment for bin Laden, stating that he was insulted by the Saudi government's agreement to "work with the infidel" over his group, fueling his "turn to megalomania and use of terror."[91] Bin Laden continued to blur the lines between his licit and illicit activities, using his business ventures to compliment his support for organized violence.

Like Escobar's relationship with his accountants, when the need for greater loyalty increased within the Al Qaeda group, bin Laden required the development of more reliable ties than those that bound the majority of Arab jihadists, many of whom joined on an ad hoc basis. Jamal Ismail explains the tie between Al Qaeda's focus on objectives beyond Afghanistan and this increased necessity for security:

> Al Qaeda is different from other organizations. Their target is to spread the soul and idea of jihad among Muslims, … which means fighting infidels and to establish a truly Islamic government all over the world. They were recruiting people from different countries, from Saudi, Yemen, Sudan, Iraq, Egypt, Palestine, Jordan, elsewhere, but they were very, very, very careful about choosing or recruiting anyone.[92]

This need for a particularly close network led to bin Laden establishing the training camp for men inducted into Al Qaeda as separate from the main base.[93] An anecdote regarding Mohammed Atef, Al Qaeda's military commander, helps clarify the differences between those in the more centralized parts of bin Laden's firm and network and those of a more ad hoc employment status. According to Abu Jandal, bin Laden's personal bodyguard, "Atef was a serious man, a disciplined man. He was not the gregarious type who could live with the young mujahedeen and understand and solve their problems and address their concerns like Osama bin Laden. Perhaps this was due to his military position in the organization. His work and activities sometimes compelled him to avoid people and keep away from others."[94] Like Escobar's accountants, the structural form of bin Laden's Al Qaeda is not exclusive to organized crime or terrorism but, rather, the exact dynamic of firm development elucidated by Ronald Coase in 1937.

Importantly, even within this tightly bound group, bin Laden still had to offer material benefits. The men were provided salaries of $1,000 a month ($1,500 if they were married), health care, and vacation time.[95] When bin Laden later moved his men to Sudan, he paid those members of Al Qaeda a bonus on top of what he paid other employees.[96] These benefits, common to many licit businesses, demonstrate that radical ideology and supernatural promises were insufficient rewards on their own, even among bin Laden's inner circles.

Once again we can see that exchanges within the marketplace impacted the conditions of organized violence. Escobar faced a similar challenge: he could build upon family ties and, to some extent, ideology to bind his accountants to him, but he also had to offer massive salaries and the promise of substantial benefits to ensure their loyalty. As Jacob Shapiro points out, "What is true for Walmart is true for al Qaeda: Managers need to keep tabs on what their people are doing and devote resources to motivate their underlings to pursue the organization's aims."[97] As we have seen several times, the need for organizational loyalty drives not just bin Laden and Escobar, but also terrorist and insurgent entrepreneurs from varied arenas to provide salaries and monitor exchanges and thereby deter defection and promote effectiveness of the firm.

Following another trip back to Pakistan, in 1991 bin Laden moved his family from Saudi Arabia to Sudan, where he continued to engage in licit business activity and expand his personal fortune. Bin Laden continued to work for his family's construction business, and conducted construction for the Sudanese government.[98] At the same time, he sponsored moving former fighters in Afghanistan to Sudan and used proceeds from his businesses to fund their ongoing salaries.[99] In their discussion of bin Laden's move to Sudan, the 9/11 Commission specifically notes the reinforcing relationship between bin Laden's terrorist and licit activities, writing, "Bin Ladin moved to Sudan in 1991 and set up a large and complex set of intertwined business and terrorist enterprises. In time, the former would encompass numerous companies and a global network of bank accounts and nongovernmental institutions."[100]

Bin Laden made a calculated decision to relocate Al Qaeda to Sudan based on the deteriorating market in Afghanistan for certain non-Afghan international jihadists. Although the decision to relocate was driven by the firm's leadership, at the individual level, employees recognized the limited opportunities in Afghanistan. Sayf al Adel, who became Al Qaeda's military commander, explained the decision to move to Sudan:

> After God granted the Muslim mujahedeen in Afghanistan victory against the Russians and when disagreements began to emerge among factions of the Arab mujahedeen, many of our Arab brothers were thinking of returning to their native countries, including the Saudis, Yemenis, and Jordanians, who had no problems with the security services in their homeland. On the other hand we, the Egyptians, and our Syria, Algerian, and Libyan brothers had no alternative other than to stay in Afghanistan, fight on the frontlines of jihad, or got to safe places where there were no powerful central Governments. Therefore, we chose Sudan, Somalia, and some underprivileged African counties.[101]

Jamal Fadl, a Sudanese member of Al Qaeda, further highlighted the role of labor market dynamics: "I remember in a guesthouse for al Qaeda members, they start[ed] talking 'In Afghanistan we don't have too much work because the Russians, they left.' And they talk[ed] about the government change in Sudan, and [how] the Islamic National Front runs the government over there, and [that] they [are] very good."[102]

From Sudan, bin Laden continued to centralize his control over the global jihadist movement, expanding his market share among the many active firms. Bin Laden brought existing jihadist organizations and individuals under his formal control while his firm built casual alliances with others. The move to Sudan allowed bin Laden to grow Al Qaeda into "a relatively structured enterprise with a central leadership, functionally differentiated committees, and a salary system."[103] As the 9/11 Commission Report states regarding bin Laden's activities while in Sudan:

> He enlisted groups from Saudi Arabia, Egypt, Jordan, Lebanon, Iraq, Oman, Algeria, Libya, Tunisia, Morocco, Somalia, and

Eritrea. Al Qaeda also established cooperative but less formal relationships with other extremist groups from these same countries; from the African states of Chad, Mali, Niger, Nigeria, and Uganda; and from the Southeast Asian states of Burma, Thailand, Malaysia, and Indonesia. Bin Laden maintained connections in the Bosnian conflict as well. The groundwork for a true global terrorist network was being laid.[104]

The 9/11 Commission Report also notes the continued existence of a competitive market and the varied levels of connections between people involved in global terrorist operations, including the 1993 World Trade Center bombing, and bin Laden's expanding firm:

By this time, Bin Laden was well-known and a senior figure among Islamist extremists, especially those in Egypt, the Arabian Peninsula, and the Afghanistan-Pakistan border region. Still, he was just one among many diverse terrorist barons. Some of Bin Ladin's close comrades were more peers than subordinates. For example, Usama Asmurai, also known as Wali Khan, worked with Bin Ladin in the early 1980s and helped him in the Philippines and in Tajikistan. The Egyptian spiritual guide based in New Jersey, the Blind Sheikh, whom Bin Ladin admired, was also in the network. Among sympathetic peers in Afghanistan were a few of the warlords still fighting for power and Abu Zubaydah, who helped operate a popular terrorist training camp near the border with Pakistan. There were also rootless but experienced operatives, such as Ramzi Yousef and Khalid Sheikh Mohammed, who-though not necessarily formal members of someone else's organization-were traveling around the world and joining in projects that were supported by or linked to Bin Ladin, the Blind Sheikh, or their associates.[105]

However, the market was centralizing. As the Commission would caution, "In now analyzing the terrorist programs carried out by members of this network, it would be misleading to apply the label 'al Qaeda operations' too often in these early years. Yet it would also be misleading to ignore the significance of these connections. And in this network, Bin Laden's agenda stood out."[106]

This dynamic recalls Coase's discussion on how, in order to advance their power, entrepreneurs use both individuals with strong ties to the organization, as well as individuals with more casual bonds who are often employed on a temporary basis. Analysis that divorces bin Laden's story from economic theory, focusing instead on his theology and ignoring Al Qaeda's role as a firm acting in a competitive market, again fails to provide useful insight.

Instead, using an economic lens demonstrates that if insurgency, crime, or terrorism is feasible and profitable, individuals will engage in it. Destroying one organization or individual without touching market incentives merely removes the competition and allows another entrepreneur to emerge. Ayman al-Zawahiri, bin Laden's successor following his death, expressed this exact view when he discussed Egypt's killing of Sayyid Qutb, "The Nasserite regime thought that the Islamic movement received a deadly blow with the execution of Sayyid Qutb and his comrades ... but the apparent surface calm concealed an immediate interaction with Sayyid Qutb's ideas and the formation of the nucleus of the modern Islamic Jihad movement in Egypt."[107] al-Zawahiri was one of the individuals who moved into the open market that remained even after Qutb's execution and, as Lawrence Wright noted, he created an underground cell that same year.[108]

Bin Laden's Safe Haven and the Market for Loyalty

While bin Laden was successfully centralizing more power and resources, the firm itself remained subject to a number of constraints, including increased international attention. Bin Laden's growing role in the marketplace from his base in Sudan soon gave rise to international pressure on the Sudanese government to curtail support for terrorism. By subjecting Sudanese government leaders to censure and sanctions, the international community attempted to raise the costs of hosting bin Laden. The 9/11 Commission points to bin Laden's support for a 1995 plot to assassinate then-Egyptian president Hosni Mubarak by members of the Egyptian Islamic Group as the "tipping point."

Just as Panama rescinded Escobar's safe haven because of the risk that the United States would offer a better deal, the rising cost to the Sudanese government eliminated bin Laden's sanctuary. Bin Laden's suspicions were first raised when the Sudanese informed him that the Libyan government had requested them to expel bin Laden's contingent of Libyan jihadists. Wright notes that when he recognized that his safe haven was no longer safe, bin Laden was forced to inform the Libyan group that he could no longer support it.[109] As Sudanese officials met with other governments to discuss possible routes to ease sanctions, bin Laden realized that security was quickly dwindling. On May 19, 1996, bin Laden decamped for Afghanistan, a place where he was confident that international attempts to outcompete his offer for sanctuary would fail.

Statements from various individuals involved in bin Laden's network and the Sudanese government this time reveal the profoundly individual and economic nature behind the considerations of whether to leave Sudan. Although Sudan's leadership had painted religious reasons for offering sanctuary (some clerics believe providing refuge is a holy obligation), bin Laden's presence provided real economic benefits.[110] Ibrahim Mohammed al Sanoussi, an adviser to Hassan al Turabi, Sudan's de facto leader at the time, explained the benefits Sudan received in exchange for bin Laden's presence, stating, "Bin Laden came to the Sudan offering his help making roads and they assigned him to make a road north of Khartoum. And he began to make canals and cultivating soil, and sunflower oil. It was very successful."[111] Al Turabi's wife recalls a similar exchange: "[My husband] didn't bring bin Laden to the Sudan. Bin Laden thought that the Sudan was attractive to him and [he could] use his money for building the Sudan. He was planting, he was making chicken farms. He was building roads for the Sudanese people."[112] She continued, "He built the Port Sudan airport and he was supposed to be given money [for that] by the government."[113] Al Turabi himself referred to bin Laden as "the great Islamic investor" at a reception in his honor.[114] Before bin Laden left, he met with al Turabi to try and convince him to let him stay, citing his investments, but al Turabi would only let bin Laden stay if he stopped his violent activity abroad.[115]

While al Turabi's associates could be accused of having personal incentive to downplay bin Laden's role and the political nature of his presence in Sudan, the economic logic is also expressed by those who accuse al Turabi of playing an active role in bringing bin Laden to Sudan. Jamal Fadl, for example, states, "The Sudan government extended an invitation for [bin Laden]. They opened the borders for Arabs and Muslims to invest and visit Sudan. And I think Sudanese, especially Dr. al Turabi, played a very, very important role in convincing

[Sudanese president] Omar Bashir [to] bring Osama because by bringing Osama, others will come with him, Ayman al Zawahiri and al Jihad group. And you don't have anyone better than Osama at that time to raise funds and to help the government."[116] In other words, even a political explanation depicts the desire of Sudanese officials to benefit via exchange within the jihadist marketplace. Al Fadl also provides a good explanation of how the economic frame of exchange was a prerequisite to any supposedly separate political agenda, stating, "[bin Laden] say [sic] our agenda is bigger than business. We [sic] not going to make business here, but we need to help the government, and the government help [sic] our group, and this is our purpose."[117] Furthermore, when sanctions increased the cost of providing protection to bin Laden, the Sudanese abandoned him and his men, demonstrating the existence of a rational calculation of interests and highlighting the economic underpinnings of bin Laden's Sudanese sanctuary.

Bin Laden's Sudanese safe haven, like Escobar's in Panama, reinforces an important aspect of the organizational analysis of violence: how competition among firms influences the behavior of the individual. Bin Laden's firm was not the only active organization in Sudan at the time, and, more importantly, there was often interaction and crossover between the individuals working for those firms. In one example, Ali Mohammed, a member of Egyptian Islamic Jihad and Al Qaeda who was involved in the 1998 Embassy Bombings, describes meetings between Al Qaeda personnel and Hezbollah operatives, including a meeting between bin Laden and Hezbollah's Imad Mughniyeh to exchange training for bin Laden's men for weapons.[118] Despite this early cooperation, men associated with bin Laden and Mughniyeh's firms would be at each other's throats in Iraq and Syria years later. There, Hezbollah backed Shi'a forces against Sunni insurgents, who had aligned themselves with Al Qaeda and later ISIS. This dynamic recalls Escobar's war with men working for M-19 and the Cali cartel when he had previously cooperated with both to varying degrees. To focus only on a firm alone misses the importance of key exchanges over calculation of costs and benefits at the individual level, as people shift their allegiances or cooperate across disparate ideologies.

Furthermore, within bin Laden's organization, some individuals calculated their interests would be best served through another path. The defection of Jamal Fadl, a Sudanese-born Arab, provides a useful example through which to examine this dynamic. Fadl was angered over his low salary, particularly when compared to the better-paid Egyptians, and ended up skimming money from the firm, eventually leading to his defection and decision to become an informant for the United States.[119] Fadl's complaint about salary also reiterates that ideological appeals for loyalty alone are often insufficient.

Nor were financial woes solely a problem for bin Laden's firm, and al-Zawahiri's Egyptian group also suffered financial hardship at the time. Lawrence Wright writes:

> Money for Al-Jihad was always in short supply. Many of Zawahiri's followers had families and they all needed food and housing. A few had turned to theft and shakedowns to support themselves. Zawahiri strongly disapproved of this; when members of al-Jihad robbed a German military attaché in Yemen, he investigated the incident and expelled those responsible. But the money problem remained.[120]

Paying a workforce for their labor is an inherent aspect of running a firm, and even for those with ideological goals with other-worldly ends, not paying your workers is a quick way to find your organization torn apart by defection. Al-Zawahiri would eventually resolve this money problem by placing his men on bin Laden's payroll. As he explained to an associate, paying his men through bin Laden's firm was "the only solution to keeping the Jihad organization abroad alive."[121]

Once in Afghanistan, Bin Laden provided both monetary and non-monetary benefits to Mullah Omar and the Taliban in exchange for his sanctuary, including the stature and pride that sheltering bin Laden granted the Taliban.[122] Michael Scheuer writes, "Simply having bin Laden agree to live under Mullah Omar's authority and protection increased the Taleban regime's standing in the Muslim world. Indeed, it is fair to argue that the decision to host bin Laden put the Taleban on the Islamic world's radar and led to the Taleban leaders' first glimmer of recognition that there might be a role for them beyond local Afghan affairs."[123] According to Prince Turki, Mullah Omar had described bin Laden as "a very honorable man that we should work with."[124] This benefit cannot be reduced to a pure religious devotion or connection. Instead, sheltering bin Laden also had or was perceived to have had significant political ramifications for the Taliban's potential survival, something that Scheuer notes various jihadist and conservative Muslim leaders were saying during the 1990s.[125]

Additionally, bin Laden also provided very clear monetary and material benefits to his Taliban hosts, just as he had done in Sudan. Scheuer writes,

> In more measurable terms, bin Laden substantially aided the Taleban. In the 1996–1997 period, he lent Mullah Omar veteran al-Qaeda insurgents who provided a leaven of combat experience and leadership to undertrained Taleban units. He also supplied funding for the Taleban's successful bribing of some of Massoud's commanders around Kabul to either switch sides or stand down as the Taleban moved toward the city. Further, bin Laden persuaded Jalaluddin Haqqani, Yunis Khalis's most senior and powerful commander, to send veteran fighters to join the Taleban's Kabul campaign.[126]

Although it is easy to latch onto Mullah Omar's refusal to hand bin Laden over to the United States following 9/11 as motivated by religious fanaticism – not betraying a co-religionist, as even Mullah Omar indicated through his own rhetoric – we see that it was actually the result of weighing economic costs and benefits. In the end, however, Mullah Omar miscalculated, and the decision cost him control over Afghanistan following the US invasion and also led to severe criticism from many in the jihadist movement. This again shows how explaining human behavior as religiously motivated – in the absence of the market context – causes misleading conclusions.[127] Miscalculation does not disprove the power of the market; Escobar miscalculated when he thought he could coerce the Colombian government by bombing an airliner, but the decision was still the product of market interactions.

In the case of the Taliban's providing sanctuary to bin Laden, Taliban members internally debated the wisdom of the decision, and there is evidence that they tried to disassociate from Osama bin Laden in order to avoid the imposition of costs by the United States. For example, Vahid Mojdeh, a former Taliban foreign ministry official, recalls, "The Taliban was not free of internal disagreements. The disparity reached a point where Mullah Omar had to encourage these factions to set aside their differences."[128] Mojdeh recalls a specific dispute over the treatment of bin Laden, saying:

> After [Maulana] Muttawakil took the job of foreign minister he tried his best to perform differently. But the situation with Osama bin Laden had really tied his hands. He believed if the Taliban wished to be accepted by the world community, they should not take actions that would antagonize it. For this reason, while he was in Kandahar, he ordered that Osama be placed under surveillance and not be permitted to do whatever he wished. When Muttawakil took charge at the foreign ministry he asked Mullah Omar to restrict Osama's activities more closely.[129]

A declassified State Department document records multiple meetings between American and Taliban officials regarding bin Laden in which, while the Taliban refused to turn him over, they insisted they had placed restrictions on his activity. Another declassified document, reporting skepticism regarding the possibility that the Taliban might turn over bin Laden, notes internal disagreement between Mullah Omar, who supported bin Laden's presence in Afghanistan, and Mullah Mohammad Rabbani, who opposed it.[130] Ultimately, however, the United States could never offer a sufficiently promising deal to the Taliban. Even as the United States prepared to invade Afghanistan, the Taliban refused to turn bin Laden over.

To understand this decision, it is necessary to acknowledge the role of the Taliban leadership's cultural and religious views. Mullah Omar, for example, famously cited the prohibition on turning over a guest.[131] At the same time, as Bergen notes, the cost in religious terms of turning over a guest was inseparable from the cost of more material goods, because the Taliban liberally employed religious rhetoric in justification for their rule. Some Taliban officials were quite explicit on this point. Mullah Akhtar Mohammed Osmani, who met with CIA station chief Robert Grenier regarding the possibility of handing over bin Laden or killing him in exchange for the Taliban maintaining some power, told Grenier that bin Laden "has become synonymous in Afghanistan with Islam. The Taliban can't hand him over publicly any more than they can publicly reject Islam. Neither Omar nor the rest of the *shura* like the Arabs."[132] Although this position may indicate solely religious attitudes driving the Taliban's decision-making, Osmani's willingness to continue engaging with the Americans and interest in potentially turning over bin Laden – as long as it was done quietly – demonstrates that this decision was firmly rooted in the market.[133]

While religious and politico-religious views did affect the negotiations, other Taliban leaders appear to have been calculating that they could survive the US invasion. Jaluddin Haqqani, for example, stated:

> We will retreat to the mountains and begin a long guerrilla war to reclaim our pure land from the infidels and free our country again like we did against the Soviets. We are eagerly awaiting the American troops to land on our soil. The Americans are creatures of comfort. We have so far held to our defenses. There is no retreat anywhere. The military strikes have failed to inflict any serious or crippling damage. Mullah Omar, Osama bin Laden, and all other commanders are safe and sound and carrying out their duties.[134]

Given Haqqani's close ties to Al Qaeda, his statement supporting the idea of America being too weak to survive a long war, and his relatively strong position as guerrilla war emerged, the decision to shelter bin Laden seems less rooted in religious belief than in a desire to protect the many benefits the Taliban received in exchange for providing bin Laden sanctuary. Indeed, regarding the failure to strike a deal for turning over bin Laden during the 1990s, the 9/11 Commission would note, "Through his relationship with Mullah Omar – and the monetary and other benefits that it brought the Taliban – Bin Ladin was able to circumvent restrictions; Mullah Omar would stand by him even when other Taliban leaders raised objections."[135]

Nor was it only the Taliban and Mullah Omar's views that prevented a deal, since it is a core principle of economics that a voluntary trade benefits all parties. Grenier recalls that his meetings with Taliban officials and the negotiations over bin Laden's fate were also constrained by political forces in the United States, a lack of interest in negotiating with the Taliban, and the growing interest in the option of invading Afghanistan.[136] What these stories reveal is that, far from being a religious objection, the Taliban refusal to hand over bin Laden is best understood as a series of negotiations over a market transaction – bin Laden for non-intervention – in which the two parties were not able to come to an agreement.

Marketing and the Violent Firm

Having examined the key economic issues, including the individuals' exchanges and the organizational dynamics that allowed bin Laden to build Al Qaeda in the run-up to the 9/11 attacks, we now turn to motivations for the attacks themselves. On what rational basis could a group of individuals choose to murder thousands of civilians? Many believe that the explanation must be rooted in mental illness or religious fanaticism. Yet these explanations promise false comfort against the realization that the market can incentivize individuals to rationally calculate that their interests will be advanced through mass murder and terrorism.

We risk our safety and security when ascribing individuals' inconsistent behavior to uncontrollable forces, or to religious or psychological impulses, rather than to the influence of market dynamics on personal aspirations. We may perceive that bin Laden was driven by religious fervor, but, as Peter Bergen writes, "Woven deep into the fabric of bin Laden's religious zeal was the fact that his family owed a good deal of its fortune and standing in society to its role for decades as the principal contractor renovating and expanding the holy sites of Mecca and Medina."[137] Market forces encouraged bin Laden to employ religious rhetoric because it was good for business.

Bin Laden's 1996 declaration of war against the United States certainly invokes religious language.[138] As discussed in the first chapter, Hirshleifer explained that ideological narratives can be viewed as an expression of kinship and group creation, capable of being analyzed in economic terms as components of the conduct of war. In fact, one does not have to get too far into bin Laden's declaration of war before he shifts from religious pronunciation to a direct economic indictment of the Arab societies upheld by American support:

> People are struggling even with the basics of everyday life, and everyone talks frankly about economic recession, price inflation, mounting debts, and prison overcrowding. Low-income government employees talk to you about their debts in the tens or hundreds of thousands of riyals, whilst complaining that the riyal's value is declining dramatically. Domestic debts owed by the government to its citizens have reached 340 billion riyals, and are rising daily due to usurious interest,

let alone all the foreign debt. People are wondering: are we really the biggest source of oil in the world? They feel that God is bringing this torture upon them because they have not spoken out against the regime's injustice and illegitimate behavior, the most prominent aspects of which are its failure to rule in accordance with God's law, its depriving of legal rights to its servants.[139]

The 1996 declaration of war, rather than being purely religious, reveals the same combination of material and non-material incentives that violent entrepreneurs in context after context use to buy the labor and services of individuals for their firms. Bin Laden's medley of financial, religious, spiritual, and other justifications for violence reveals his understanding that individuals are often motivated by many factors. Rather than focusing solely on religion, bin Laden recalled common grievances in order to summon recruits and strengthen his group, and he formed an "us"-versus-"them" dynamic. Bin Laden was certainly aware of the varied incentives when he wrote, "I say to the youth of Islam who have waged jihad in Afghanistan and Bosnia-Herzegovina, with their financial, spiritual, linguistic, and scholarly resources, that the battle is not yet over."[140]

By citing more than one benefit, bin Laden increased the potential rewards available in exchange for services, increasing the number of people who took up his offer. As highlighted in the discussion of Stathis Kalyvas' work in Chapter 2, the overall master cleavage, or narrative, put forth does not actually represent individuals' interests and reasons for joining a conflict. Although the master narrative – in bin Laden's case, religious war – provides a frame for violence, leaders incite and invoke cleavages and grievances at localized levels to further recruitment by appealing to individuals' interests. We have seen both Kony and Escobar use similar tactics, providing material and non-material rewards to recruits. We've also noted that writers for the *Harvard Business Review* counsel managers to use this same approach and reduce monetary costs of employment by promising more intangible, psychological, and emotional rewards, such as feelings of fulfillment or kinship.[141]

As individuals have their own reasons for joining, their religious beliefs or understandings might not even conform to the master narrative. An individual's membership may be for reasons entirely separate from leadership efforts, and he may be completely unaware of this cleavage, as each individual remains focused on his own experience. Among fighters in Afghanistan, only some joined Al Qaeda, and of those only a smaller portion supported the decision or even knew about bin Laden's plan to conduct the 9/11 operation. A prime example is Abu Jandal, bin Laden's former bodyguard who provided information to Ali Soufian, an FBI agent, following 9/11. Soufian convinced Jandal that the attacks violated his jihadist ethics, demonstrating a deviation from the overall religious narrative.[142]

A similar pattern reveals itself in the 1998 World Islamic Front Statement issued by bin Laden, Ayman al-Zawahiri, and others, asserting that it is an individual religious duty to kill Americans, whether military or civilian.[143] The statement again recalls the master narrative, the religious war, by opening with:

> Praise be to Allah, who revealed the Book, controls the clouds, defeats factionalism, and says in His Book: "But when the forbidden months are past, then fight and slay the pagans wherever ye find them, seize them, beleaguer them, and lie in wait for them in every stratagem (of war)"; and peace be upon our Prophet, Muhammad Bin-'Abdallah, who said: "I have been sent with the sword between my hands to ensure that no one but Allah is worshipped, Allah who put my livelihood under the shadow of my spear and who inflicts humiliation and scorn on those who disobey my orders."[144]

If one would stop there it would appear bin Laden's religious motivations were pure; however, the very next line presents a clearly earthly depiction of scarcity:

> The Arabian Peninsula has never – since Allah made it flat, created its desert, and encircled it with seas – been stormed by any forces like the crusader armies spreading in it like locusts, eating its riches and wiping out its plantations. All this is happening at a time in which nations are attacking Muslims like people fighting over a plate of food. In light of the grave situation and the lack of support, we and you are obliged to discuss current events, and we should all agree on how to settle the matter.[145]

It is apparent here that bin Laden's use of religious language addressees' affiliative instinct – Muslims have an obligation to stand with bin Laden to address scarcity caused by "the other," in this case taking the form of the West.

To prioritize radical Islam at the expense of market logic will not provide much analytic purchase and overlooks other complex factors. As Lawrence Wright points out regarding the Afghan jihad, there are both Quranic passages that appear to support jihadist violence and others that oppose it, resulting in different interpretations that split Muslim communities and even families.[146] He writes:

> Yet the declaration of jihad was tearing the Muslim community apart. There was never a consensus that the jihad in Afghanistan was a genuine religious obligation. In Saudi Arabia, for example, the local chapter of the Muslim Brotherhood refuted the demand to send its members to jihad, although it encouraged relief work in Afghanistan and Pakistan. Those who did go were often unaffiliated with established Muslim organizations and therefore more open to radicalization. Many concerned Saudi fathers went to the training camps to drag their sons home.[147]

Even within bin Laden's close circles there was disagreement over the interpretation of Quranic scriptures and their application to violence. Trying to assume behavior, therefore, from looking to the Quran as a study in theology will be fruitless without an understanding of the particular context in which individuals are making decisions. Economic forces were clearly at play in bin Laden's decision-making. Thus the challenge to those who would look only to religious texts for explanation becomes magnified when one considers that bin Laden deliberately appealed to individuals both with material incentives and non-religious, non-material incentives.

Importantly, focusing on only the religious piece of bin Laden's story tends to insinuate that his terrorist activities were somehow unique to Islam, rather than stemming from market logic. Our discussions of Escobar and Kony have proved this notion utterly false; the supposed secular drug dealer and extremist Christian insurgent committed very similar acts of violence, for political motivations, against civilian populations. As we have seen, these actions stemmed from rational calculations in competitive markets. For example, Escobar thought it would serve his interests to bomb buildings and an airplane to coerce the Colombian government. These actions are neither unique to Islam nor to the contexts we have discussed in this book.

6 THE RISE OF THE ISLAMIC STATE IN AL QAEDA'S MARKET

The Emergence of ISIS in the Market

Terrorism did not die with bin Laden, and many of the same discussions that confused and consumed our energy regarding bin Laden now focus on the Islamic State of Iraq and the Levant (ISIS/ISIL) and that group's leader, Abu Bakr al Baghdadi. ISIS has become almost synonymous with an image of a radical, religious death cult – with commenters falling into many of the same traps that precluded thorough analysis of Al Qaeda. Discussion of the November 2015 attacks in Paris, for example, include language such as "slaughter for its own sake," or, in President Obama's words, "an attack on all of humanity."[1] These comments ignore the rational economic logic behind the attacks and disregard the roots of the attacks in individual decision-making in conditions of scarcity. In order to really understand ISIS, and therefore develop effective policies to defend ourselves and our interests, it is again necessary to view ISIS as a firm in a competitive marketplace.

The emergence of ISIS in Iraq and Syria and its ability to pass the feasibility threshold – transitioning from a terrorist group, to insurgency, and eventually to a conventional force – depended on the same market dynamics underlying the success of the firms of Pablo Escobar, Joseph Kony, and Osama bin Laden. Rather than labeling ISIS as a unique religious ideology, we can trace its origins to the market. Specifically, the US and coalition forces created scarcity in the governing space when fighting Saddam Hussein and later Al Qaeda in Iraq, and a leader subsequently emerged under the brand of ISIS. As

Steve Coll has noted, "If the United States is returning to war in the region, one might wish for a more considered vision than Whack-a-Mole against jihadists."[2] The marketplace in Iraq also facilitated the rise of the Islamic State because the Shi'a-led government's policies in 2012 created a renewed market for ISIS within Iraq, allowing forces it had built in Syria to return. As the Shi'a government rose in power, it provided an incentive for a Sunni-led group to counter that power. They did so by organizing their efforts in Syria and then returning to Iraq as the Islamic State.

Coll reinforces a crucial point here in economic terms: focus on the marketplace itself and not just the currently popular entrepreneur acting within it. To defeat these groups, approach them as businesses and counter them in the marketplace. Put them out of business and promote competing firms able to dominate the marketplace in ways consistent with our interests. Each leader and violent group not only fits into market models, but makes the most sense when thought of in this way: starting from counterterrorism versus COIN, etc., is like holding a hammer to what might look like a nail. We lose clear sight of our goal. To continue the analogy, hammering in nails alone will not build a house.

Following 9/11, the United States vastly expanded its efforts against Al Qaeda and reshaped the marketplace. In Chapter 3 on organized crime, we noted how the United States offered bounties in Somalia for Al Qaeda militants, creating a market for such bounties. Similarly, during the surge in Iraq, the United States provided funding and other support to tribal leaders in exchange for their support against Al Qaeda, creating the "awakening." The United States threatened to increase the costs of support or even tacit allowance of Al Qaeda while promising to provide support to those groups that joined the fight against Al Qaeda. President Bush declared, "You're either with us or against us."[3] The formulation should be familiar: it is the same basic concept as Escobar's *plata o plomo*, and the "no better friend, no worse enemy" phrase articulated by General James Mattis, with a lineage dating back to the Romans.[4] The market opened by the United States' call for bounties in Somalia produced a rush of entrepreneurs seeking to sell to individuals, regardless of their connection to Al Qaeda, just as Escobar's offering of bounties for the killing of Colombian police officers produced a wave of unregulated violence that did not serve his ends. In both cases, the actors who created the market found themselves in need of regulation and governance. The same exchanges that occurred in Iraq have their counterparts in Central Africa, where the United States paid militias to counter poaching, as seen in the previous chapter. It is also the same as purchasing safe havens, or the lack of a safe haven, as was the case for bin Laden in Sudan prior to Afghanistan and for Escobar in Panama.

However, it is essential to remember that markets are not unitary and people paid on an ad hoc basis and not bound by tight kinship ties are susceptible to switching teams for a better deal. In Iraq, changes in the Iraqi government's relation with Sunnis, in the United States' presence, and the geopolitical situation in neighboring countries – most importantly in Syria – helped shift many individuals' calculations, bringing ISIS into power at least for a short time in parts of Iraq. Although much counterinsurgency literature focuses on "winning hearts and minds," the US-backed Sunni militias known as the "Sons of Iraq," for example, were not won over solely by the pleasantries of US troops and the great merits of representative democracy. America imported another lesson learned from its own democracy: when you can't convince someone to support you based solely on the merits of your ideas, you must then pay them to endorse your idea as their own. If you can't "win" their hearts and minds, you buy them instead. Only now, having withdrawn from Iraq, Americans realized that we neither "won" nor "bought" the hearts and minds of Iraqis; we only rented them.[5]

US strategy requires moving beyond an organizational focus, because while organizations may come and go, the underlying problem will remain. Pursuing a whack-a-mole effort against ISIS will end the same way as our efforts against Al Qaeda in Iraq did – with the emergence of related actors espousing the same grievances under a different banner.

How We Perceive ISIS

Similar to common interpretations of Al Qaeda, analysis of ISIS has thus far been primarily contained with a perspective overly focused on the significance of religion and organization. Let's recall the core perspectives that dominated security and policy discussions around Al Qaeda: a focus on radical religious thought; a "war on terror"; and an organizational focus. We can see the same frameworks dominating the discussion on how to counter ISIS. In March 2015, Graeme Wood argued in the cover story of *The Atlantic Monthly* that ISIS constituted an Islamic group whose actions must be analyzed in terms of its religious beliefs.[6] The story introduced itself with the tagline, "The Islamic State is no mere collection of psychopaths. It is a religious group with carefully considered beliefs, among them that it is a key agent of the coming apocalypse."[7] Politicians have furthered this strain of thinking, using increasingly alarming Islamophobic rhetoric that ascribes inherent problems in Islam as the primary motivation for the rise of ISIS.

ISIS' use of religious overtures should be familiar rather than seen as a reflection of a purely ideological organization. Wood designates ISIS as a truly religious cult, even more so than Al Qaeda. This distinction, however, ignores that both ISIS and Al Qaeda leaders, similar to Joseph Kony and Mafia leaders, use religion as an organizing and control mechanism for their firms. Indeed, Al Qaeda and its precursors in the Afghan jihad had made many of the same religious overtures and used similar ideological narratives to further the cause. In fact, Lawrence Wright uses similar language when he notes that Azzam traveled the world drumming up imagery of martyrdom and writes that this "created the death cult that would one day form the core of al-Qaeda."[8] Yet, as we saw in the previous chapter, bin Laden purposefully downplayed martyrdom when actually managing the organization – for example, by using both monetary and non-monetary reward systems – to effectively run an organization that engaged and competed in competitive markets.

Similar to bin Laden, al Baghdadi uses religion as an organizing principle to recruit members and manage the firm effectively. Although Wood states that their fighters display a seemingly distinct apocalypticism, their willingness to die recalls the Arabs fighting in Afghanistan, one of whom proclaimed to a reporter, "We want them to bomb us ... We want to die!"[9] Additionally, Wood's focus on religious references in ISIS propaganda such as the magazine *Dabiq* to demonstrate ISIS' coherent ideology ignores the purpose of that ideology. Rather than a dogma to which its members fully and blindly adhere, ISIS' religious narrative provides a brand for the group that strengthens its ability to recruit and act in a competitive marketplace. We've seen bin Laden and Kony act similarly. Bin Laden, for example, named a guesthouse he established in the 1980s "Beit al-Ansar" in reference to the individuals who helped the Prophet in his flight from Mecca; he also called one of his Afghan training camps "Al-Badr," after one of the Prophet Mohammed's famous battles. Religious imagery was consistently woven into the organization's everyday operations.[10] Contrary to Wood's arguments, however, we have seen that these proclamations and symbolic imagery, while undoubtedly religious, do not provide a convincing motivation for insurgent or terrorist activity.

The second framework, understanding ISIS simply and solely as a terrorist group, also poses several limitations. Recalling President Bush's declaration of a "war on terror," media pundits and politicians continue to lump ISIS into the "terror" that we need "to stop ... eliminate ... and destroy it where it grows."[11] Fox News host Bill O'Reilly provides an unedited version of this thought process when he says: "We have to wipe out ISIS. Every American should know this. We have to kill them all."[12] This attitude highlights a core flaw in the way we think about ISIS: terrorism is a tactic that ISIS uses, but the group is not solely comprised of full-time terrorists. We have seen that the difference between an insurgent and a terrorist is not the motivation but the feasibility. ISIS has surpassed the feasibility threshold for entry into the market for large-scale civil violence in a way unmatched by its predecessor. As Daniel Byman states, ISIS "has gone beyond terrorism and even insurgency, establishing an army and state-like structures in the vast territory it controls."[13]

This brings us to the third framework, viewing ISIS as an organization distinct from market dynamics. Wood's analysis highlights this perspective when he argues, "Bin Laden viewed his terrorism as a prologue to a caliphate he did not expect to see in his lifetime. His organization was flexible, operating as a geographically diffuse network of autonomous cells. The Islamic State, by contrast, requires territory to remain legitimate, and a top-down structure to rule it."[14] This statement seems to hold a lot of truth; it makes sense intuitively and recalls the point that ISIS has made strides toward a more conventional force. However, such analysis leads Wood to the policy conclusion that "one way to un-cast the Islamic State's spell over its adherents would be to overpower it militarily and occupy the parts of Syria and Iraq now under caliphate rule. Al Qaeda is ineradicable because it can survive, cockroach-like, by going underground. The Islamic State cannot."[15]

By concentrating strictly on ISIS as an organization, this policy recommendation ignores the competitive and institutional dynamics surrounding ISIS and its leadership. While ISIS – a firm – may collapse, the individuals behind the group will not disappear, and can, and likely will, shift back to form or join another Al Qaeda-like organization. In *The Godfather*, Don Vito's rise and death do not correspond to the start and end of violence; to the contrary, he takes power from others as he ascends, and passes on power to Sonny and then to Michael. When Pablo Escobar was killed, drug trafficking did not cease to exist in South America. Joseph Kony's organization may have shrunk, but violence and civil unrest continues in Eastern and Central Africa. We focus on the organization (Al Qaeda, ISIS, the Corleone family, the Medellín cartel, the Lord's Resistance Army), and miss the critical dynamics – the market in which these firms can succeed.

In fact, this phenomenon is exactly what we saw before in Iraq that led to the formation of ISIS. When the United States and the tribal groups it supported occupied northern Iraq during the surge, its governance (rules and associated enforcement) suppressed Al Qaeda's potential power, making it infeasible to sustain an insurgency-level of violence and forcing the leaders underground and toward terrorist tactics. As soon as pressure was removed, however, insurgency again became feasible and the same individuals who had made up Al Qaeda in Iraq reemerged as ISIS. Bernard Haykel, whom Wood relies upon to make his ideological case regarding ISIS, points out this problem in an interview, stating, "I would argue even if you were to destroy IS – which is possible; I mean if America and other countries were to send troops on the ground, they could defeat IS militarily – it would not end the phenomena, the structural feature of the Arab Muslim world that creates this kind of movement."[16] While Haykel's commentary on the Arab Muslim world may not make sense, he rightly identifies the need to address the market's structures.

Those same market dynamics were at play when ISIS split from Jabhat al-Nusra in 2013. The split was at its core a dispute between leaders, Abu Bakr al Baghdadi and Abu Mohammad al-Julani, over who should receive profits from firm activity. When organizations weaken or split in this way, it is because there is a failure to maintain cohesion. The dynamics of cohesion are different when considering rival goods, like wealth – which can only be owned by one person at a time – versus non-rival goods, like a religious ideology, which can benefit multiple people at once. The conflict over profits, a rival good, eventually eroded the cohesion of the firm.[17,18]

Relying on limited perspectives holds serious implications for our policy. If we refuse to see ISIS' actions as anything but delusional religious fervor, we ascribe to them a level of irrationality that cannot be countered. How do you argue with true believers? Similarly troubling, diminishing members of ISIS as merely "criminals" or "terrorists" does not provide a thorough analysis of the group and limits our policy options. Last, focusing on ISIS as an organization that can be eliminated overlooks the dynamics that gave rise to the firm in the first place. The national security community has to understand these nuances, or it will continue attempting to eradicate the recurring religious, social, or organizational symptoms of the problem without ever addressing its economic roots.

Abu Bakr al Baghdadi

Little is known about ISIS' leader, Abu Bakr al Baghdadi, in comparison to our highly notorious cast of the previous chapters. What does emerge from depictions of al Baghdadi's life, however, resembles what we have seen in the stories of Pablo Escobar, Joseph Kony, or Osama bin Laden: a relatively normal but ambitious man who became an entrepreneur of organized violence. Once again, we need to turn our focus to the individual level. Al Baghdadi was not born a terrorist, nor can we dismiss him as the latest "big bad" dominating the market for organized violence and capturing news headlines with his organization's brutal activities. Al Baghdadi played an instrumental role in developing ISIS' capabilities, and his carefully shrouded persona, religious credentials, and supposed descent from the prophet have all factored into ISIS' narrative and strength.

Before he became the self-proclaimed Caliph of the Islamic State, however, al Baghdadi was born Ibrahim Awad Ibrahim al-Badri in Samarra, Iraq in 1971. Acquaintances and neighbors recall al Baghdadi as a quiet youth, religious but not an outspoken fanatic, and an avid soccer player. A former teammate and fellow worshiper at a local mosque recalled al Baghdadi as their best player, stating, "He was the Messi of our team."[19] Al Baghdadi, as was Osama bin Laden, is highly educated and received his PhD from the Islamic University in Baghdad. His religious credentials far exceed those of bin Laden or other predecessors in the jihadist movement, assets that would prove beneficial when crafting ISIS' narrative. Despite his religious training, few remember him as being particularly radical in his youth. A former acquaintance of al Baghdadi named Abu Ali, for example, stated, "He wasn't a preacher," and although al Baghdadi occasionally led the mosque in prayer when the Imam traveled, he "did not give any sermons."[20] Ali added that al Baghdadi "didn't show any hostility to the Americans," and a classmate who claimed to be well acquainted with Iraq's jihadi scene stated that al Baghdadi was "insignificant … no one noticed him."

Camp Bucca and Radicalization

In 2004, US forces detained al Baghdadi at Camp Bucca, a place that quickly became a hotbed for jihadist recruitment and an opportunity for al Baghdadi to begin building the early foundations of what would later become ISIS. Labeled a "civilian detainee," his captors described him as not a "particularly dangerous threat," and by some accounts he even got along with those detaining him.[21] Prison was the perfect opportunity for al Baghdadi to begin forming his network. Recall the discussion of radicalization and prison gangs from Chapter 2. Similar to what occurs in American prisons, prisoners aligned with radicals in order to establish governance amidst a breakdown within the prison, hastened by vastly expanding numbers of incarcerated individuals.

Detainees at Camp Bucca developed bonds based on the affiliative instinct – the human nature to divide the world between "us" and "them." Their majority religion, Islam, provided kinship, an in-group, and a sense of belonging. Furthermore, if the religious leader in a prison subscribes to an extremist interpretation that encourages violence, then the other members of that kinship group will similarly align their views in order to strengthen the group's bonds. For example, James Skylar Gerrond, a compound commander at Camp Bucca in 2006 and 2007, explained how prisoners sought support from one another that they couldn't get from others. This allowed for extremist entrepreneurs to offer such organized support in exchange for loyalty:

> There was a huge amount of collective pressure exerted on detainees to become more radical in their beliefs. Obviously, this was supported by the fact that the detainees were being

held against their will in a facility with minimal communication with their family and friends. This led to detainees turning to each other for support. If there were radical elements within this support network, there was always the potential that detainees would become more radical in their beliefs.[22]

A former inmate at Camp Bucca also recounts this dynamic, stating that when a new prisoner arrived, the others would "teach him, indoctrinate him, and give him direction so he leaves a burning flame."[23] This kinship group began to grow into a firm, with the inmate even calling Camp Bucca "a factory." Lieutenant Junior Grade Kevin Taylor also noted the role of the extremists' sharia courts inside the prison in establishing rules, saying, "Sharia courts enforce a lot of rules inside the compounds."[24] Such a development has echoes not only in Afghanistan, where Taliban courts challenged legitimate governance, but also in American prisons. Moreover, it ought to have sounded the warning bells that rather than a strategic victory, the surge led to tens of thousands of people being funneled through prisons and detention centers where extremists were known to be outcompeting the authorities in the labor market, setting and enforcing rules.[25] Unfortunately, while many sought to confront prison radicalization in Iraq, it did not affect the largely supply-side-focused aspects of the surge, which continued to kill and arrest militants without changing the incentive structures that produced terrorism – even at the heart of where state authority ought to have reigned.

This, however, is not a unique story. Before al Baghdadi and other ISIS leaders built their firm out of prisons in Iraq, Abu Musab al-Zarqawi, for example, spent time in a Jordanian prison during which he grew Al Qaeda in Iraq, the precursor to ISIS. Just as organized criminals like Pablo Escobar were able to buy or coerce influence from prisoners and guards alike, so was Zarqawi.[26] One Pentagon counter-terrorism official explained the similarities between organized criminals' use of prison to establish gangs and al-Zarqawi's use of prison to build his own networks. Michael Weiss and Hassan Hassan, authors of *ISIS: Inside the Army of Terror*, compare al-Zarqawi's time in prison with that of Boston mobster Whitey Bulger: "We sent him to the Harvard of American penitentiaries. He was a wily criminal who had a little IQ and put together some good streams of income. He comes out of the pen with great street cred that helped him form his own gang, which ran Boston for four or five years. Same with al-Zarqawi. Prison was his university."[27]

Where incentives encourage such violent firm formation, gangs will undoubtedly form. The effort to classify the firm as "criminal" or "terrorist,"' "Islamist" or not, misses the larger story of entrepreneurs and firms in the competitive marketplace.

Al Baghdadi's Rise and the Emergence of ISIS

When US forces released al Baghdadi, he had created a network of future recruits. Having written each other's phone numbers in the elastic of their underwear, the Bucca inmates were determined to remain in contact.[28] Al Baghdadi subsequently joined the Islamic State of Iraq – an umbrella organization primarily dominated by Al Qaeda in Iraq. During this time al Baghdadi utilized his connections with the jihadist movement and Iraqi tribes to assist foreign fighters in crossing the Syrian border to join the insurgency in Iraq.[29] Al Baghdadi served under both Abu Musab al-Zarqawi and his successor, Abu Ayyub al-Masri, who transformed the group from a branch of Al Qaeda to an independent, but affiliated, firm known as the Islamic State. Throughout al-Masri's tenure, Baghdadi gained managerial experience in the firm through his appointment to the Islamic State's Coordination Committee – a small council that would lead the selection and supervision of the group's commanders of Iraqi provinces.[30] Following al-Masri's death in 2010, al Baghdadi took up the mantle just prior to the group's expansion into Syria.

Al Baghdadi's crucial ally at this time was Samir Abd Muhammad al-Khlifawi, also known as Haji Bakr, the head of the Islamic State's military council, who ensured firm loyalty to al Baghdadi through patronage and coercion. Haji Bakr highlighted al Baghdadi's religious credentials and played up his supposed descent from the prophet, recalling members' kinship affiliations and engendering support. For those who doubted al Baghdadi or remained unconvinced, Haji Bakr "settled scores and eliminated rivals through intimidation and assassination."[31]

Al Baghdadi's rise through Al Qaeda in Iraq's ranks corresponded with the increasing tensions and eventual outbreak of the Syrian civil war, presenting an opportunity for the entrepreneurial leader to rise. As Byman states, al Baghdadi "cleverly exploited the

Syrian civil war to rebuild his organization, using the fighting there to develop a haven and attract new recruits and support."[32] Recognizing an opening in the market for political power, al Baghdadi expanded his firm across borders – capitalizing on legitimate grievances in Syria and Iraq to increase his own operations. Hardly an irrational move driven by insatiable blood lust, the Islamic State's expansion into Syria was the result of a calculation of costs and benefits to the group and its leaders.

The Religious Narrative, Focality, and Recruitment

Although ISIS' governance in Syria has been marked by its brutal violence and religious justifications – leading many to fall into the trap of regarding the group as either irrational religious terrorists or psychopathic thugs – the group shares many similar characteristics to other organized violent firms. Recent internal documents have revealed organizational patterns and secular, clearly market-based reasoning similar to Al Qaeda and other militant groups. For example, documents from Haji Bakr, the man who planned much of ISIS' early operations in Syria, are almost devoid of apocalyptic religious statements.[33] Instead, the documents reveal familiar methods of recruitment along kinship lines, for example, the identification of key families to coerce or incentivize support of ISIS, and the blackmailing of individuals who committed crimes according to sharia law. Additionally, Haji Bakr's descriptions relied not on religious language, but secular words. As *Der Spiegel* reports, "Even the word that Bakr used for the conversion of true Muslims, *takwin*, is not a religious but a technical term that translates as 'implementation,' a prosaic word otherwise used in geology or construction."[34]

The documents also reveal the kind of exchange that one would expect to see in the labor market of a huge bureaucratic enterprise, including identifying information on foreign fighters who joined ISIS and their informants in other rebel groups and towns. *Der Spiegel* reports, "Personnel files of the fighters were among them, including detailed letters of application from incoming foreigners, such as the Jordanian Nidal Abu Eysch. He sent along all of his terror references, including their telephone numbers, and the file number of a felony case against him. His hobbies were also listed: hunting, boxing, bomb building."[35] Additionally, the documents showed that the fighters had very practical requests and needs having very little, if anything, to do with their religious devotion. "The files from Aleppo also included a list of 34 fighters who wanted wives in addition to other domestic needs. Abu Luqman and Abu Yahya al-Tunis, for example, noted that they needed an apartment. Abu Suheib and Abu Ahmed Osama requested bedroom furniture. Abu al-Baraa al Dimaschqi asked for financial assistance in addition to a complete set of furniture, while Abu Azmi wanted a fully automatic washing machine."[36] This recalls Raab's analysis of the Mafia that "each member was an individual entrepreneur who had to be an earner and a producer to survive, prosper, and advance."[37]

Additionally, the ISIS leadership manages martyrdom – an act deeply associated with religious fanaticism – as an economic activity; these acts garner attention, attract foreign fighters, and support organizational fundraising campaigns. Al Baghdadi and his commanders have carefully crafted ISIS' brand around a particularly radical vision of Islam that permits mass murders, sexual violence, and torture. Although there may be members of ISIS, including al Baghdadi himself, who consider themselves true believers, their religious narrative is a tool to further the organization's goals. Although al Baghdadi primarily remains in the shadows, he consistently uses religious and historical narratives to bolster his legitimacy and garner loyalty. For example, the leader chose the *nom de guerre* Abu Bakr after the first Muslim caliph. He also paraphrased the caliph's words during a rare public appearance: "I was appointed to rule you, but I am not the best among you."[38] By describing his role in powerful symbolism, al Baghdadi brands himself as the legitimate leader of Islam, playing to his audience's affiliative instinct and seeking its loyalty. Similarly, ISIS uses violent spectacles to create a focal narrative that generates attention. For example, ISIS has claimed that its targeted destruction of cultural and archaeological artifacts is done for ideological reasons. In reality, these attacks serve as spectacle, an opportunity to shock the world, show power, and demonstrate the group's capacity for violence.[39]

These citations of larger narratives and use of spectacle are not unique to ISIS; they are an economic tool that has been used at least as far back as the Roman practice of "bread and circuses," and are presently used in modern militaries' nationalist displays or festivities, in exchange for dangerous labor.[40] Tyler Cowen highlights four reasons that terrorists develop these focal narratives: "First, they may value propagation of the ideology per se. Second, propagation of the ideology may enhance their control over material resources. In particular being focal may ease fundraising. Third, holding or creating a focal ideology may cement political power. Fourth, spectacles may make it easier to motivate subsequent terrorists."[41] As Lawrence Wright notes, after bin Laden lost much of his monetary wealth after being kicked out of Sudan, "publicity was the currency bin Laden was spending, replacing his wealth with fame and it repaid him with recruits and donations."[42] As such, producing spectacles via television interviews or eventually major terrorist attacks, including 9/11, became essential to his relevance and his firm's continued survival. Similarly, ISIS relies on the spectacle of religiously motivated brutality because it brings in recruits, gives the organization greater fundraising power, and provides other material benefits. If it didn't fulfill those functions there would likely still be radical Islamists in Syria and Iraq preaching such brutality, but they would not have been able to organize the firm of ISIS.

This focal narrative has become the centerpiece of the ISIS image, which is just as much a brand as the donut shops in our small-town example in Chapter 5. There are many jihadist terrorist groups and many donut shops, but by implementing this form of branding the firm is able to compete in a crowded market. This is a universal story, whether the brand is ISIS versus Al Qaeda, or Dunkin Donuts versus Starbucks. Just as ISIS has built an identity and brand distinct from Al Qaeda's in order to branch off, one of its rival groups in Syria, Jabhat al Nusra, has done the same to distinguish itself from ISIS. As ISIS becomes increasingly brutal in its governance, Nusra has attempted to soften its image in order to appeal to potential recruits and external funders put off by ISIS' extreme branding.

Although ISIS' core narrative centers on its religious conviction, individuals in the firm hold varying motivations for joining that may be unrelated to its focal ideology. Viewing ISIS' whole fighting force as consisting only of the religiously convinced further neglects the group's use of child soldiers and conscripts to fill out its ranks.[43] Those who willingly join the ranks also come from a variety of backgrounds. This is exactly the mixture of motives that Kalyvas refers to when describing the disparity between local and master cleavages. While many members may be motivated by their drive for affiliation based upon religion, others fighting with ISIS may do so for fundamentally material reasons. In order to sustain power, the leadership must engage in exchanges with religiously motivated, materially incentivized and the seekers of revenge and justice.

This practice is not exclusive to ISIS, and the adoption of religiosity for pragmatic reasons by many in the Syrian conflict is also demonstrated by an anecdote relayed by Michael Weiss and Hassan Hassan of a Free Syrian Army fighter they met who "drank alcohol and smoked marijuana and professed to want to see a democratic state emerge in the wake of Assadism. However, his battlefield photo showed a long-bearded Islamic militant."[44] Weiss and Hassan provide a simple economic explanation for the seeming dissonance: "a little-explored facet of the Syrian Civil War was how a highly competitive bidding war for arms by fighters naturally inclined toward nationalism or secularism accelerated their radicalization, or at least their show of *having been* radicalized."[45] In other words, in a competitive market where start-up money came from religious-organization affiliated donors, we do not know who truly believes the jihadist radical narrative and who does not; we only know that the best way to get paid is by appearing radical.

Another prominent example of such a dynamic is the central role of ISIS officials who were previously officials in Saddam's Ba'athist government, a secular ideology.[46] These Ba'athists have clashed with more religious ISIS members.[47] A Kurdish intelligence officer, for example, told Fox News "as an effective fighting force alone, ISIS would never have been able to hold such large territories, ... but with the help of Baathists [united under the banner of the Naqshbandi army], they have been able to keep the momentum going."[48] In exchange for inclusion in ISIS' success pushing back Shi'a and Iraqi government forces, the Ba'athists provide their experienced military training and ability to tap kinship networks.[49] Among these, for example, is Abu Abdul-Rahman al-Bilawi, who, before he was killed during the taking of Mosul, was al Baghdadi's chief of ISIS' general military council. Prior to that, however, he served as a captain in Saddam Hussein's army.[50] Another individual, Ab Ali al-Anbari, who led ISIS operations in Syria, had also served in Saddam's army and had been kicked out of the Ansar al-Islam group after accusations of financial impropriety.[51]

In addition to the Ba'athists, many other Iraqis and Syrians, as well as foreigners, joined the fight for their own diverse reasons – some religiously motivated, some not. Weiss and Hassan write how after interviewing ISIS members, "We found that what draws people to ISIS could bring them to any number of cults or totalitarian movements, even those ideologically contradictory to Salafist Jihadism."[52] For example, they note the case of one reported ISIS supporter, Saleh al-Awad, a former secular lawyer and critic of ISIS, who once told Weiss and Hassan, "We're tired, every day they [ISIS] cut off four or five heads in our town" only to, months later, become a supporter seeing the group as the only challenge to Kurdish expansionism.[53] Additionally, ISIS' foreign-fighter ranks consist of individuals who may be adventurers, risk seekers, and people looking for a radical alternative to Western societies.[54] Similar to Weiss and Hassan's findings, Thomas Hegghammer has suggested that "it is fundamentally the same malaise that is also inspiring the far-left activists."[55] That is, rather than an attraction to ISIS' specific ideology, many may join ISIS over another group due to opportunity and accessibility, facilitated by the group's impressive marketing.

These recruits, with varying motivations and ideologies, pose a managerial problem for ISIS commanders. Just as we've seen with other leaders of organized violence, ISIS needs to provide both material and immaterial rewards to its members in order to control them. When an ISIS commander engages with a zealot subordinate, like bin Laden to Sheikh Tameem, by allowing him to run amok or taking actions consistent with zealotry, it does not prove the commander's religious fanaticism but rather his economic incentive to appease his subordinates. Viewing this scenario in economic terms is similar to Kony's allowing his men to loot and rape as compensation. In fact, ISIS has also engaged in similar behavior with its development of markets for enslaved women, an act that it also tries to portray as being derived from scripture but that is best understood as a market compounded by the benefit ISIS leadership derives from its relationship to its brand. This dual nature of ISIS' use of sexual violence and enslavement is simply another form of the more universal economic story of coercion and rents to ensure governance. A United Nations report makes the economic nature of ISIS' sexual violence clear, stating that the UN "received a number of reports that an office for the sale of abducted women was opened in the al-Quds area of Mosul city. Women and girls are brought with price tags for the buyers to choose and negotiate the sale. The buyers were said to be mostly youth from the local communities. Apparently ISIL was 'selling' these Yezidi women to the youth as a means of inducing them to join their ranks."[56]

None of this is to say that it is not important to examine how religion impacts and informs terrorist groups. Fulfillment of religious goals can be a form of non-monetary payment. It is important to acknowledge that simply because the payment does not take the form of currency does not mean it is not an economic exchange. As we've seen, leaders can use religion as a tool to increase trust, reduce transaction costs, and bind the members of a firm through shared identity. This is not exclusive to ISIS or Al Qaeda, and it is found in other Islamist-nationalist groups like Hamas, Catholic-influenced criminal gangs like the Sicilian Mafia, and right-wing Christian groups in the United States. The Mafia developed a blood-oath ritual structured around Catholicism to retain its members' loyalty. Hamas adopted a similar strategy, using religion and religious institutions to screen its operatives and ensure organizational discipline.[57] Jacob Shapiro notes the use of this strategy and its similarity to tactics used in the business world, writing:

> An alternative screening strategy is to demand the kind of lengthy ideological debates between prospective members and their recruiters which are an old screening tactic of militant organizations, one practiced by GSPC, the Red Brigades, ETA, and others. Essentially, weeks or months of late-night debates about fine doctrinal distinctions are too laborious for anyone not extremely committed to the cause. This is analogous to the role of education as a screening mechanism for business firms.[58]

These examples reveal that the starting point of scholarly and policy analysis of violent terrorism must be the market and individual exchange, rather than ideological reasoning. Although understanding the theology of a group is necessary when engaging in a contextualized economic analysis, we must recognize that beginning and ending with religion will contribute little to the analysis of sub-state violent actors. Importantly, failure to look beyond religious dynamics will mislead policymakers and lead to continued failure when countering sub-state threats.

IS Implications for Policy

The post-9/11 history of Al Qaeda and the rise of ISIS illuminate the lack of a coherent basis for differentiating terrorism from other forms of activity, therefore calling into question the current approaches to counter-terrorism. The national security community's key flaw in the War on Terror is its tendency to focus on the different identity-category manifestations of violence and to use definitions of those manifestations as a point of departure for policy. The vast majority of Al Qaeda's efforts today take the form of insurgency and in some cases traditional conventional warfare, yet we limit their label to, "Islamic terrorist group."[59] Leaders of Al Qaeda-affiliated groups have shifted in the other direction, from insurgency to terrorism. Brian Fishman, for example, noted that Al Qaeda in Iraq, after suffering setbacks during the surge, moved from being an insurgency to relying on terrorist tactics. Our discussion on ISIS has described the group's expansion into Syria, where it once again crossed the feasibility threshold, moving from insurgency to providing governance and maintaining a standing militia. These moves are often obscured by citation of data on sectarian violence and territorial control, trumpeting the success of the surge while concealing continued conflict.[60] As noted above, when a number of factors conspired to create a marketplace more conducive to Al Qaeda in Iraq – which had since become ISIS – it reemerged at first as an insurgency and, over time, a conventional military force. That terrorist groups can morph their tactics between insurgency and what is traditionally considered terrorism reveals the radical insufficiency of subfields, such as counter-terrorism or counterinsurgency, and policies that are so labeled.

An economic perspective provides a depth of insight into the ways in which groups like Al Qaeda in Iraq, ISIS, and Al Qaeda-affiliated groups move between different expressions of need and power. With this understanding, policymakers can better understand implications for policy – something that a simplistic focus on the identity-category would not provide. For one thing, economic theory reveals that rhetorical tools articulating goals – removing a strong US presence from the Middle East, for example – are commodities that can be created, bought, and sold. Therefore, a focus on particular tactics, or even on the concept of terrorism, can miss substitution effects in which preventing one manifestation of organized violence shifts the entrepreneur's activity to another form.[61] Indeed, using the tools of economic analysis, Walter Enders and Todd Sandler have argued that, following the War on Terror crackdown, we witnessed no substantial change in the amount of terrorism but a substitution effect where bombings of soft targets replaced more complex hostage operations.[62]

Another lesson of the economic literature for counter-terrorism emerges out of the understanding of terror groups as firms that face the problem of managing workforces. As Nuno Garoupa et al. argue, drawing upon economic studies of corporate and organized crime, law enforcement's destruction of larger networks can have the adverse effect of encouraging terrorist groups to become smaller entities that then have less difficulty managing their workforces.[63] Reducing the management challenge can actually make terrorist groups more dangerous. As Fishman argues, this helps explain how individuals who were formerly part of Al Qaeda in Iraq kept the group going during the surge, allowing it to reemerge later as ISIS. It is this type of risk that non-economic analyses and Graeme Wood's religious-organizational dissection tend to miss.

Nor are terrorism and insurgency the only forms between which terrorist organizations can morph, as they can also often transform into criminal enterprises. This is a pattern we have seen with insurgencies, as the discussion of FARC's narco-trafficking in Chapter 3 or wildlife poaching in Chapter 4 demonstrated; the pattern can also occur in reverse, as it did with Escobar's decision to bomb an airliner. In fact, much of the insurgency in Iraq during the early 2000s was driven by a Ba'athist organized crime network that smuggled cars into Iraq and was led by Izzat Ibrahim al-Douri, who built the network with Saddam Hussein's support before the Iraqi government fell. The members of the network later received state support from Syria to disrupt American policy in Iraq. Were they criminals, terrorists, insurgents, or rebels? Yes. Does it help to label them as just one? No. After the invasion, the vertically integrated criminal firm began not only to import cars, but to create vehicular improvised explosive devices via the same structures.[64] These transitions highlight how organized violence groups take advantage of conditions in the marketplace, recognizing opportunities for either crime, terrorism, or insurgency.

The Abu Sayyaf Group further demonstrates how groups choose to engage in particular forms of organized violence based on market conditions. As bin Laden formed his Al Qaeda firm in the late 1980s and early 1990s, he reached out to a Filipino militant Abdurajak Janjalani, whom he had befriended when the two fought against the Soviets in Afghanistan.[65] Zachary Abuza notes that bin Laden helped fund Janjalani's group, the Abu Sayyaf Group, which was foraying into terrorism. One of the connections was the Bojinka plot by Ramzi

Yousef, who had been introduced to the Abu Sayyaf Group through his bin Laden ties. As Abuza illuminates, the plot would have involved the bombing of multiple US airliners, in a glimpse of what was to come on 9/11, as well as a series of bombings against Christian targets in the Philippines.

However, Abuza notes, with the breakup of the Bojinka plot and other forms of police and military pressure – including the death and capture of key leaders – the group's ties with Al Qaeda suffered, and it devolved into a kidnapping gang, ceasing its use of bombings, to push a political agenda through terrorism. The group transitioned to an organized crime group, but that was not the end of the story. In the early 2000s, the Abu Sayyaf Group restarted a bombing campaign with seemingly political motivations. Part of the reason for the shift back to terrorism appears to have been the opening of an opportunity for Khaddafy Janjalani, the younger brother of Abdurajak who had trained in Afghanistan, thus having close ties to terrorists. Abuza highlights how, with an entrepreneurial spirit, he consolidated authority for himself, rebuilding a firm producing terrorism and relying on links to his brother's ideological effort for legitimacy. Emphasizing the importance of individual exchanges in the market, Khaddafy's rise was enabled by the clearing of competition when Filipino security forces killed other leaders who were more interested in the profits of kidnapping.

We have also already seen how bin Laden's firm of Al Qaeda was integrated into the licit economy through much of the 1990s, and we've seen the integration of Victor Bout's arms trade business. However, it is important to note as well that, in addition to involvement in licit markets, terrorist groups also find themselves exercising governance. This can take many forms. For example, terrorist groups have in the past turned into licit political parties, such as Sinn Fein's integration into democratic Irish politics or Hizballah's growth into Lebanon's most powerful political party. Governance can also take the form of terrorist groups turning tactical success into recognition by the world community, as occurred with many anti-colonial movements that utilized terrorism – for example, Algeria's National Liberation Front became the country's primary political party following independence from France. Governance can also occur when terrorists take territory, but the world community does not recognize their legitimacy. Jihadist terrorists have had such experiences in Iraq, Somalia, Mali, and Yemen since the collapse of Taliban rule in Afghanistan.[66]

Importantly, governance is a challenge in which the governing party has to provide public goods while extracting rents – and it is a challenge that jihadist groups have often found difficult.[67] I note the difficulty because it provides another illustration of the market's central role within even the most supposedly ideological terror groups. For example, a letter from Abdelmalek Droukdel, the leader of Al Qaeda in the Islamic Maghreb, includes recommendations to avoid losing the chance to govern by pushing overly ideological goals too quickly.[68] That challenge, of course, would have been familiar to bin Laden, who had to manage hotheaded ideologues in Afghanistan and urge them to moderate their religious zeal when it contradicted his managerial ends.

The ability of terrorist organizations to exercise governance or even become recognized governments, and the challenges of the process, would not surprise an individual with even a cursory background in economics. After all, Mancur Olson's classic economic explanation of the rise of government is a story of roving, violent, non-state actors who find themselves in stabilized market interactions with subjects as a way of reducing costs, but in doing so they also have to provide public goods. Whether its Olson's roving bandits or the Islamic State, it is a universal economic story.

We have now seen, through the examination of specific cases of organized crime, insurgency, and terrorism, that efforts to analyze each of these subjects in isolation, or to focus on particular contextual factors – religious motives, for example – fail to explain events and ignore the foundational similarities of individuals making exchanges in markets. The question then emerges: what would security efforts look like if they adopted an economic analysis, and what changes should be made to the way security affairs are currently being conducted?

7 CONCLUSIONS AND PRESCRIPTIONS

Where Violence Comes From

The enemy? His sense of duty was no less than yours, I deem. You wonder what his name is, where he came from. And if he was really evil at heart. What lies or threats led him on this long march from home. If he would not rather have stayed there in peace. War will make corpses of us all.

J.R.R. Tolkien, *The Lord of the Rings*

With fictional narratives, we have the opportunity to personally identify with some of the profound ideas explaining the origins of violence. In the course of this book, we've shared some experiences with Don Vito Corleone and Bonasera, with Robinson Crusoe, Tyler Durden, and with Moss and Blake from *Glengarry Glen Ross*. We conclude with a reference to LOTR, otherwise known as J.R.R. Tolkien's *The Lord of the Rings*. In the quotation above, Faramir finds common cause with Frodo Baggins, a relationship that captures the essence of organized violence. Tolkien acknowledges the humanity of the just-killed soldier and poignantly asks us to consider the source of violence when we read Faramir's question, "What lies or threats led him on this long march from home?" Through the power of storytelling and the craft of Tolkien's writing, consider for a moment that the soldier could have been you. We can thus imagine the enemy combatant as someone with friends, a love for and need to take care of a family, a desire to succeed professionally, and whose appearance on a battlefield is a function of both choices and opportunities, or lack thereof.

Although we know the master narrative of the battle, we cannot assume to know the motivations of each belligerent.[1] Was he "all in" for the evil Sauron, or just temporarily supportive? The enemy soldier was not always the enemy – a personal threat to Frodo; he was not always a soldier. He may or may not even agree with the larger narrative of the battle – he may not support Sauron's attempts to rule Middle Earth. But here we find him, on the battlefield prepared to kill our protagonist. Tolkien does not tell us why, but through the fictitious narrative we understand the flawed logic of assigning the same motive to each belligerent. We must transfer this same lesson to the real world of non-fiction national security.

When we see the fallen soldier's corpse in the context of the human experience, we can imagine so much more than simply a *Southron* soldier on a remote battlefield.

This book argues for a social-science-based approach to national security to improve the status quo. The communities of national security professionals must move beyond shallow identity-category foreign policy and move toward more science-based practices. We must abandon the rigid use of labels – *criminal, insurgent, terrorist, Muslim, Christian, Israeli, Palestinian* – when looking for the causes of violence, and refer instead to the language of economics – *firm, entrepreneur, institution, brand, recruit, governance*. The use of identity-category foreign policy facilitates the continuation of the limited kinetic-thinking of warfare and limits the development of broader human-behavior-based methods to combat violent acts and the people who commit them.

Violence occurs in conditions of scarcity, in which humans are incentivized to make exchanges in competitive markets. Using an economist's lens, we see the continuum of organized violence as an easily understandable human phenomenon. In today's headlines we see the brands of some violent firms: Islamic State, Al Qaeda, the Lord's Resistance Army, Boko Haram, the Ku Klux Klan, and Hezbollah, each reflecting fundamentally the same human behavioral dynamics. Only the specific firms and their entrepreneurs differ. By dispensing with the buzzwords of the modern press, we can better describe, understand, and counter organized violence. When we read about terrorists, insurgents, and criminals, and see the carnage brought about by their destructive acts, we must see more than a *radical religious zealot*, an *ethnic nationalist*, or an *illicit trafficker*. We must see them as humans, with families, friends, and individual motivations and perceptions of scarcity.

The challenge of the past decade of our great conflicts – the wars in Iraq, Afghanistan, and Syria – is that the combatants are not uniformed soldiers arrayed across well-marked borders, as in earlier conflicts, or fictional literature. Instead, we fight *amongst the people* – as insurgents and counterinsurgents, as terrorists and counter-terrorists, or as transnational criminals and law enforcement.[2] In crowded marketplaces, in the absence of uniforms, we do not know who takes what side. So we go to the next simplest forms of visual identity: skin color and signals of ethnicity, religion, and tribal affiliation. This is wrong. We must do better.

Instead, economic science suggests that we see entrepreneurs, firms, and workers competing over scarcities in markets that are subject to rules and enforcement. Issues of identity impact firms in markets, no doubt. But to combat organized violence, we must defeat the firms and redirect the energies of the entrepreneurs who oppose us. And to compete successfully, we must understand and influence the marketplace: we must govern or support those who support the rules that we support.

Violence comes from individual perceptions of scarcities and actions among the groups of people who form marketplaces for the alleviation of scarcities. Individuals affiliate with others to reconcile and resolve wants and needs in markets. Groups of people require governance – rules and enforcement of those rules. Entrepreneurs lead groups, and may thrive or challenge the rules of the marketplace. The challenging of rules may occur through legal or extra-legal means, and may include the sustained provision of violence and coercion. Through an economist's lens we can conclude that the antecedents to violence occur everywhere, so illicit violence occurs in markets where governance (rules and enforcement) allows for illicit violence.[3]

Violence does not come from religious zealotry, or a particular religious dogma, or the split between rich and poor, or the differences between ethnicities. In social science literature, scholars have come up with a nice simplification to explain the motivations to insurgency: they say that people are motivated by greed, power, or grievance, but regardless of specific motivation, insurgency occurs when insurgency is feasible.[4] This formulation makes sense across all of organized violence.

Violence can be motivated by greed – we see this, for example, in the actions of bank robbers and drug kingpins. Violence can also be motivated by power – we see this among many guerilla leaders and political figures. And we see violent acts motivated by grievance when rebel leaders exact revenge or retribution for past injustices. Greed, power, and grievance, while important to understanding violence, do not explain why we see violence some places but not most places in the world.[5]

Economic science also suggests that we consider the human tendency toward affiliation in our analysis of organized violent groups.[6] Humans demonstrate strong propensities toward group identities. We demonstrate loyalties to our blood relatives and also form familial-type relationships with others. Mafias and drug cartels, for example, use family-like terms in describing co-members. Pablo Escobar, Joseph Kony, and Osama bin Laden each used concepts of fictive kinship in their organizational designs. In our own lives, we identify with sports teams, political parties, fraternities, and universities. This affiliative instinct is not limited by age, geographic location, religion, ethnicity, or time in history. But affiliation alone is not enough to engender violence. People may use ethnicity, religion, and wealth for affiliative purposes, but these identities do not create violence; they simply help draw the teams – the boundaries between "us" and "them."

Economists describes human interaction, including violence, in terms of trade taking place in markets with rules and enforcement. Wealth seems positively correlated with markets, so we are better off when we have access to markets. And affiliations are valuable because in a group we can divide our time and efforts, specialize, and create higher-value skills and things to trade. If a market is well governed, with clear rules over property rights and contract sanctity, then wealth will increase. If, however, a market lacks good governance, then theft and violence may occur, as some will use coercion to appropriate the goods and services of others.

Affiliations and motivations (greed/power/grievance), and disaggregating individual from group rhetoric, explain organized violence. Successful violent groups use identity for sound business purposes, and are led by entrepreneurs seeking to maximize something (greed, power, or grievance). The successful entrepreneur manages to recruit and retain workers, who remain for multiple and often differing reasons.

Furthermore, the entrepreneur chooses her tactic – violent theft, insurgency, or terrorism – based upon factors such as probability of success, consequences of failure, and strength of peer competitors. She may not seek to maximize identity (religious dogma or the color of her skin) but simply to maximize success in the marketplace.

The terms "war with radical Islam" and "War on Terror" chafe at an economic understanding of organized violence. We are engaged in a conflict with leaders who have found the ability to use religious and ethnic identities as fundamental parts of a successful branding campaign, enabling the threat and use of violence to consolidate political power and wealth. These entrepreneurs often succeed in population centers where governance is otherwise weak, so the competitive barriers to entry are low. Through increasing power and wealth, they govern, setting and enforcing rules that constrain human behavior for those they govern. We have to think of our national security professionals and our own government institutions as brands of their own, competing with brands like the Medellín cartel, the Lord's Resistance Army, or ISIS. To combat criminals, to win our wars, to counter insurgencies, and to counter terrorism, we must put our rivals out of business and make reconstitution economically unviable. To combat organized violence, we must employ the science of economics.

How to Improve Security

How, then, once we understand the theories that lie behind organized violence, can we prevent it? To achieve security goals, we need to govern the markets that enable and constrain human interaction. Instead of aiming to end violence and coercion, we need to take ownership of it by setting and enforcing the rules of the marketplaces. We must fight to minimize the powers of adversaries so that allies can govern. Succeeding in national security, not unlike commercial success in businesses, entails exercising sufficient power to prevent those with opposing interests from exercising market power. National security professionals must use social science to achieve security goals.

Three concrete actions will improve national security. First, analyze adversaries like a business executive. Second, define success appropriate to modern violence and markets. Finally, fight like an entrepreneur.

1 Analyze Like a Business Executive

To defeat adversaries, we must first develop sound economic analysis of their firms. We have to understand the markets in which they operate, and what in those market allows them to succeed. An analyst following publicly traded companies, or a venture capitalist tracking start-up companies, tracks important aspects of these companies in order to make forecasts of future success and failure. National security decision-makers and experts should use the below ten topics to analyze the "firms" they are hoping to defeat.

1. **Mission.** Does the firm have a stated mission? Is it coherent, and do firm actions and marketing rhetoric align? Can you use public relations, such as paid and earned media, to discredit "the story"? How can Military Information Support Operations (MISO) most effectively undermine the credibility of your adversary? Can you separate the center from the periphery – the core narrative from the many motivations of the firm's workers and the funders of that firm? What is the perception of the rival firm's brand and how might you use that perception to influence potential recruits and current employees?

2. **Leadership.** Are the key members critical to mission success? Can targeting the firm's leadership help to weaken the firm, or might it strengthen the firm or create multiple offshoots? Can this targeting best be accomplished through information (e.g., public relations campaigns to erode trust and confidence) or via kinetic operations (e.g., kill or capture)?

3. **Offering.** What is the key value the firm brings to the market? Can you compete against the firm for that offering, on price or quality for the product or service? Or can you offer a fundamentally different good that accomplishes the same or a related mission? Can you provide similar goods but also offer club benefits the firm is not offering? What aspect of the production process does the rival firm outsource, and can you identify weaknesses in the rival's supply chain that would impair the firm's ability to bring its goods to market?

4. **Competitors.** Who are the competitors in the marketplace selling rival goods, and how might these other firms complement your mission and undermine your rival's mission? Instead of competing directly with your rival, can you support other market participants – your rival's rival?

5. **Finances.** What is the state of the firm's finances? Does it have wealth? Free cash flow? Is it profitable on a daily, weekly, or quarterly basis? Is its revenue smooth or lumpy? Are its costs smooth or lumpy? Where does the firm derive most of its revenue and profits? Does it have fixed and variable costs other than payroll that must be met? What is the

firm's monthly spending and monthly revenue? Do the subsidiaries, if any, report finances to the corporate headquarters, or are the subsidiaries operating under a franchise model? Does the firm have access to credit, stable currency, regulated and sound banking, or safe ways to move and spend money?

6. **Traction.** What is the firm's current market share? What is the growth (positive or negative) over the past year(s)? What is the total addressable market? What adjacent markets might the firm try to enter in the next one to two years?

7. **Human resources.** What are the firm's top recruiting methods? How do they retain their most valuable talent? How might you impact their ability to recruit and retain ideal workers?

8. **Time horizon.** Do your rivals have an unusually short time horizon to meet certain goals? For example, do they have a competitor readying to enter the market in the next six months, or do they appear unrivaled for the foreseeable future? Can you cause an event to force an action they might prefer to avoid?

9. **Knowledge.** Does the firm have information asymmetries that you can exploit? For example, do you know things the leaders do not? Do they exploit information asymmetries among customer and worker populations that you can also exploit?

10. **Culture.** Does the firm face high costs of enforcement of internal rules and norms of behavior? Does it create strong bonds of fictive kinship? Can you take actions to drive up these costs of maintaining loyalty?

2 Define Victory in Market Terms

There is no such thing as a permanently secure area, so successful interventions will ensure benevolent firms succeed over malevolent firms. Counterinsurgency strategies have focused on a "clear, hold, and build" approach that emphasizes eliminating insurgent influence from an area (clear) before restoring governance, often by the counter-insurgent (hold), and supporting the local population (build).[7] However, the idea that simply clearing an area of opposing forces with a surge of military force will earn lasting loyalty from locals seems naive. The surge "cleared" substantial parts of Iraq, but the insurgent network of entrepreneurs and firms continued to operate and reemerged when the incentive structure of the market changed. Illicit entrepreneurs routinely manage to establish violent networks and continue activity from the very heart of state authority (e.g., the cartel leaders who successfully operate from prison; ISIS rising where Al Qaeda in Iraq departed; Pablo Escobar's Medellín cartel replaced by the Rodriguez brothers and their Cali cartel). We must focus on the markets of an area in order to obtain security.

On the other hand, the challenge of permanent security means that illicit actors face the challenge of permanent insecurity. The inevitability of sustained exchange can be made into an advantage for the security professional: we can trade our way toward security. The illicit entrepreneur must deal with the uncertain loyalty of an ad hoc workforce and the ease with which a safe haven can turn into contested terrain. US and Colombian government efforts forced Escobar to flee to Panama, and then the US president offered Panamanian president Noriega better relations and funding in exchange for the kingpin. Osama bin Laden fled Sudan when the Sudanese government leadership was offered the easing or non-imposition of sanctions for his expulsion.

In traditional warfare, we pit military force against military force, and when one side's leaders no longer believe they can achieve a military victory, then the conflict ends. But this logic only considers military-on-military violence. The competition in the marketplace, and the factors that facilitated the violence, often persist. The kinetic battlespace remains only an aspect of the market. Tracking the group's headquarters or the fate of a particular insurgent or terrorist leader is a misleading oversimplification when it ignores the marketplace. Coalition forces defeated the insurgency in Iraq following the "surge" because the opposition was battered and lost substantial ground. However, the market for organized violence continued throughout those years. Coalition forces killed and captured combatants and made market dominance for a group of enemy leaders unfeasible, but this did not change the underlying incentives; local entrepreneurs sought some combination of greed, power, or grievance, and waited for the US-led Coalition COIN forces to depart. When the dominant firm exited the market, other entrepreneurs of violence predictably emerged. The institutions of violence moved from one organizational form to another when the economic prospects for a particular firm or business models changed. When Coalition forces defeated Iraqi insurgents, focus shifted, and we did not foresee that the market that enabled Osama bin Laden would facilitate ISIS' formation under Abu Bakr al Baghdadi.

We have inherited a definition of "victory" as the particular moment when the enemy surrenders – General Robert E. Lee's surrender to Ulysses S. Grant at Appomattox on April 9, 1865; the Japanese signing of surrender aboard the USS *Missouri* on September 2, 1945; the German surrender at Reims on May 7, 1945. When it comes to modern violent actors, this kind of official surrender is unlikely. As Peter Bergen writes regarding the war on Al Qaeda:

> To end World War II, Franklin D. Roosevelt, Winston Churchill and Joseph Stalin demanded an unconditional surrender from the Nazis. But there will be no such surrender from al Qaeda. The group is not a state that is capable of entering into such an agreement, even if it wanted to do so, which seems highly unlikely.[8]

Seeing organized violence through the economic lens illustrated in this book – the actions of firms led by entrepreneurs in competitive marketplaces – we can better understand that there will be no picture-perfect surrender – not because of the doctrines of a particular sect of Islam, but because market dynamics make violence a continuum and not a binary. One might even question whether the old tales of signed victories were ever true. After all, it took almost a century after Robert E. Lee's surrender for the Civil Rights Act of 1964 to enforce many of those rights supposedly been won during the war, and out of the "defeated" confederacy emerged the Ku Klux Klan, a terrorist group.

A hazier form of victory, but an alternative to surrender, is the acquisition/merger outcome. An acquisition/merger of firms, in which the competing firms merge or one buys its competitor, is a way for violence to end. In a merger, one firm essentially offers the other an alternative to surrender. Examples of successful mergers include the FARC finding a mutually agreeable set of terms with the Colombian government; the merger between the insurgency in Nepal and the government-backed army; and the peace talks in Northern Ireland between the British and Irish governments. In contrast, the rise of the Islamic State out of the ashes of Al Qaeda in Iraq is an example of a merger gone wrong. When the Shi'a government in Iraq failed to abide by the terms of its merger with the Sunni population, the Sunnis brought violence back into the region – a consequence of breach of contract.

Ultimately, victory will not last when market power remains up for grabs. Power goes to those who set and enforce rules – though comparative advantage or by actually setting the terms in the marketplace. If peace treaty-style victory is unattainable, perhaps instead of envisioning those working in the security field as soldiers seeking total surrender from a unified collective of individuals, we need to envision the national security workforce as enforcers of rules. Victory for a military force, for example, could be defined as seeing some set of "desired" rules adopted and enforced by indigenous firms in a functioning marketplace that makes illicit violence infeasible. Adopting a language of *rules and enforcement* will place battlefield successes in the context of success in a market. Understanding the enemy and redefining what victory means are essential, but victory also requires taking actions like an entrepreneur.

3 Fight Like an Entrepreneur

Entrepreneurs take risks in making resource allocation decisions, and good entrepreneurs adapt to the markets they seek to dominate. To successfully combat organized violence, we must build agile, not rigid, institutions of national security. Successful violent groups display agility; they evolve. These groups in Iraq and Afghanistan have adapted better than the political leaders of the United States and her allies, for example.

Non-state purveyors of violence lead unitary organizations that collapse the distinctions between terrorism, insurgency, and crime. From 2014 through 2016, ISIS demonstrated the effectiveness of this approach when it swept across northern Iraq. It employed insurgent tactics when convenient; routinely used terror to attract attention, draw recruits, and demoralize its opponents; and relied on a bureaucracy to govern population centers. It supplemented these actions with sophisticated cyber operations to disseminate narratives supportive of its marketing campaigns, and to recruit foreign fighters. Leaders used the rhetoric of the caliphate when appropriate, but also governed in purely sectarian ways, providing goods in the here-and-now, and a reassuring social safety net, when deemed appropriate. To call the group an Islamic state does them a service – we add value to the brand created by the ISIS entrepreneurs – and also fails to appreciate the full dynamism of this adversary. The firm known as ISIS today represents a hybrid organization: sometime terrorist, sometimes insurgent, and sometimes state. This hybridity worked to al Baghdadi's advantage.

In contrast, the counterinsurgency and counter-terrorism solutions the United States and coalition forces have employed since

9/11/2001 have taught us a great deal about the inability of the national security communities to hybridize. The US government addresses its national security through an interagency (IA) process that fails to create hybridization. Our rigidity hinders our ability to act on our analysis. Part of this rigidity lies in the process of allocating monetary resources within the government. As senior government leaders, we face incentives to fight for a share of the overall federal budget. We seek to get our institution "plussed up," and the leaders receive rewards for growing budget share relative to sister agencies. We don't compensate agency leaders effectively for actual contributions to all-of-government initiatives that undermine illicit violence. The leadership at the time of 9/11, to our credit, realized this problem and sought to create more collaborative environments, resulting in the creation of new agencies like the Office of the Director of National Intelligence (ODNI), the Department of Homeland Security (DHS), and the National Counterterrorism Center (NCTC). I served in the first generation of Senior Executive Service leaders at DHS. A decade and a half into this reformed environment, however, turf battles remain – rigidities persist and entrepreneurs are scarce.

So how do the leaders in the national security community counter evolving, illicit, and violent firms when policy in the United States, for example, emerges from a large bureaucracy of institutions competing for funds from a powerful chief executive and co-equal legislature?

During the 2014–2015 academic year, I worked with two groups, under the sponsorship of the US Department of Homeland Security Science and Technology Directorate, to address the need for national security institutions to adapt their approach to effectively counter non-state organized violence.[9] The first group was comprised of national security experts, many with several decades of experience, and included current and former members of the US Departments of Defense, Homeland Security, Treasury, and Justice, as well as intelligence agencies, academia, and the private sector. Many members of this group had served as the architects for post-9/11 national security policies.

The second group included graduate students from Georgetown University. Here, the median years of work experience were about three. These students all entered their professional careers after 9/11. While the interests of the two groups overlapped significantly, the graduate students displayed little emotional attachment to the status quo institutions of national security. They maintained weak encumbering ties to the equities of existing departments and agencies and valued the ends over the means – accomplishing true change, even if it meant going against accepted and traditional practices. While the group of senior leaders displayed greater pragmatism, they defended in particular the interagency process, whereas the graduate students displayed greater creativity in addressing today's threats, understanding more easily the dynamic – hybrid – nature of organized violent groups.

Combining the talents and experience of both senior experts and early-career professionals, we concluded that: 1) people who run illicit organizations that specialize in violence for political ends must control costs to fund their activities, as well as hire managers to recruit and train members and capable individuals that can execute the leadership's plans. 2) Just like their licit counterparts, violent entrepreneurs must find ways of generating revenue, creating or accessing lawyers, law enforcement, and banks to establish and enforce contracts and store and move money. And, therefore, 3) the issue when it comes to hybrid organization is not so much about how to use kinetic force to destroy these groups but instead about how US national security institutions can undermine what sustains these organizations. Such an approach would demand attacking their sources of funding, their managerial capabilities, and their ability to recruit.

However, the US security establishment often has trouble executing a preferred strategy when faced with the realities on the ground. For example, in drafting responses to Al Qaeda and ISIS, policymakers assumed that poverty was the key factor driving radicalization and recruitment, and in response launched large development projects in countries buffeted by terrorism. The countries that received the most aid were Iraq and Afghanistan, but the United States also provided support to the Philippines, Colombia, and Sri Lanka. The outcome varied depending on the country largely because not every place faced the same type of terrorist group or even a terrorist threat in the first place. For example, large economy-boosting activities like dam building generally increased the number of terrorist attacks in a particular region; in such cases, money tended to bring violence rather than reduce it. A greater awareness of local markets – how investments and security forces displace and empower local populations and political elites – might have led to different aid tactics on a neighborhood-by-neighborhood basis.

Our working group developed several pragmatic solutions to combat calcification in government agencies that might prevent both creating and executing innovative solutions to organized violence.

1. Strengthen the ties between the private and public sectors. Given that many of today's innovations originate in the private sector rather than the other way around, the private sector might offer unique and creative solutions; government leaders should seek advice from leaders of industry.
2. Create or augment economic institutions similar to the US National Security Council (NSC) that could advise the president on how to safeguard the country from business entrepreneurs' perspectives.
3. Increase cooperation and collaboration among the interagency (IA). Few government employees are exposed to different agencies, how they function, and how they make decisions. National security employees should be rewarded for solving problems in collaboration with employees of other agencies. The system as it functions right now is one where different parts of the national security bureaucracy exist in perpetual competition with one another for resources and talent to work on the same problems. Incentives should be used to foster cooperation.

In short, the leaders of our national security organizations must be able to govern – that is, establish and enforce rules – amidst the varying challenges in crowded marketplaces anywhere in the world. To achieve this, national security professionals must work together to hybridize efforts to defeat hybrid threats

FINAL THOUGHTS

As I think back to those days at my US Senate desk from 1997 to 2000, frustrated by my inability to address the threat of suicide terrorism, two major trends seem apparent and relevant. The national security community emphasized a style of warfare ill-suited to non-state organized violence, and, therefore, the technology of national security would, in my lifetime, lag behind the threats I would witness. Our successes in the 1990 Gulf War and our failure to decisively win our wars in Iraq and Afghanistan since 2003 proves this point, and the economic approach to organized violence explained in this book explains why. The technology of violence would go from the "shock and awe" successes of the Gulf War to the frustrations of war *among* the people in Iraq and Afghanistan. The next frontier in scientific advancement for national security must build on this economist's views of violence. National security requires investment in and understanding of the social and behavioral sciences.

I was trained as a Surface Warfare Officer in the US Navy. I learned the Soviet Navy's Order of Battle: what ships, submarines, and aircraft they possessed and how we believed they would deploy them in combat environments. I learned the military insignias of the People's Liberation Army. And I received tremendous training in anti-submarine warfare: how to use towed arrays of hydrophones to listen for enemy submarines, and how to actively deploy hull-mounted sonars for active submarine and mine hunting. During the Gulf War of 1990–1991, I learned the power of the combined forces of the US and her allies. Along with the rest of the world, I witnessed the power associated with air superiority – controlling the skies over Iraq. The key first step in this battle plan was the proper use of Tomahawk missiles to take out Iraqi air defenses from hundreds of miles away. Once the Tomahawk shooters completed their missions, then tactical bombers, fighter jets, and command-and-control aircraft moved in to complete the domination of the skies, enabling the launch of the invasion by land, and the quick route of the Iraqi military. The US military of the Vietnam War had been rebuilt into the US military of the Gulf War. We witnessed "shock and awe," and it worked. But it worked in the *Gulf War*. From my perch in the US Senate in 1997, however, I could not see how to use Tomahawk missiles and associated technologies – technologies I knew so well – to address terrorism in crowded markets.

Warfare can change like fashion, with some styles persisting, and others rotating with seasons or generations. Over the past 19 years, we've been engaged in wars where combatants do not wear uniforms. We need science to contribute to national security, now as much as ever, but the scientific contribution must go beyond advances in kinetic warfare; national security needs to benefit from the science of human behavior.

The impressive display of military might in my lifetime did not happen overnight, and reflects a long trend of scientific contribution to the military.[1] In the days since the Great War of 1914, the interwar period, and the Second World War, and through today, scientific advances in support of military and defense have become institutionalized. We've seen the developments of rockets, drones, proximity fuses, jet fighters, submarines, nuclear weapons, radar and sonar, electronic computers, GPS, stealth, and voice-to-text technologies. We've seen increasingly closer collaborations between defense, academia, and industry. And we have seen the institutionalization of defense-funded research, independent and separate from research done by the military services, to seek to achieve revolutionary gains in the science of military combat.

My thought in 1997 may have been that Tomahawk cruise missiles and the impressive array of other technological advances could not have stopped radical Islamic suicide terror attacks. Today, we wonder why overwhelming military force in Iraq from the US-led invasion of March 2003 did not prevent the rise of ISIS a decade later. I go further and ask how we might have inadvertently facilitated the rise of Islamic State.

In 2009, I was given the opportunity to work as a behavioral scientist on a DARPA project, and my world view started to change. Invited into a typical DARPA program, I was initially a single behavioral scientist in a room full of engineers. The program soon brought on more social scientists, and we developed methods for finding foreign fighters in Afghanistan while sitting at computers in Arlington, Virginia. I worked on DARPA programs for about six years before starting a social science-led company called Giant Oak, Inc., intended to transition technologies based upon the craft of social and behavioral science, married with computer science and engineering, to the national security and law enforcement communities.

What makes the science of human behavior more possible today than in past generations are the advances in computing, data, and storage, and the so-called "big data" world we live in. We have opportunities for revolutionary advances in the science of human behavior; in fact, I would argue that we are witnessing these advances in knowledge each time we look at our smartphones. If one considers science a process of observing the world with the goal of understanding it, big data enables amazing opportunities for the observation of human behavior never before possible in the history of the world. Our personal digital devices and our online behaviors create a digital wake as we proceed through our days. In the past, business marketers would create broad demographics for targeting sales efforts; but today, it is the Amazon-, Google- and Facebook-type data companies that allow for the understanding and predicting of our purchasing habits.

It is time for the military-defense-academia alliance, which so successfully advanced the science of the atom bomb and the computer, to participate in the science of human behavior. In the past, we generalized the target by their geographic location, the uniform they wore; in today's modern warfare of hybrid organizations and crowded marketplaces, we cannot target by location and uniform, because most people in the crowded marketplace do not intend us harm. Therefore, we need to use science and data to determine the small percentage of people who represent legitimate targets. Like online marketers, we must move from broad demographics to person-specific targeting.

Addressing violence means addressing where violence comes from, the marketplace in which people make decisions in conditions of scarcity. Markets have discoverable sets of rules – rules made by people – and associated enforcement. People behave in predictable ways, and these behaviors can be understood in the context of the institutional constraints that influence their behaviors. Understanding individuals informs the use of coercive power, and substitutes for kinetic force. Cruise missiles and other elements of overwhelming military force, therefore, can play useful roles in combatting organized violence, but coercive power must be seen in context. We cannot be distracted by veils of identity. The answers, instead, lie in the market. We may not be able to have permanent or enduring peace. But, by focusing on behaviors instead of identities as we expect and plan for conflict and violence, we can set the rules of the game.

GLOSSARY OF TERMS

Acquisition or Merger: A transaction in which competing firms merge to form a new, joint firm, or one firm buys another. For example, two drug gangs can merge into a larger gang, or one gang leader can acquire the assets of a peer, through coercion or economic goods.

Affiliations: The connections or ties formed between members of a social or familial group or unit, such as kinship ties. Affiliations can form on the basis of religion, race, language, or other factors.

Affiliative instinct: Economist Jack Hirshleifer defines this concept as "a readiness to divide the world between 'us' and 'them.'" People form affiliation groups based on social class, language, race, or other factors, with the purpose of ensuring survival, trading, or gaining protection from looting or physical violence.

Cohesion: A bond that links members of a group together and creates a sense of belonging. Infighting decreases cohesion; kindship ties increase cohesion.

Collective action: Action taken as a unit by a group of individuals to achieve a common goal.

Comparative advantage: In a market, or in the presence of opportunities for trade, people and firms will be better off when they produce goods at the lowest opportunity cost. When Person A can produce a good more efficiently and at a lower opportunity cost than Person B, Person A has the comparative advantage.

Contact enforcement: The ability to enforce contracts, laws, and rules is essential for a functional marketplace. Contract enforcement is equally as important to the success of illicit economies as it is to licit economies. Without enforcement, people in markets have little incentive to abide by rules, so institutions require both rules and associated enforcement.

Cost-benefit analysis: A decision-making tool that determines the economic advantages and disadvantages of various alternatives. Cost-benefit analysis calculates the benefits of an action or decision and subtracts the costs associated with it.

Division of labor: The separation of tasks into component parts so that individuals may specialize in specific tasks, often based on capabilities or preferences. based on their own capabilities. Adam Smith explained this concept in *The Wealth of Nations* by describing the process of making pins: whereby one person could produce about 20 pins per day, ten people could produce 48,000 pins – each person therefore contributing the equivalent of 4,800 pins per day.

Entrepreneur: An individual who makes resource allocation decisions, usually considered to be a risk taker.

Expected benefits: Prior to taking an action, a person makes choices based upon the benefits he expects to receive from these choices. After the choice is made, the actual benefits may or may not align with expectations.

Firm: As described by Ronald Coase in "The Nature of the Firm," people come together to form partnerships in order to minimize transactions costs that would normally occur should transactions take place in markets.

Individual preferences and constraints: Individuals have goals and desires but often face constraints in achieving them. Individuals make choices based on these desires and constraints. Constraints can include: wealth, time, information, and institutions.

Institutions: Human-made rules and associated enforcement of those rules. The rules can be formal and informal, such as cultural prohibitions. Markets are institutions, with rules constraining the behavior of firms, entrepreneurs, and individuals.

Kinship: A network of social and familial bonds, and one of the core drivers of human behavior. Most people feel a propensity for belonging. When we lack bonds with family or blood relatives, or some other incentive causes us to change, we create kinships that are non-genetic but that can be just as powerful.

Labor market: In a labor market, individuals sell their time and capabilities (sometimes called "human capital") for a wage, and firms compete for these labor hours. Violent firms compete in labor markets, often competing against licit firms and the state.

Operating under imperfect information: In a marketplace, people make decisions based on the information available to them – decisions that, given that information, they believe are in their best interests. When the information is imperfect, or the perception in flawed, the outcome may not be as expected or desired.

Production possibility: The outermost productive capacity of an economy at any moment in time. This range defines the greatest productive output from a combination of activities. For example, a person alone on an island can spend his time fishing, harvesting bananas, or a combination of the two.

Rational choice: An economic theory that assumes individuals make logical, non-random choices, often in their own self-interest. Rational choices may be right or wrong, but they are made with purpose and intention. Failure does not make a choice irrational; rather, it can mean an individual was acting on wrong information.

Rational economic exchange: An economic transaction in which goods or services are bought and sold to the perceived economic benefit of both parties.

Repeated exchange: In a repeated exchange, incentives change because of the dimension of a time horizon. The lifetime value of a repeat customer, for example, far exceeds that of the one-time customer. In the context of violence, if there is an enduring marketplace for violence and coercion, a firm can incentivize its members to engage in that marketplace.

Revealed preference: The preference of a person as revealed by behavior. This can differ from a stated preference, which is a person's verbalized preference. For example, while a person might state that he prefers coffee, his revealed preference – what he drinks every morning – might show that he actually prefers tea.

Scarcity: Arises from the state of having or perceiving one has fewer goods than one needs or wants. We live in a world of scarcity; this concept drives much of human behavioral science. When analyzing any human condition or interaction, including violence, ask yourself first, "what is the scarcity?".

Time inconsistency: A decision becomes time-inconsistent when a person makes a rationally optimal choice today but faces different constraints in the future, making the initial choice no longer optimal.

Transaction costs: The costs associated with trade and exchange in marketplaces, such as setting prices, and creating and enforcing contracts. The lower the transaction costs, the more wealth we likely possess and create.

NOTES

Introduction

1 Serge Schmemann, "3 Bombers in Suicide Attack Kill 4 On Jerusalem Street in Another Blow to Peace," *New York Times*, September 5, 1997. See also START. umd.edu, Global Terrorism Database incident IDs 199707300002 (Mahane Yehuda Market) and 199709040001 (Ben Yehuda Street).

2 Janell Ross, "Dylann Roof Reportedly Wanted a Race War. How Many Americans Sympathize?" *The Washington Post*, June 19, 2015.

1 Violence

1 Gretchen Peters, *Seeds of Terror: How Drugs, Thugs, and Crime Are Reshaping the Afghan War* (New York: Thomas Dunne Books, 2009), p. 8.

2 Robert M. Gates, *Duty: Memoirs of a Secretary at War*, Kindle Edition (New York: Knopf Doubleday Publishing Group, 2014), p. 341.

3 *Ibid.*, p. 374.

4 *Ibid.*, p. 384.

5 Gretchen Peters, "Crime and Insurgency in Afghanistan/Pakistan" (guest lecture, Georgetown University, Washington, DC, March 17, 2014).

6 David Kilcullen, *Out of the Mountains: The Coming Age of the Urban Guerrilla* (New York: Oxford University Press, 2013), pp. 12–14.

7 Kilcullen, *Out of the Mountains*, p. 13.

8 Kilcullen, *Out of the Mountains*, p. 16.

9 Jane Perlez, "Chinese Plan to Kill Drug Lord With Drone Highlights Military Advances," *New York Times*, February 20, 2013, www.nytimes.com/2013/02/21/world/asia/chinese-plan-to-use-drone-highlights-military-advances.html?_r=0.

10 "Deadly Attacks Since 9/11," *New America Foundation*, http://securitydata.newamerica.net/extremists/deadly-attacks.html.

11 Mark Bowden, *Killing Pablo: The Hunt for the World's Greatest Outlaw*, reprint edition (New York: Grove Press, 2015), pp. 80–81.

12 Benjamin Lessing, "Logics of Violence in Criminal War," *Journal of Conflict Resolution*, 59, no. 8 (December 2015).

13 Matthew Levitt, "South of the Border, a Threat from Hezbollah," *Journal of International Security Affairs* (Spring 2013), p. 78.

14 Gary M. Shiffman, "It's Strictly Business: Understanding the Evolution of Violence in Mexico," Prepared Testimony to the House Committee on Foreign Affairs, Subcommittee on the Western Hemisphere, September 13, 2011, http://archives .republicans.foreignaffairs.house.gov/112/shi091311.pdf, and www.nytimes.com/ 2011/12/14/world/middleeast/beirut-bank-seen-as-a-hub-of-hezbollahs-financing .html?pagewanted=all&_r=0.

15 Boaz Ganor, "*The Hybrid Terrorist Organization and Incitement*," Jerusalem Center for Public Affairs (JCPA), November 1, 2012.

16 Matthew Levitt, "Hizbullah Narco-Terrorism," *IHS Defense, Risk and Security Consulting* (Washington, DC: The Washington Institute for Near East Policy, September 2012), www.washingtoninstitute.org/uploads/Levitt20120900_1.pdf.

2 The Human Condition

1 Matt Ford and Adam Chandler, "'Hate Crime: A Mass Killing at a Historic Church," *The Atlantic*, June 19, 2015, www.theatlantic.com/national/archive/2015/ 06/shooting-emanuel-ame-charleston/396209/.

2 Michael Pearson, "ISIS Claims Responsibility for Fatal Mosque Attack in Kuwait," *CNN*, June 26, 2015, www.cnn.com/2015/06/26/world/kuwait-mosque-attack/.

3 See for example, Robert M. Solow, "A Contribution to the Theory of Economic Growth," *The Quarterly Journal of Economics* 70, no. 1 (1956), pp. 65–94; K. J. Arrow H. B. Chenery, B. S. Minhas and R. M. Solow, "Capital-Labor Substitution and Economic Efficiency," *The Review of Economics and Statistics*, 43, no. 3 (August 1961); Solow, "Technical Progress, Capital Formation, and Economic Growth," *The American Economic Review*, 52, no. 2; Papers and Proceedings of the Seventy-Fourth Annual Meeting of the American Economic Association, May 1962; Robert E. Lucas Jr., "On the Mechanics of Economic Development," *Journal of Monetary Economics*, 22, no. 1 (July 1988); Paul M. Romer, "Endogenous Technological Change," *Journal of Political Economy*, 98, no. 5 (October 1990); N. Gregory Mankiw, David Romer, and David N. Weil, "A Contribution to the Empirics of Economic Growth," *The Quarterly Journal of Economics*, 107, no. 2 (May 1992), pp. 407–437.

4 Robert M. Gates, "Remarks as Delivered by Secretary of Defense Robert M. Gates, Gaylord Convention Center, National Harbor, Maryland," May 3, 2010, www .defense.gov/speeches/speech.aspx?speechid=1460.

5 *Ibid.*

6 Jack Hirshleifer, "The Bioeconomic Causes of War," *Managerial and Decision Economics*, 19 (1998).

7 *Ibid.*, p. 458.

8 *Ibid.*, p. 458.

9 Jack Hirshleifer, "The Bioeconomic Causes of War," *Managerial and Decision Economics*, 19 (1998).

10 Smith as quoted in *ibid.*, p. 461.

11 David Skarbek, *The Social Order of the Underworld: How Prison Gangs Govern the American Penal System* (New York: Oxford University Press, 2014), p. 77.

12 Robert S. Fong and Salvador Buentello, "Detection of Prison Gang Development: An Empirical Assessment," *Federal Probation*, 55, no. 1 (March 1991).

13 Skarbek, *Social Order*, p. 160.

14 *Ibid.*, p. 161.

15 *Ibid.*, p. 9.

16 Peter Neumann, *Prisons and Terrorism: Radicalization and De-Radicalization in 15 Countries* (London: International Centre for the Study of Radicalisation and Political Violence, 2010), p. 33, http://icsr.info/2010/08/prisons-and-terrorism-radicalisation-and-de-radicalisation-in-15-countries/.

17 *Ibid.*, p. 34.

18 Ronald Coase, "The Nature of the Firm," *Economica*, 4 (1937), p. 388.

19 *Ibid.*, p. 392.

20 *Ibid.*, p. 23.

21 Stathis N. Kalyvas, "The Ontology of 'Political Violence': Action and Identity in Civil Wars," *Perspectives on Politics*, 1, no. 3 (2003), p. 87.

22 *Ibid.*

23 The following section relies on Mancur Olson, "Dictatorship, Democracy, and Development," *The American Political Science Review*, 87, no. 3 (September 1993). It details Olson's description of roving and stationary bandits to demonstrate how governance emerges.

24 *Ibid.*

25 *Ibid.*, Chapter 2.

26 Ronald Wintrobe, *The Political Economy of Dictatorship* (Cambridge: Cambridge University Press, 2000).

27 Gary M. Shiffman and James J. Jochum, *Economic Instruments of Security Policy: Influencing Choices of Leaders* (London: Palgrave Macmillan, 2011), p. 25.

28 For example, see Douglass C. North, John Joseph Wallis, and Barry R. Weingast, "Violence and the Rise of Open-Access Orders," *Journal of Democracy*, 20, no. 1 (January 2009), pp. 55–68; also, Douglass C. North, *Institutions, Institutional Change and Economic Performance* (Cambridge: Cambridge University Press, 1990).

29 Daniel Byman and Kenneth Pollack, "Let Us Now Praise Great Men: Bringing the Statesman Back In," *International Security*, 25, no. 4 (Spring 2001), pp. 107–146, http://belfercenter.ksg.harvard.edu/files/bymanetalvol25no4.pdf.

3 Organized Crime

1 Francis Ford Coppola and Mario Puzo, *The Godfather*, 1972.

2 Gary S. Becker, "Crime and Punishment: An Economic Approach," *Journal of Political Economy*, 76 (1968), p. 170.

3 *Ibid.*, p. 176.

4 Mark Bowden, *Killing Pablo: The Hunt for the World's Greatest Outlaw*, reprint edition (New York: Grove Press, 2015), pp. 16–17.

5 *Ibid.*, p. 15.

6 *Ibid.*

7 *Ibid.*, p. 17.

8 Roberto Escobar, *The Accountant's Story: Inside the Violent World of the Medellín Cartel*, Kindle Edition (New York: Grand Central Publishing, 2009), p. 234.

9 Author Interview with Greg Passic, "Pablo Escobar and Combatting Drug Trafficking in Colombia," Washington, DC, 2015.

10 Escobar, *The Accountant's Story*, pp. 3033–3034.

11 Bowden, *Killing Pablo*, p. 18.

12 *Ibid.*, p. 19.

13 *Ibid.*, p. 20.

14 *Ibid.*, p. 19.

15 *Ibid.*, p. 20.

16 *Ibid.*

17 John Dickie, *Cosa Nostra: A History of the Sicilian Mafia* (New York: Palgrave Macmillian, 2004).
18 *Ibid.*
19 *Ibid.*, 40.
20 *Ibid.*
21 *Ibid.*
22 *Ibid.*, p. 42.
23 *Ibid.*, p. 43.
24 *Ibid.*, pp. 49–50.
25 *Ibid.*, p. 59.
26 *Ibid.*, p. 58.
27 *Ibid.*, p. 59.
28 Bowden, *Killing Pablo*, p. 18.
29 *Ibid.*, p. 21.
30 Author Interview with Greg Passic, "Pablo Escobar and Combatting Drug Trafficking in Colombia," Washington, DC, 2015.
31 Escobar, *The Accountant's Story*, pp. 491–494.
32 Mauricio Rubio, "Social Capital: Some Evidence from Colombia," *Journal of Economic Issues*, 31, no. 3 (September 1997).
33 *Ibid.*, p. 807.
34 *Ibid.*, p. 812.
35 Guy Gugliotta and Jeff Leen, *Kings of Cocaine: Inside the Medellín Cartel – An Astonishing True Story of Murder, Money, and International Corruption*, Kindle Edition (New Orleans, LA: Garrett County Press, 2011), pp. 265–266.
36 *Ibid.*
37 Rubio, "Social Capital," p. 812.
38 Author Interview with Greg Passic, "Pablo Escobar and Combatting Drug Trafficking in Colombia," Washington, DC, 2015.
39 *Ibid.*
40 Escobar, *The Accountant's Story*, p. 736.
41 *Ibid.*, pp. 684–685.
42 Author Interview with Greg Passic, "Pablo Escobar and Combatting Drug Trafficking in Colombia," Washington, DC, 2015.
43 Bowden, *Killing Pablo*, p. 21.
44 *Ibid.*, p. 22.
45 PBS, "Interview, Jorge Ochoa," *Frontline*, 2000, www.pbs.org/wgbh/pages/frontline/shows/drugs/interviews/ochoajorge.html.
46 Bowden, *Killing Pablo*, p. 23.
47 *Ibid.*
48 Gugliotta and Leen, *Kings of Cocaine*, pp. 1217–1219.
49 *Ibid.*, pp. 1233–1235.
50 *Ibid.*, p. 1235.
51 Bowden, *Killing Pablo*, p. 24.
52 Gugliotta and Leen, *Kings of Cocaine*, pp. 1230–1232.
53 M-19, or the 19th of April Movement, was a Colombian guerrilla group active in the 1970s and 1980s. With roots in the nationalist and revolutionary socialist movement, the group led several attacks against the Colombian government and engaged in kidnapping schemes. The group eventually demobilized at the end of the 1980s, turning to politics in the next decade. See: Roman D. Ortiz, "Insurgent Strategies in the Post-Cold War: The Case of the Revolutionary Armed Forces of Colombia," *Studies in Conflict and Terrorism*, 25 (2002).
54 Jorge Pablo Osterling, *Democracy in Colombia: Clientelistic Politics and Guerrilla Warfare* (Livingston, NJ: Transaction Publishers, 1988), p. 303.
55 Escobar, *The Accountant's Story*, pp. 840–841.

56 Bowden, *Killing Pablo*, p. 33.
57 Escobar, *The Accountant's Story*, pp. 840–841.
58 *Ibid.*, p. 811.
59 Bowden, *Killing Pablo*, p. 33.
60 Escobar, *The Accountant's Story*, pp. 844–845.
61 *Ibid.*, pp. 848–851.
62 Gugliotta and Leen, *Kings of Cocaine*, pp. 1353–1356.
63 Escobar, *The Accountant's Story*, pp. 807–809.
64 *Ibid.*, pp. 1883–1885.
65 Gugliotta and Leen, *Kings of Cocaine*, p. 1356.
66 Escobar, *The Accountant's Story*, pp. 215–216.
67 Bowden, *Killing Pablo*, p. 29.
68 *Ibid.*
69 Sylvia Ann Hewlett, "Attract and Keep A-Players with Nonfinancial Rewards," *Harvard Business Review* (May 24, 2012), http://blogs.hbr.org/2012/05/attract-and-keep-a-players-wit/.
70 *Ibid.*
71 Escobar, *The Accountant's Story*, pp. 1216–1217.
72 *Ibid.*, pp. 1220–1221.
73 *Ibid.*, pp. 974–975.
74 For more on why organized crime sometimes adopts decentralized and networked structures, see Phil Williams, "Transnational Criminal Networks," in John Arquilla and David Ronfeldt (eds), *Networks and Netwars: The Future of Crime, Terror, and Militancy* (Santa Monica, CA: RAND, 2001).
75 Author Interview with Greg Passic, "Pablo Escobar and Combatting Drug Trafficking in Colombia," Washington, DC, 2015.
76 *Ibid.*
77 Bowden, *Killing Pablo*, p. 29.
78 *Ibid.*
79 *Ibid.*
80 Major General J.N. Mattis, "Eve of Battle Speech," *Free Republic*, April 1, 2003, www.freerepublic.com/focus/f-news/881955/posts.
81 "North: No Better Friend, No Worse Enemy," *Bearing Arms*, March 31, 2013, www.humanevents.com/2013/03/31/north-no-better-friend-no-worse-enemy.
82 Bowden, *Killing Pablo*, p. 30.
83 *Ibid.*
84 Gugliotta and Leen, *Kings of Cocaine*, pp. 200–203.
85 Dickie, *Cosa Nostra*, p. 42.
86 *Ibid.*, pp. 44–46.
87 *Ibid.*, p. 47.
88 Bowden, *Killing Pablo*, p. 28.
89 Douglass C. North, "Economic Performance Through Time," *The American Economic Review*, 84, no. 3 (June 1994), pp. 359–368. From his lecture upon receiving the 1993 Nobel Memorial Prize in Economic Science.
90 Bowden, *Killing Pablo*, pp. 28–29.
91 *Ibid.*, p. 30.
92 *Ibid.*, p. 31.
93 *Ibid.*
94 Escobar, *The Accountant's Story*, pp. 1463–1466.
95 *Ibid.*, pp. 1458–1459.
96 Bowden, *Killing Pablo*, p. 35.
97 *Ibid.*
98 *Ibid.*
99 Gugliotta and Leen, *Kings of Cocaine*, pp. 1474–1475.

100 Bowden, *Killing Pablo*, p. 35.
101 *Ibid.*, p. 36.
102 *Ibid.*, p. 38.
103 Escobar, *The Accountant's Story*, pp. 1551–1552.
104 Gugliotta and Leen, *Kings of Cocaine*, pp. 1648–1650.
105 Bowden, *Killing Pablo*, p. 38.
106 *Ibid.*, p. 39.
107 *Ibid.*, p. 40.
108 *Ibid.*
109 *Ibid.*, p. 43.
110 *Ibid.*
111 Escobar, *The Accountant's Story*, p. 1574.
112 *Ibid.*
113 For a timeline, see PBS, "Thirty Years of America's Drug War," *Frontline*, www
    .pbs.org/wgbh/pages/frontline/shows/drugs/cron/.
114 Gugliotta and Leen, *Kings of Cocaine*, p. 2155.
115 *Ibid.*
116 PBS, "Interview with Fernando Arenas," *Frontline*, 2000, www.pbs.org/wgbh/
    pages/frontline/shows/drugs/interviews/arenas.html.
117 Bowden, *Killing Pablo*, p. 44.
118 PBS, "Interview with Fernando Arenas," *Frontline*, 2000, www.pbs.org/wgbh/
    pages/frontline/shows/drugs/interviews/arenas.html.
119 Bowden, *Killing Pablo*, p. 44.
120 Gugliotta and Leen, *Kings of Cocaine*, pp. 2626–2628.
121 Robert L. Jackson, "Pilot Says Noriega Got $100,000 a Load in Drug Flight
    Payoffs," *Los Angeles Times,* September 27, 1991, http://articles.latimes.com/
    1991-09-27/news/mn-2916_1_drug-flights.
122 *Ibid.*
123 Associated Press, "Witness Says Noriega Aide Received $4-Million Payoff," *Los
    Angeles Times*, October 26, 1991, http://articles.latimes.com/1991-10-26/news/
    mn-191_1_medellin-cartel.
124 PBS, "Interview with Fernando Arenas," *Frontline*, 2000, www.pbs.org/wgbh/
    pages/frontline/shows/drugs/interviews/arenas.html.
125 Bowden, *Killing Pablo*, pp. 45–46.
126 Escobar, *The Accountant's Story*, pp. 1745–1747.
127 *Ibid.*
128 Bowden, *Killing Pablo*, p. 48.
129 *Ibid.*
130 Escobar, *The Accountant's Story*, pp. 1748–1749.
131 *Ibid.*
132 Escobar, *The Accountant's Story*, pp. 1783–1784.
133 *Ibid.*, p. 1803.
134 *Ibid.*, pp. 1800–1801.
135 *Ibid.*
136 *Ibid.*, p. 1828.
137 *Ibid.*, pp. 1830–1834.
138 *Ibid.*, pp. 1860–1861.
139 Gugliotta and Leen, *Kings of Cocaine*, pp. 3771–3774.
140 Bowden, *Killing Pablo*, p. 51.
141 *Ibid.*, p. 52.
142 Escobar, *The Accountant's Story*, pp. 1876–1878.
143 Bowden, *Killing Pablo*, p. 52.
144 *Ibid.*, p. 53.
145 Bowden, *Killing Pablo*, p. 53.

146 *Ibid.*, p. 55.
147 Escobar, *The Accountant's Story*, pp. 2030–2031.
148 *Ibid.*, pp. 2031–2034.
149 "Counter-Terrorism in Somalia: Losing Hearts and Minds?" *Africa Report*, 95 (July 11, 2005), www.somaliatalk.com/2005/oct/crisisgroup.pdf.
150 Bowden, *Killing Pablo*, p. 58.
151 *Ibid.*; Anastasia Moloney, "Drug Baron's Ally on Trial for Killing of Political Rival," *The Independent*, July 12, 2006, www.independent.co.uk/news/world/americas/drug-barons-ally-on-trial-for-killing-of-political-rival-407731.html.
152 Bowden, *Killing Pablo*, p. 58.
153 *Ibid.*, p. 92.
154 *Ibid.*, p. 100.
155 PBS, "Interview with Jorge Ochoa," *Frontline*, 2000, www.pbs.org/wgbh/pages/frontline/shows/drugs/interviews/ochoajorge.html.
156 Lessing, "Logics of Violence," p. 1.
157 William Cran, "The Godfather of Cocaine," *Frontline*, March 25, 1997, www.pbs.org/wgbh/pages/frontline/shows/drugs/archive/godfathercocaine.html.
158 Bowden, *Killing Pablo*, p. 115.
159 Escobar, *The Accountant's Story*, pp. 2850–2852.
160 Raab, *Five Families*, pp. 1167–1169.
161 *Ibid.*, pp. 1170–1173.
162 Bowden, *Killing Pablo*, p. 12.
163 Jeff "the Dude" Lebowski, in Joel Coen and Ethan Coen, *The Big Lebowski*, 1998.
164 *Ibid.*, p. 117.
165 Bowden, *Killing Pablo*, p. 122.
166 *Ibid.*, p. 122.
167 *Ibid.*, p. 123.
168 *Ibid.*, pp. 126–127.
169 *Ibid.*, pp. 130–133.
170 *Ibid.*, p. 125.
171 *Ibid.*, p. 143.
172 *Ibid.*, p. 144.
173 *Ibid.*
174 Robert J. Bunker and John P. Sullivan, "Cartel Car Bombings in Mexico," *The LeTort Papers* (Carlisle, PA: Strategic Studies Institute and US Army War College, August 2013), p. 4, www.strategicstudiesinstitute.army.mil/pdffiles/PUB1166.pdf.
175 Bowden, *Killing Pablo*, p. 168.
176 Escobar, *The Accountant's Story*, pp. 3394–3396.
177 Elaine Shannon Washington, "Cover Stories: New Kings of Coke," *Time*, June 24, 2001, http://content.time.com/time/magazine/article/0,9171,157350,00.html.
178 *Ibid.*
179 *Ibid.*
180 Gugliotta and Leen, *Kings of Cocaine*, p. 2929.
181 Peter Kerr, "Cocaine Glut Pulls New York Market Into Drug Rings' Tug-of-War," *New York Times*, August 24, 1988, www.nytimes.com/1988/08/24/nyregion/cocaine-glut-pulls-new-york-market-into-drug-rings-tug-of-war.html.
182 Lloyd D. Johnston, Patrick M. O'Malley, Jerald G. Bachman, and John E. Schulenberg, *Monitoring the Future National Survey Results on Drug Use, 1975–2011: Volume I, Secondary School Students* (Ann Arbor, MI: Institute for Social Research, The University of Michigan, June 2012), p. 39, www.monitoringthefuture.org/pubs/monographs/mtf-vol1_2011.pdf.
183 "The Price and Purity of Illicit Drugs: 1981 Through the Second Quarter of 2003" (Washington, DC: Executive Office of the President, 2004), p. v., www.ncjrs.gov/ondcppubs/publications/pdf/price_purity.pdf.

184 Kerr, "Cocaine Glut."
185 *Ibid.*
186 *Ibid.*
187 *Ibid.*
188 Alan Riding, "Drug Rings Wage War For Control: Colombian Cocaine Cartels Inform On Or Kill Rivals," *SunSentinel*, August 23, 1988, http://articles.sun-sentinel .com/1988-08-23/news/8802180677_1_cali-cartel-medellin-cartel-two-cartels.
189 Kerr, "Cocaine Glut."
190 William C. Rempel, *At the Devil's Table: The Untold Story of the Insider Who Brought Down the Cali Cartel*, Kindle Edition (New York: Random House Publishing Group, 2011), p. 146.
191 *Ibid.*, p. 198.
192 *Ibid.*, p. 202.
193 Ortiz, "Insurgent Strategies in the Post-Cold War," p. 133.
194 Rempel, *At the Devil's Table*, pp. 215–216.
195 *Ibid.*, p. 224.
196 "Killing Pablo," *CNN Presents*, May 25, 2003, http://edition.cnn.com/TRANSCRIPTS/ 0305/25/cp.00.html.
197 Rempel, *At the Devil's Table*, p. 2029.
198 James Brooke, "Drug Spotlight Falls on an Unblinking Cali Cartel," *New York Times*, December 17, 1993, www.nytimes.com/1993/12/17/world/drug-spotlight-falls-on-an-unblinking-cali-cartel.html.
199 Central Intelligence Agency, "Colombia: Extralegal Steps Against Escobar Possible," April 30, 1993, www2.gwu.edu/~nsarchiv/NSAEBB/NSAEBB243/ 19930400-cia.pdf.
200 "Killing Pablo," *CNN Presents*, May 25, 2003, http://edition.cnn.com/TRANSCRIPTS/ 0305/25/cp.00.html.
201 Brooke, "Drug Spotlight Falls on an Unblinking Cali Cartel."
202 Bert Ruiz, *The Colombian Civil War*, Kindle Edition (Jefferson, NC: Mcfarland & Co., Inc. Publishers, 2001), p. 204.
203 Bowden, *Killing Pablo*, p. 269.

4 Insurgency

1 James C. McKinley Jr., "Uganda's Christian Rebels Revive War in North," *New York Times*, April 1, 1996.
2 For example, Kony is commonly referred to as an irrational "madman" (see "Obama Continues Effort Against 'Madman' Kony," *CNN*, April 23, 2012, www.cnn.com/2012/04/23/us/obama-kony/), while campaigns to bring Kony to justice have characterized him as leading a mindless evil force; see Polly Curtis and Tom McCarthy, "Kony 2012: What's the Real Story?" *Guardian*, March 8, 2012, www.theguardian.com/politics/reality-check-with-polly-curtis/2012/mar/ 08/kony-2012-what-s-the-story.
3 Emma Mutaizibwa, "The Roots of War: How Alice Lakwena Gave Way to Joseph Kony," *The Observer*, August 11, 2011, www.observer.ug/index .php?option=com_content&view=article&id=14678:the-roots-of-war-how-alice-lakwena-gave-way-to-joseph-kony&catid=57:feature.
4 *Ibid.*
5 Christopher Blattman and Jeannie Annan, "On the Nature and Causes of LRA Abduction: What the Abductees Say," in Tim Allen and Koen Vlassenroot (eds), *The Lord's Resistance Army: Myth and Reality* (London: Zed Books, 2010), p. 135.

6 "The Remains of Kony's Father Reburied in his Ancestral Home," *Acholi Times*, March 19, 2012.

7 Mutaizibwa, "The Roots of War."

8 "The Remains of Kony's Father."

9 Tim Allen and Koen Vlassenroot, "Introduction," *The Lord's Resistance Army: Myth and Reality* (London: Zed Books, 2010), p. 6.

10 Aili Mari Tripp, *Museveni's Uganda: Paradoxes of Power in a Hybrid Regime (Challenge and Change in African Politics)* (Boulder, CO: Lynne Rienner Publishers, 2010), p. 47.

11 Allen and Vlassenroot, *The Lord's Resistance Army*, p. 7.

12 *Ibid.*

13 Tripp, *Museveni's Uganda*, p. 48.

14 Lawrence E. Cline, *The Lord's Resistance Army* (Santa Barbara, CA: Praeger, 2013), p. 9.

15 Heike Behrend, *Alice Lakwena and the Holy Spirits: War in Northern Uganda, 1986–97* (Athens, Ohio: Ohio University Press, 2000), p. 173. Museveni's offer of amnesty for all Acholi insurgents ultimately brought about the UPDA's demise. Okello was in favor of a peace agreement with Museveni and urged his troops to accept the terms of the government-proffered amnesty agreement. Conversely, Latek refused to end his fight against the government and urged the forces that remained loyal to him to follow him and join with the LRA.

16 Adam Branch, "Exploring the Roots of LRA Violence: Political Crisis and Ethnic Politics in Acholiland" in Allen and Vlassenroot (eds), *The Lord's Resistance Army: Myth and Reality*, p. 38. Shortly after his rise to power, Museveni renamed his forces the Uganda People's Defence Force (UPDF), a name that exists to this day.

17 "Alice Lakwena," *The Economist*. January 2007. www.economist.com/node/8584604.

18 Tim Allen, "Understanding Alice: Uganda's Holy Spirit Movement in Context," *Africa: Journal of the International African Institute*, 61, no. 3 (1991), p. 375.

19 Peter Eichstaedt, *First Kill Your Family: Child Soldiers of Uganda and the Lord's Resistance Army* (Chicago: Lawrence Hill Books, 2013), p. 208.

20 Allen and Vlassenroot, *The Lord's Resistance Army*, p. 8.

21 *Ibid.*

22 Behrend, *"Alice Lakwena and the Holy Spirits,"* p. 110.

23 Gary M. Shiffman and James J. Jochum, *Economic Instruments of Security Policy: Influencing Choices of Leaders* (London: Palgrave Macmillan, 2011).

24 Behrend, *Alice Lakwena and the Holy Spirits*, p. 179

25 Allen and Vlassenroot, *The Lord's Resistance Army*, p. 10; Behrend, *Alice Lakwena and the Holy Spirits*, pp. 86–87.

26 Behrend, *Alice Lakwena and the Holy Spirits*, pp. 91–93.

27 Branch, "Exploring the Roots of LRA Violence," p. 39.

28 Shiffman and Jochum, *Economic Instruments of Security Policy*, p. 26; Ronald Wintrobe, "The Tinpot and the Totalitarian: An Economic Theory of Dictatorship," *The American Political Science Review*, 84, no. 3 (September 1990).

29 Cline, *The Lord's Resistance Army*, p. 12.

30 *Ibid.*, p. 29.

31 *Ibid.*, p. 28.

32 James Bevan, "The Myth of Madness: Cold Rationality and 'Resource' Plunder by the Lord's Resistance Army," *Civil Wars*, 9, no. 4 (December 2007), p. 345.

33 *Ibid.*, p. 351.

34 Cline, *The Lord's Resistance Army*, p. 29.

35 Reproduced from Tim Allen and Koen Vlassenroot, *The Lord's Resistance Army: Myth and Reality* (London: Zed Books, 2010).

36 Paul Collier, "Rebellion as a Quasi-Criminal Activity," *Journal of Conflict Resolution*, 44, no. 6 (2000), p. 839.

37 *Ibid.*, p. 841.

38 *Ibid.*, p. 846.

39 Sam Farmer, "I Will Use the 10 Commandments to Liberate Uganda," *The Times*, June 28, 2006, www.thetimes.co.uk/tto/news/world/article1982845.ece.

40 Human Rights Watch, "No Place for Children: Child Recruitment, Forced Marriage, and Attacks on Schools in Somalia," February 20, 2012, www.hrw.org/report/2012/02/20/no-place-children/child-recruitment-forced-marriage-and-attacks-schools-somalia.

41 *Ibid.*

42 *Ibid.*, p. 21.

43 *Ibid.*, p. 23.

44 *Ibid.*

45 *Ibid.*, p. 20.

46 William Booth and Steve Fainaru, "Mexican Drug Cartels Increasingly Recruit the Young," *Washington Post*, November 3, 2009, www.washingtonpost.com/wp-dyn/content/article/2009/11/02/AR2009110203492.html.

47 *Ibid.*

48 *Ibid.*

49 "Report on the Youth Labor Force," *Bureau of Labor Statistics* (2002), p. 3, www.bls.gov/opub/rylf/pdf/chapter2.pdf.

50 *Ibid.*, p. 138.

51 *Ibid.*, p. 145; Bernd Beber and Christopher Blattman, "The Logic of Child Soldiering and Coercion," *International Organization*, 67, no. 1 (January 2013), p. 67.

52 Blattman and Annan, "On the Nature and Causes of LRA Abduction," pp. 145–148.

53 Maria Micaela Sviatschi, "Making a Narco: Childhood Exposure to Illegal Labor Markets and Criminal Life Paths," Job Market Paper, Columbia University, January 1, 2017.

54 Erin Baines, "Forced Marriage as a Political Project: Sexual Rules and Relations in the Lord's Resistance Army," *Journal of Peace Research*, 51, no. 3 (2014), p. 409.

55 *Ibid.*, p. 414

56 *Ibid.*, p. 406.

57 Grace Akello, "Experiences of Forced Mothers in Northern Uganda: The Legacy of War," *Intervention*, 11, no. 2 (September 2013), p. 149.

58 *Ibid.*, p. 150.

59 Baines, "Forced Marriage," p. 405.

60 *Ibid.*, p. 412.

61 Dara Cohen, "Explaining Rape during Civil War: Cross-National Evidence (1980–2009)," *American Political Science Review*, 107, no. 3 (2013), pp. 461–477.

62 Jacob N. Shapiro, *The Terrorist's Dilemma: Managing Violent Covert Organizations*, Kindle Edition (Princeton, NJ: Princeton University Press, 2013), p. 76.

63 Human Rights Watch, "No Place for Children: Child Recruitment, Forced Marriage, and Attacks on Schools in Somalia."

64 *Ibid.*, p. 54.

65 Aki Peritz and Tara Maller, "The Islamic State of Sexual Violence," *Foreign Policy*, September 16, 2014, www.foreignpolicy.com/articles/2014/09/16/the_islamic_state_of_sexual_violence_women_rape_iraq_syria.

66 Kathleen Geier, "R.I.P., Gary Becker," *Washington Monthly*, May 4, 2014, www.washingtonmonthly.com/political-animal-a/2014_05/rip_gary_becker050194.php.

67 *Ibid.*

68 Jeremy M. Weinstein, *Inside Rebellion: The Politics of Insurgent Violence (Cambridge Studies in Comparative Politics)*, Kindle Edition (Cambridge: Cambridge University Press, 2006), p. 7.
69 *Ibid.*
70 *Ibid.*
71 Muhsin Hassan, "Understanding Drivers of Violent Extremism: The Case of Al-Shabab and Somali Youth," Combating Terrorism Center, August 23, 2012, www.ctc.usma.edu/posts/understanding-drivers-of-violent-extremism-the-case-of-al-shabab-and-somali-youth.
72 Benjamin W. Bahney, Radha K. Iyengar, Patrick B. Johnston, Danielle F. Jung, Jacob N. Shapiro, and Howard J. Shatz, "Insurgent Compensation: Evidence from Iraq," *American Economic Review*, 103, no. 3 (2013), http://patrickjohnston.info/materials/InsurgentCompensationEvidenceFromIr_preview.pdf.
73 Joanne Salop and Steven Salop, "Self-Selection and Turnover in the Labor Market," *The Quarterly Journal of Economics*, 90, no. 4 (November 1976), p. 622.
74 Gretchen Peters, *Seeds of Terror: How Drugs, Thugs, and Crime Are Reshaping the Afghan War* (New York: Thomas Dunne Books, 2009), p. 146.
75 Peters, *Seeds of Terror*, p. 153.
76 Weinstein, *Inside Rebellion*, p. 9.
77 *Ibid.*
78 *Ibid.*, pp. 10–12.
79 *Ibid.*, p. 20.
80 John Nagl, *Learning to Eat Soup with a Knife: Counterinsurgency Lessons from Malaya and Vietnam* (Chicago: The University of Chicago Press, 2005), p. 213.
81 *Ibid.*, p. 214.
82 Fred Kaplan, *The Insurgents: David Petraeus and the Plot to Change the American Way of War* (New York: Simon & Schuster, 2013); Tom Ricks, *The Gamble: General Petraeus and the American Military Adventure in Iraq* (New York: Penguin, 2009).
83 Nagl, *Learning to Eat Soup*, p. 15.
84 *Ibid.*, p. 15.
85 *Ibid.*, p. 28.
86 "Insurgencies and Countering Insurgencies," Headquarters, Department of the Army, Washington, DC (June 2, 2014), p. I-9, http://fas.org/irp/doddir/army/fm3-24.pdf.
87 Robert Taber, *The War of the Flea* (Lincoln, NE: Potomac Books, 1957), p. 109.
88 James Weir and Hekmatullah Azamy, "The Taliban's Transformation From Ideology to Franchise," *Foreign Policy*, October 17, 2014, http://foreignpolicy.com/2014/10/17/the-talibans-transformation-from-ideology-to-franchise/.
89 Richard A. Oppel Jr., "Iraq's Insurgency Runs on Stolen Oil Profits," *New York Times*, March 16, 2008, www.nytimes.com/2008/03/16/world/middleeast/16insurgent.html?pagewanted=all.
90 *Ibid.*
91 Bahney et al., "Insurgent Compensation."
92 John Nagl, *Knife Fights: A Memoir of Modern War in Theory and Practice*, Kindle Edition (London: Penguin, 2014), p. 1176.
93 *Ibid.*, p. 1179.
94 *Ibid.*, p. 1188.
95 *Ibid.*, p. 1446.
96 Martin Plaut, "Behind the LRA's Terror Tactics," *BBC News*, February 17, 2009, http://news.bbc.co.uk/2/hi/africa/7885885.stm.
97 *Ibid.*

98 *Ibid.*

99 *Ibid.*

100 James Ciment, *World Terrorism: An Encyclopedia of Political Violence from Ancient Times to the Post 9/11 Era* (New York: Routledge, 2015), p. 486.

101 International Criminal Court, "ICC-02/04-01/05: The Prosecutor v. Joseph Kony, Vincent Otti, Okot Okhiambo, and Dominic Ongwen," www.icc-cpi.int/en_menus/icc/situations%20and%20cases/situations/situation%20icc%200204/related%20cases/icc%200204%200105/Pages/uganda.aspx.

102 United States Department of State, "Lord's Resistance Army: Fact Sheet," Office of the Spokesperson, Washington, DC, March 23, 2012, www.state.gov/r/pa/prs/ps/2012/03/186734.htm.

103 Bruce Hoffman, *Inside Terrorism* (New York: Columbia University Press, 2006), p. 43.

104 *Ibid.*

105 Kasper Agger and Jonathan Hutson, "Kony's Ivory: How Elephant Poaching in Congo Helps Support the Lord's Resistance Army," *Enough Project*, June 2013, www.enoughproject.org/files/KonysIvory.pdf.

106 *Ibid.*

107 *Ibid.*

108 Jeffrey Gettleman, "Elephants Dying in Epic Frenzy as Ivory Fuels Wars and Profits," *New York Times*, September 3, 2012, www.nytimes.com/2012/09/04/world/africa/africas-elephants-are-being-slaughtered-in-poaching-frenzy.html?pagewanted=all.

109 *Ibid.*

110 *Ibid.*

111 Jeffrey Gettleman, "To Save Wildlife, and Tourism, Kenyans Take Up Arms," *New York Times*, December 29, 2012, www.nytimes.com/2012/12/30/world/africa/to-save-wildlife-and-tourism-kenyans-take-up-arms.html?pagewanted=1&_r=2&smid=re-share.

112 *Ibid.*

113 *Ibid.*

114 Barbara Crossette, "Sierra Leone Rebel Leader Reportedly Smuggled Gems," *New York Times*, May 14, 2000, www.nytimes.com/2000/05/14/world/sierra-leone-rebel-leader-reportedly-smuggled-gems.html.

115 Dickie, *Cosa Nostra*, p. 21.

116 Dickie, *Cosa Nostra*, p. 56.

117 *Ibid.*, p. 64.

118 *Ibid.*, p. 72.

119 *Ibid.*, p. 77.

120 *Ibid.*, p. 134.

121 *Ibid.*, pp. 148–150.

122 *Ibid.*, pp. 99, 106.

123 *Ibid.*, p. 161.

124 *Ibid.*, p. 195.

125 *Ibid.*, p. 243.

126 *Ibid.*, p. 250.

127 *Ibid.*, p. 248.

128 *Ibid.*, p. 252.

129 *Ibid.*, p. 255.

130 *Ibid.*, p. 256.

131 *Ibid.*, p. 285.

132 *Ibid.*, p. 286.

133 *Ibid.*, p. 290.

134 *Ibid.*, p. 305.

135 *Ibid.*, p. 315.

136 *Ibid.*, p. 326.

5 Terrorism

1 James Foley, *Glengarry Glen Ross*, 1992.
2 Chuck Palahniuk, *Fight Club* (New York: W. W. Norton & Company, 1996).
3 "President Bush Addresses the Nation," *Washington Post*, September 20, 2001, www.washingtonpost.com/wp-srv/nation/specials/attacked/transcripts/bushaddress_092001.html.
4 Dan Bilefsky and Maïa de la Baume, "French Premier Declares 'War' on Radical Islam as Paris Girds for Rally," *New York Times*, January 10, 2015, www.nytimes.com/2015/01/11/world/europe/paris-terrorist-attacks.html?_r=0.
5 Joseph Lieberman, "A Global War on Radical Islam," *Wall Street Journal*, January 12, 2015, www.wsj.com/articles/joseph-lieberman-a-global-war-on-radical-islam-1421106699.
6 Michael Rubin, "Why So Many Suicide Bombers if Islam Prohibits Suicide?" *American Enterprise Institute*, January 12, 2015, www.aei.org/publication/many-suicide-bombers-islam-prohibits-suicide/.
7 Julian E. Zelizer, "Bush Was Right: We're Not at War with Islam," *CNN.com*, September 13, 2010, www.cnn.com/2010/OPINION/09/13/zelizer.bush.muslims/.
8 Peter Beinart, "The GOP's Islamophobia Problem," *The Atlantic*, February 13, 2015, www.theatlantic.com/national/archive/2015/02/anti-islam/385463/.
9 George W. Bush, "State of the Union Address," *Guardian*, September 21, 2001, www.theguardian.com/world/2001/sep/21/september11.usa13.
10 *Ibid.*
11 Susan Jones, "WH Chief of Staff: We're In a War Against Al Qaeda and ISIL," *cnsnews.com*, January 26, 2015, http://cnsnews.com/news/article/susan-jones/wh-chief-staff-were-war-against-al-qaeda-and-isil.
12 Michael Scheuer, *Osama Bin Laden*, Kindle Edition (New York: Oxford University Press, 2011), p. 39.
13 *Ibid.*, p. 40.
14 *Ibid.*
15 *Ibid.*, p. 21.
16 Lawrence Wright, *The Looming Tower: Al Qaeda and the Road to 9/11* (New York: Vintage, 2006).
17 Scheuer, *Osama Bin Laden*, p. 35.
18 *Ibid.*, p. 33.
19 *Ibid.*, p. 49.
20 Peter L. Bergen, *The Osama Bin Laden I Know: An Oral History of al Qaeda's Leader* (New York: Free Press, 2006), p. 60.
21 Wright, *Looming Tower*, p. 95.
22 *Ibid.*
23 *Ibid.*
24 See anthropologist Scott Atran's work for interesting comments on the importance of going to war, Scott Atran, *Talking To the Enemy: Faith, Brotherhood, and the (Un)Making of Terrorists* (New York: Ecco, 2010).
25 Bergen, *Bin Laden I Know*, p. 53.
26 Scheuer, *Osama Bin Laden*, p. 50.
27 *Ibid.*
28 *Ibid.*, p. 54.
29 *Ibid.*
30 Scheuer, *Osama bin Laden*, p. 54.
31 *Ibid.*
32 *Ibid.*
33 Bergen, *Bin Laden I Know*, p. 34.
34 *Ibid.*

35 Benjamin W. Bahney, Radha K. Iyengar, Patrick B. Johnston, Danielle F. Jung, Jacob Shapiro, and Howard J. Shatz, "Insurgent Compensation: Evidence from Iraq," *American Economic Review: Papers and Proceedings*, 103 (2013), pp. 512–517.

36 Wright, *Looming Tower*, p. 154.

37 *Ibid.*, p. 155.

38 Scheuer, *Osama Bin Laden*, p. 58.

39 Wright, *Looming Tower*, p. 155.

40 Scheuer, *Osama Bin Laden*, p. 58.

41 Bergen, *Bin Laden I Know*, p. 75.

42 Scheuer, *Osama Bin Laden*, pp. 61–62.

43 *Ibid.*, p. 60

44 *Ibid.*

45 Edward L. Glaeser, "The Political Economy of Hatred,", *The Quarterly Journal of Economics*, February 2005, p. 79, the President and Fellows of Harvard College and the Massachusetts Institute of Technology.

46 Khaleel Mohammed, *Islam and Violence* (Cambridge: Cambridge University Press, 2018).

47 Laurence R. Iannaccone, "The Market for Martyrs" (presented at the Meetings of the American Economic Association, San Diego, CA, 2004), http://isites.harvard.edu/fs/docs/icb.topic107502.files/Iannaccone.Market_for_Martyrs.pdf.

48 Eli Berman and Laurence R. Iannaccone, "Religious Extremism: The Good, the Bad, and the Deadly" (NBER Working Paper No. 11663, September 2005), www.nber.org/papers/w11663.pdf.

49 *Ibid.*

50 *Ibid.*

51 *Ibid.*

52 I define technology as knowledge of a process, or a recipe for how to do something. In this definition, technology need not be physical. Multiple people can own the same technology simultaneously. It is not rival.

53 Iannaccone, "Market for Martyrs."

54 *Ibid.*

55 *Ibid.*

56 Scheuer, *Osama Bin Laden*, p. 62.

57 Bergen, *Bin Laden I Know*, p. 60.

58 Scheuer, *Osama Bin Laden*, p. 65.

59 Wright, *Looming Tower*, p. 132.

60 *Ibid.*

61 *Ibid.*, p. 133.

62 *Ibid.*

63 Scheuer, *Osama Bin Laden*, pp. 62–63.

64 See chapter 3, Jacob N. Shapiro, *The Terrorists Dilemma: Managing Violent Covert Organizations* (Princeton, NJ: Princeton University Press, 2015).

65 Jacob N. Shapiro, "The Business Habits of Highly Effective Terrorists," *Foreign Affairs*, August 14, 2013, www.foreignaffairs.com/articles/139817/jacob-n-shapiro/the-business-habits-of-highly-effective-terrorists.

66 Eli Berman, *Radical, Religious, and Violent: The New Economics of Terrorism* (Cambridge, MA: MIT Press, 2009).

67 *Ibid.*

68 Berman and Iannaccone, "Religious Extremism."

69 Iannaccone, "Market for Martyrs."

70 Thomas Hegghammer, "The Recruiter's Dilemma: Signaling and Rebel Recruitment Tactics," *Journal of Peace Research*, 50 no. 1 (2013), pp. 3–16.

71 *Ibid.*

72 Bergen, *Bin Laden I Know*, p. 76.

73 *Ibid.*, p. 79.
74 *Ibid.*
75 *Ibid.*, p. 81.
76 Prince Turki bin Faisal al Saud, "Economics of Substate Violence" (guest lecture, Georgetown University, Washington, DC, October 26, 2015).
77 Aryn Baker, "Who Killed Abdullah Azzam," *Time*, June 18, 2009, http://content.time.com/time/specials/packages/printout/0,29239,1902809_1902810_1905173,00.html.
78 Wright, *Looming Tower*, p. 154.
79 *Ibid.*, p. 164.
80 *Ibid.*, p. 146.
81 Bergen, *Bin Laden I Know*, p. 83.
82 *Ibid.*
83 Wright, *Looming Tower*, p. 154.
84 Prince Turki bin Faisal al Saud, "Economics of Substate Violence."
85 Baker, "Who Killed Abdullah Azzam."
86 Wright, *Looming Tower*, p. 157.
87 Scheuer, *Osama bin Laden*, p. 79.
88 *Ibid.*, p. 80.
89 Wright, *Looming Tower*, p. 174.
90 *Ibid.*
91 Prince Turki bin Faisal al Saud, "Economics of Substate Violence" (guest lecture, Georgetown University, Washington, DC, October 26, 2015).
92 Bergen, *Bin Laden I Know*, p. 82.
93 Wright, *Looming Tower*, p. 162
94 Bergen, *Bin Laden I Know*, p. 229.
95 Wright, *Looming Tower*, p. 162.
96 *Ibid.*, p. 191.
97 Shapiro, "Business Habits."
98 Scheuer, *Osama Bin Laden*, pp. 88–89.
99 *Ibid.*, p. 86.
100 The National Commission on Terrorist Attacks Upon the United States, "The Foundation of the New Terrorism," August 21, 2004, http://govinfo.library.unt.edu/911/report/911Report_Ch2.htm.
101 Bergen, *Bin Laden I Know*, p. 121.
102 *Ibid.*
103 Thomas Hegghammer, *Jihad in Saudi Arabia: Violence and Pan-Islamism since 1979* (New York: Cambridge University Press, 2010), p. 100.
104 Commission on Terrorist Attacks.
105 *Ibid.*
106 *Ibid.*
107 Wright, *Looming Tower*, p. 44.
108 *Ibid.*
109 Wright, *Looming Tower*, p. 250.
110 Prince Turki bin Faisal al Saud, "Economics of Substate Violence."
111 Bergen, *Bin Laden I Know*, p. 124.
112 *Ibid.*, p. 122.
113 *Ibid.*
114 Wright, *Looming Tower*, p. 190.
115 *Ibid.*, p. 252.
116 Bergen, *Bin Laden I Know*, p. 122.
117 *Ibid.*, p. 129.
118 Matthew Levitt, *Hezbollah: The Global Footprint of Lebanon's Party of God*, Kindle Edition (Washington, DC: Georgetown University Press, 2013), pp. 7460–7461; and Wright, *Looming Tower*, p. 197.

119 Commission on Terrorist Attacks; for more on the Al Fadl case and its relationship to the larger organizational dilemmas facing terrorist organizations, see Shapiro, *The Terrorist's Dilemma.*

120 Wright, *Looming Tower*, p. 207.

121 *Ibid.*, p. 210.

122 Scheuer, *Osama Bin Laden*, pp. 123–124.

123 *Ibid.*, p. 123.

124 Prince Turki bin Faisal al Saud, "Economics of Substate Violence."

125 Scheuer, *Osama Bin Laden*, p. 123.

126 *Ibid.*, p. 124.

127 For more on this point, see Bergen, *Bin Laden I Know.*

128 Bergen, *Bin Laden I Know*, p. 250.

129 *Ibid.*

130 State Department Memo, Secret, Circa September 1998, www2.gwu.edu/~nsarchiv/NSAEBB/NSAEBB97/tal26.pdf.

131 Bergen, *Bin Laden I Know*, p. 315

132 Robert L. Grenier, "What If America Had Never Invaded Afghanistan?" *The Atlantic*, February 1, 2015, www.theatlantic.com/international/archive/2015/02/what-if-america-had-never-invaded-afghanistan/385026/.

133 *Ibid.*

134 Bergen, *Bin Laden I Know*, p. 322.

135 National Commission on Terrorist Attacks.

136 Grenier, "What If America Had Never Invaded Afghanistan?"

137 Peter L. Bergen, *The Longest War: The Enduring Conflict Between America and al Qaeda* (New York: Free Press, 2011), p. 12.

138 "Osama bin Laden's Declaration of Jihad Against Americans," *Milestone Documents in World History*, salempress.com, http://salempress.com/store/pdfs/bin_laden.pdf.

139 "Osama bin Laden's Declaration."

140 *Ibid.*

141 Sylvia Ann Hewlett, "Attract and Keep A-Players with Nonfinancial Rewards," *Harvard Business Review*, May 24, 2012, https://hbr.org/2012/05/attract-and-keep-a-players-wit/; Simon C.Y. Wong, "Aligning CEO Incentives with a Company's Long-Term Agenda," *Harvard Business Review*, October 11, 2011, https://hbr.org/2011/10/aligning-a-companys-incentive.

142 Wright, *Looming Tower*, pp. 410–413.

143 Osama bin Laden, "Jihad Against Jews and Crusaders: World Islamic Front Statement," February 23, 1998, www.fas.org/irp/world/para/docs/980223-fatwa.htm.

144 *Ibid.*

145 *Ibid.*

146 Wright, *Looming Tower*, p. 125.

147 *Ibid.*, p. 126.

6 The Rise of the Islamic State in Al Qaeda's Market

1 Adam Gopnik, "Terror Strikes in Paris," *The New Yorker*, November 14, 2015, www.newyorker.com/news/news-desk/terror-strikes-in-paris; "Statement by the President on the Situation in Paris," *White House Office of the Press Secretary*, November 13, 2015, www.whitehouse.gov/the-press-office/2015/11/13/statement-president-situation-paris.

2 Steve Coll, "In Search of a Strategy," *The New Yorker*, September 8, 2014, www.newyorker.com/magazine/2014/09/08/return-war.

3 "Bush Says Its Time for Action," *CNN*, November 6, 2001, http://edition.cnn.com/2001/US/11/06/ret.bush.coalition/index.html.

4 Major General J.N. Mattis, "Eve of Battle Speech," *Free Republic* (April 2003), www.freerepublic.com/focus/f-news/881955/posts.
5 Clint Watts, "You Don't Win Hearts and Minds, You Rent Them – Reigniting Sunni Tribes Against ISIS," *Geopoliticus: The Foreign Policy Research Institute Blog*, November 17, 2014, www.fpri.org/geopoliticus/2014/11/you-dont-win-hearts-and-minds-you-rent-them-reigniting-sunni-tribes-against-isis.
6 Graeme Wood, "What ISIS Really Wants," *The Atlantic*, March 2015, www.theatlantic.com/features/archive/2015/02/what-isis-really-wants/384980/.
7 *Ibid.*
8 Wright, *Looming Tower*, p. 124.
9 *Ibid.*
10 Bergen, *The Longest War*, p. 29.
11 Bush, "State of the Union."
12 "O'Reilly: 'ISIS Isn't Going to Stop, We Have to Kill Them All,'" *FoxNews.com*, August 20, 2014, http://insider.foxnews.com/2014/08/20/oreilly-isis-isnt-going-stop-we-have-kill-them-all.
13 Daniel Byman, *Al Qaeda, The Islamic State, and the Global Jihadist Movement: What Everyone Needs to Know* (New York: Oxford University Press, 2015), p. 170.
14 Wood, "What ISIS Really Wants."
15 *Ibid.*
16 Bernard Haykel, "The Rise of the Islamic State," *YouTube.com*, November 14, 2014, www.youtube.com/watch?v=qcDTP-7nleA.
17 Joby Warrick, *Black Flags: The Rise of ISIS* (New York: Doubleday, 2015).
18 Muhammad al-'Ubaydi, Nelly Lahoud, Daniel Milton, and Bryan Price, "The Group That Calls Itself a State: Understanding the Evolution and Challenges of the Islamic State," The Combating Terrorism Center at West Point, December 2014.
19 Ruth Sherlock, "How a Talented Footballer Became the World's Most Wanted Man, Abu Bakr al Baghdadi," *The Telegraph*, November 11, 2014, www.telegraph.co.uk/news/worldnews/middleeast/iraq/10948846/How-a-talented-footballer-became-worlds-most-wanted-man-Abu-Bakr-al-Baghdadi.html.
20 *Ibid.*
21 Byman, *Al Qaeda, The Islamic State*, p. 165.
22 Jenna McLaughlin, "Was Iraq's Top Terrorist Radicalized at a US-Run Prison?" *Mother Jones*, July 11, 2014, www.motherjones.com/politics/2014/07/was-camp-bucca-pressure-cooker-extremism.
23 William McCants, "The Believer," *The Brookings Institution*, September 1, 2015, www.brookings.edu/research/essays/2015/thebeliever.
24 Jason McCammack, "Camp Bucca: Inside the Wire," *All Hands*, January 2008, www.navy.mil/ah_online/archpdf/ah200801.pdf.
25 Terrence McCoy, "How the Islamic State Evolved in an American Prison," *Washington Post*, November 4, 2014, www.washingtonpost.com/news/morning-mix/wp/2014/11/04/how-an-american-prison-helped-ignite-the-islamic-state/.
26 Michael Weiss and Hassan Hassan, *ISIS: Inside the Army of Terror* (New York: Regan Arts, 2015), p. 9.
27 *Ibid.*, p. 10.
28 McCants, "The Believer."
29 *Ibid.*
30 *Ibid.*
31 *Ibid.*
32 Byman, *Al Qaeda, The Islamic State*, p. 165.
33 Christoph Reuter, "The Terror Strategist: Secret Files Reveal the Structure of Islamic State," *Spiegel International*, April 18, 2015, www.spiegel.de/international/world/islamic-state-files-show-structure-of-islamist-terror-group-a-1029274.html.
34 *Ibid.*

35 *Ibid.*
36 *Ibid.*
37 Raab, *Five Families*, p. 136.
38 McCants, "The Believer."
39 Amr Al-Azm, "Why ISIS Wants to Destroy Syria's Cultural Heritage," *Time*, October 8, 2015, http://time.com/4065290/syria-cultural-heritage/.
40 Tyler Cowen, "Terrorism as Theatre: Analysis and Policy Implications," *Public Choice*, 128, no. 1/2 (July 2006), p. 234.
41 *Ibid.*, p. 235.
42 Wright, *Looming Tower*, p. 297.
43 Julian E. Barnes, "U.S., Iraq Prepare Offensive to Retake Mosul From Islamic State," *Wall Street Journal*, January 22, 2015, www.wsj.com/articles/us-and-iraq-prepare-offensive-to-retake-mosul-1421949677.
44 Weiss and Hassan, *ISIS: Inside the Army of Terror*, p. 181.
45 *Ibid.*
46 Charlotte Alfred, "The Strange Irony Hidden Among the Highest Ranks of ISIS," *Huffington Post*, September 12, 2014, www.huffingtonpost.com/2014/09/12/isis-baathist-alliance_n_5792172.html.
47 *Ibid.*
48 "ISIS Joins Forces With Saddam Loyalists in Bid to Take Baghdad," *FoxNews.com*, June 23, 2014, www.foxnews.com/world/2014/06/23/isis-joins-forces-with-saddam-loyalists-in-bid-to-take-baghdad/.
49 *Ibid.*
50 Weiss and Hassan, *ISIS: Inside the Army of Terror,* p. 128.
51 *Ibid.*, p. 124.
52 *Ibid.*, p. 153.
53 *Ibid.*, p. 163.
54 Yaroslav Trofimov, "Islamic State's Scariest Success: Attracting Western Newcomers," *Wall Street Journal*, February 26, 2015, www.wsj.com/articles/islamic-states-scariest-success-attracting-western-newcomers-1424932279.
55 *Ibid.*
56 "Report on the Protection of Civilians in Armed Conflict in Iraq: 6 July–10 September, 2014," *UNHCR*, August 18, 2015, p. 15.
57 Shapiro, *Terrorists Dilemma*, p. 206.
58 *Ibid.*, p. 55.
59 J. M. Berger, "War on Error," *Foreign Policy*, February 5, 2014, http://foreignpolicy.com/2014/02/05/war-on-error/.
60 Brian Fishman, "After Zarqawi: The Dilemmas and Future of Al Qaeda in Iraq," *The Washington Quarterly*, 29, no. 4 (2006), p. 29.
61 Walter Enders and Todd Sandler, "Transnational Terrorism: An Economic Analysis," CREATE Research Archive, April 8, 2005, http://research.create.usc.edu/cgi/viewcontent.cgi?article=1125&context=nonpublished_reports.
62 Walter Enders and Todd Sandler, "After 9/11: Is It All Different Now?" abstract, January 2004, www.deu.edu.tr/userweb/onder.hanedar/dosyalar/end.pdf.
63 Nuno M. Garoupa, Jonathan Klick, and Francesco Parisi, "A Law and Economics Perspective on Terrorism," Social Science Research Network, September 9, 2005, http://papers.ssrn.com/sol3/papers.cfm?abstract_id=800705.
64 *Ibid.*
65 Zachary Abuza, "Balik-Terrorism: The Return of the Abu Sayyaf," Strategic Studies Institute, September 2005, www.strategicstudiesinstitute.army.mil/pdffiles/PUB625.pdf.
66 Daveed Gartenstein-Ross and Amichai Magen, "The Jihadist Governance Dilemma," *Washington Post*, July 18, 2014, www.washingtonpost.com/blogs/monkey-cage/wp/2014/07/18/the-jihadist-governance-dilemma/.
67 *Ibid.*

68 Abdel-malek Droukdel, "Mali-Al-Qaida's Sahara Playbook," Associated Press, http://hosted.ap.org/specials/interactives/_international/_pdfs/al-qaida-manifesto.pdf.

7 Conclusions and Prescriptions

1 Stathis Kalyvas calls this the "master cleavage" and compares this to local or private issues when discussing civil wars. See Stathis N. Kalyvas, "The Ontology of "Political Violence": Action and Identity in Civil Wars," *Perspectives on Politics* 1, no. 3 (September 2003), pp. 475–494.

2 For an interesting discussion of "war amongst the people," see Rupert Smith, *The Utility of Force: The Art of War in the Modern World* (New York: Knopf, 2007).

3 This statement is consistent with Paul Collier, Anke Hoeffler, and Dominic Rohner, "Beyond Greed and Grievance: Feasibility and Civil War," *Oxford Economic Papers*, 61 no. 1 (2009), pp. 1–27.

4 Collier, Hoeffler, and Rohner, "Beyond Greed and Grievance"; James D. Fearon and David Laitin, "Ethnicity, Insurgency, and Civil War," *American Political Science Review*, 97 (2003), pp. 75–90.

5 For more discussion on this topic, see Collier, Hoeffler, and Rohner, "Beyond Greed and Grievance," and Eli Berman and Ara Stepanyan, "*How Many Radical Islamists? Indirect Evidence from Five Countries*," University of California at San Diego, National Bureau of Economic Research, and Rice University, 2003.

6 See Jack Hirshleifer for introduction of this concept to the literature on violence. "affiliative instinct: individuals in tightly knit groups can more effectively take advantage of returns to scale in contending for ultimate biological goals." For example, Hirshleifer, "The Bioeconomic Causes of War," *Managerial and Decision Economics*, 19, no. 7/8 (November–December 1998).

7 Daniel Marston and Carter Malkasian, *Counterinsurgency in Modern Warfare* (Long Island City, NY: Osprey Publishing, 2008), p. 14.

8 Peter Bergen, "Time to Declare Victory: Al Qaeda is Defeated," *CNN.com*, June 27, 2012, http://security.blogs.cnn.com/2012/06/27/time-to-declare-victory-al-qaeda-is-defeated-opinion/.

9 The Center for Risk and Economic Analysis of Terrorism Events (CREATE) is an interdisciplinary national research center based out of the University of Southern California. For more information, see: http://create.usc.edu/. Some research for this book was supported by the United States Department of Homeland Security through the National Center for Risk and Economic Analysis of Terrorism Events (CREATE) under Cooperative Agreement 2007-ST-061-RE0001. However, any opinions, findings, and conclusions or recommendations in this document are those of the authors and do not necessarily reflect views of the United States Department of Homeland Security or the University of Southern California.

Final Thoughts

1 For a rich discussion of the history of science and defense, I recommend learning about the role played by Vannevar Bush and the team on the Manhattan Project. In particular, I recommend, Bush's *Modern Arms and Free Men* (New York, Simon and Schuster, 1949).

INDEX